To Josette,
with Gratitude
and Love

My

With Bing

by

Kathryn Crosby

Kathryn Crosby

Josette—
Nice Meeting You.
Very Best Wishes.

Mary Crosby

Collage Books Inc.
4244 Corporate Square
Naples, Florida 34104

4/25/05

Library of Congress Control Number: 2002112033
ISBN: 0-938728-09-1

Printed and bound in the United States of America

9 8 7 6 5 4 3 2

Our Hillsborough home

Bing's office

The library

The drawing room

PROLOGUE

My Life With Bing recounted my share of his experiences from our first fateful meeting when I was nineteen to the day that, as a thirty-year-old mother of three, I translated my family into our last and permanent abode in Hillsborough, California. The present narrative takes up where its predecessor left off, and recapitulates our final twelve years.

The intervening decades have seen a number of books purporting to depict my husband, some absurd, and others so well documented that only one thing is missing from their pages, namely the 95% of his life that a very private man deliberately concealed from the world.

Obviously this is not the fault of the dedicated biographers. They were familiar only with Bing's performances which, however important to his fans, never played the major role in his life.

For once again it is the tale of the blind men and the elephant. Each has his little Bing that he knows, while the giant behind the scenes, who scorned to identify with his singing, acting, writing, golfing, hunting, fishing, traveling, horse racing, etc., remains lost in the mist.

I too may fail in my appointed task, but at least I've had ample occasion to acquaint myself with my subject.

As before, I have utilized the meticulous diaries which we both kept, and have had recourse to our voluminous correspondence, to supplement my own vivid memories, and those of scores of friends. With their help, I now invite the reader once again to share those bygone days with Bing and me.

Ballerina Margot Fonteyn with chairmen Hope and Crosby

1966

The process of translating our familial effects to Hillsborough had finally come to an end, as all things must. But just as we were getting established in our new neighborhood, I received a visit from the Mother Superior of the Immaculate Heart Nuns.

Without explanation, she invited me to accompany her on a trip to Italy to interview the Pope. When it comes to traveling, I've always been Available Jones herself, but for once I took the precaution of discussing the matter with Bing before packing my valise.

To my surprise, he failed to evince his customary enthusiasm for religious pilgrimages. Did he know something that I didn't?

In any event, he soon rendered the discussion academic by reminding me that the Royal Ballet would arrive in Los Angeles on January 3rd. As he well knew, for me dignitaries of the Church are all very well in their place, but the ballet is a deeply religious experience.

The performance was a gala for the benefit of the ballet in Los Angeles. It was presented at the Chandler Music Center, a monument to the patience and perseverance of Buffy Chandler, who had spent a decade extorting the requisite funds from every celebrity in Hollywood, under the dire threat of ostracism from the pages of her husband's *Los Angeles Times*. As a consequence, it was forevermore affectionately denominated *Buffy's Tavern*.

After a cocktail party for the dancers, who were much too nervous to participate with any enthusiasm, we repaired to Buffy's box. There Bing interrupted the rampant exhibitionism to remark that he couldn't hear the music. This had a quieting effect on the other members of the group, who then found time to notice that they couldn't hear the music either.

By a bizarre mischance, Buffy's box had been located in the exact center of the sole dead spot in the superb audi-

Beautiful Inger Stevens

torium. Heretofore the occupants had been so preoccupied with engaging each other's attention that no one had found time to notice.

Trust Bing to spoil the show. He was looking so put-upon that I finally counseled him to keep his eyes firmly fixed on Margot's legs, and he grumpily agreed to make do with that. As I have had occasion to remark previously, he would make any sacrifice for the arts.

Once Bing had settled down, I, who had no need of the music, disappeared into the ecstatic haze that always accompanied any exposure to the dance, and remained blissfully oblivious of my surroundings until I found myself at the post-performance celebration.

It consisted of a formal dinner, with Margot Fonteyn seated at the head of the main table, flanked by Bing and Bob Hope. Opening my eyes a trifle wider, I discovered that Inger Stevens was ensconced on Bing's right, and that I had somehow been relegated to Lower Slobbovia. A tiny inner voice almost questioned Bing's new-found interest in the ballet, but I dismissed the thought as unworthy of me.

In any event, I rejoiced to see that my husband was not suffering. Margot had the biggest, blackest eyes I've ever seen, and they remained solemnly fixed upon him throughout the long evening. When and if he ever came up for air, he had only to turn his head to drown in Inger Stevens' enormous orbs.

This he did frequently, largely because Inger was making full use of her previous acquaintance with his idiosyncracies by copiously plying him with Scotch and water, which she knew that he preferred to Margot's champagne for serious drinking.

As the evening wore on, the battle intensified. I was at first put off by Bing's obvious stratagem of playing one temptress against the other. Then I realized that my sly old jouster had scored a tactical triumph.

As the tempo increased, the strife itself came to the fore, and the prey was forgotten in the full fury of combat. Bing was sitting back, and serenely sipping his Scotch, while the juxtaposed beauties strove to bedazzle each other.

Situated well back among the *corps de ballet,* I too found ample leisure for meditation. I could hardly blame Bing for Margot; that was one which I had definitely brought upon myself.

Inger, on the other hand, was a blonde of a different color. Bing's costar in *Man on Fire,* she had descended on him with a vengeance in 1956, and again in 1957, when I had imprudently left him to his own devices.

During a period of over a year, she had simply appeared out of the blue, at any hour of the day or night, whether at Bing's home at Pebble Beach, when he was visiting San Simeon, or when he stopped off at the fishing club, across from what later became our Rising River Ranch in Northern California.

The very week that we were married, Bing had given her a combination housewarming-and-birthday party at his new home in Palm Springs, which he subsequently decided that he had built for me. Inger, in turn, had spent Bing's birthday gift certificate on our wedding present.

When newshounds surprised Bing's sheepish look, and scented a story, Inger coyly informed them that he had always been like a father to her, and that she treasured his paternal advice.

A cotton picker returns to Texas.

While I was making *The Big Circus* in 1960, *Metro-Goldwyn-Mayer's* famed hair stylist, Sidney Guilleroff, had notified me that Inger, who had recently failed in a suicide attempt, had again fallen into a state of depression, and was in immediate need of a retreat from the world.

Recalling pictures of her at our ranch, laughing delightedly with Bing, Alice Faye, and Phil Harris, I obliged Sidney by inviting her to go there, and to stay as long as she wished. The next day, he informed me that Inger had accepted "Bing's invitation."

Not caring for the ring of that somehow, but convinced that Bing would approve of my charitable efforts, I informed him that he was about to have a guest. He turned white, red, and white again, before gulping, "Are you crazy?"

"Am I to read that as a negative?"

"Don't you know that that woman may do anything at any time?"

"No, but I'd be interested in learning just how you picked up that fascinating bit of information."

"Never mind. Just keep her away from my ranch."

And that I did, by the simple expedient of crawling back to Sidney, with my tail between my legs, and informing him that "Bing's invitation" had just been rescinded.

Thereafter we enjoyed a blessed five-year dry spell, during which I admired Inger's lovely face solely in her popular movies and highly successful television series, and endured her cold and distant glances only at occasional gatherings. It gladdened my heart to observe that she nonetheless harbored no permanent grudge against Bing, however faulty his taste in marriage partners.

Trying to think of some way in which I excelled Miss Sweden, and not coming up with much, I finally bethought me of hunting, and lured Bing off to my home turf in Refugio, Texas, near the town where I had attended high school. But oh what a change was there, my countrymen!

At the bottom of the pasture where the shoot took place, a Queen Anne mirror and leaded-glass birds were suspended from tall oak trees. Hand lotions, colognes, and exotic soaps stood beside pitchers of Victorian china, brimming with hot water. Antique tables groaned under a "picnic lunch," which would have done credit to the finest of international hotels.

Matagorda oysters and blue crabs arrived in a helicopter piloted by a billionaire, who didn't in the least mind playing errand boy, since his main joy in life was "cruisin' for coyotes" in his flying machine. I learned that his sole responsibility was equally absorbing, consisting as it did of donning his one suit, in order to attend friends' funerals.

Bing regarded the scene in blank amazement, and admitted that he was obtaining new insights into my background. "Was it really this fancy when you were a Robstown Cottonpicker?" he inquired.

"Of course," I lied blithely. "Aunt Frances cooked delicious barbecued doves, and Uncle Leon took us all on hayrides."

Upon our return to California, I resumed my home tutoring, and began writing my first book, *Bing and Other Things,* while my pupils were off at school.

Meanwhile my husband devoted the mornings to his voluminous correspondence, dropped by at noon to read what

Captain Crosby

I'd written, lunched in the men's grill at his club, spent his afternoons playing golf, and arrived home for dinner, a weary but happy man.

He carried me off to his annual tournament at Pebble Beach, where a frightful storm broke on Saturday. While I cowered in the clubhouse, Bing strode across the fairways, encouraging the desperate players.

On the 16th tee at Cypress, he encountered a bedraggled Tom Nieporte, who was later to win the Palm Springs Tournament.

Tom was 35 over par, and his playing partner, Billy Farrell, was 26 over. "Bing," they wailed, "we've never shot in the nineties in our professional careers."

"I wouldn't let a little thing like that worry you," Bing rejoined. "The way you're going today, you'll both be well into the hundreds."

On February 25th, Bing and I flew to Medway, an antebellum estate outside Charleston, South Carolina. There the famed British portrait painter, Simon Elwiss, dined with us, collared Bing, and gushed, "I visualize Kathryn in a three-quarter facial angle, with the frame stopping just above the knees."

Unmentioned was the fact that said modest effort would set the lady's husband back some $100,000.

"I gave at the office," Bing drawled.

"Er, what was that?"

"Thank you very much, but my wife has already been painted."

Then we were off to the races at Hialeah, and to an introductory voyage on George Coleman's boat, which he was devoting his life to outfitting. As a boy, George had always loved toys. As an adult of sorts, he believed in being prepared for all emergencies.

The *Aurora C,* so named in honor of George's wife, Dawn Coleman, had so much navigational equipment aboard that its gunwales were fighting to remain above water, and so much air conditioning that the overburdened exhaust leaked fumes back into the living quarters.

All in all, it was so luxurious that there was no room left for passengers. Bing eventually referred to George as Dr. Frankenstein, because he was clearly creating a monster.

In truth, my husband was in no position to be critical. When at long last, by some still-unfathomable miracle, the science-fiction craft brought its skipper to Las Cruces, Bing ministered to George's madness by bringing his own boat, the Maria Francesca, named for our daughter Mary Frances, into the fray.

Like little children, the twain would sally forth at dawn with their walkie-talkies, calling back and forth for hours, with inordinately specific and totally unintelligible advice about repairs to the abundantly useless equipment that each had installed.

They desisted only when one or the other of the radios also failed, or I called a halt for lunch.

At the Colemans, we met one of George's favorite fellow Oklahomans, Charles Wrightsman, who had been a mere stripling when his father suffered a serious heart attack, and consequently transferred most of the family property to his son, in a last-ditch effort to thwart the tax collectors.

Shortly thereafter, the father miraculously recovered, and tried in vain to rescind his bequest.

"Tough luck," our hero sympathized. "You're a poor Okie now."

Early Bing with partially flattened ears

This same humanitarian had kept his wife Jane on a very short financial leash, but had permitted her to accumulate an extensive collection of invaluable antiques, which he had prudently kept in his name.

As advancing age and crippling arthritis gradually transformed Charles' personality from merely difficult to clearly impossible, Jane began to view these *objets d'art* as her sole nest egg, and commenced to inventory them with a view to divorce.

It was at this juncture that her husband donated the entire collection to the Metropolitan Museum of Art, where they may now be viewed by a grateful public in the gallery which bears his name.

Back in San Francisco, I played nurse again, seeing a nephew through the ear repair that is called pinning.

Bing first expressed disdain, then viewed the results critically, and finally admitted, "If it really had been that simple in my day, I just might have had it done myself."

Although I had never been troubled by Bing's ears, he had suffered mightily for them. He had failed his first screen test on the grounds that he was patently "too wingy." When he was vouchsafed another chance, the studio had still insisted on gluing his ears back, until he finally achieved such stature that he could simply banish the sticky annoyance forever.

This he did in the middle of a film, leaving movie historians to revel in the climactic moment, triumphantly detailing the last of the scenes in which Bing's auricles remain plastered flat against his head, and the first in which they are gloriously unfurled, as they were to remain forevermore.

Bing's ears became the source of innumerable jokes. Bob Hope, for example, accused him of "looking like a taxi cab with both doors open," and then made capital of the other extreme by claiming that George Raft, who had submitted to having his ears pinned, "resembled a glider in full flight before the operation, and a wet whippet in a windstorm thereafter."

In spite of all the ridicule, Bing came to terms with his ears early in life, but his other cosmetic problem was to dog him to his dying day.

For my part, I must admit that, as a woman who throws on chignons, pastiches, falls, and false braids at a moments notice, without a trace of embarrassment, I experienced difficulty in identifying with his neurotic approach to hair.

A modest man, who would have gone comfortably bald if left to his own devices, Bing never succeeded in reconciling the studio's demand that he not be photographed without a hairpiece, with the requirements of social engagements and outdoor sports. As a consequence, he wore hats whenever possible, and avoided public occasions.

Bing would forego his favorite operas or dramatic works, rather than don what he termed his "scalp doily." Since I was unprepared to make similar sacrifices, this led to continual domestic dissension.

When I absolutely insisted, or when he was faced with an unavoidable professional appearance, I took it upon myself to relieve him of discomfiture by applying it for him, rather like a mother with her child's stocking cap or mittens.

April 28th found Bing in the throes of paternity. His female Labrador, Topsy, was about to whelp, while he

Later Bing with unleashed ears

paced the floor, and solicited my medical advice.

"She keeps running around in circles in her kennel," Bing insisted. "What should we do now?"

"How about a movie?"

"This is no time for levity. Topsy needs your help."

"All my nursing training has been with bipeds, but it left me with the distinct impression that puppies come naturally to dogs."

"That's easy for you to say. It's her first litter, and she might not know what to do."

"I'll try taking her temperature and pulse every half hour."

We never did get to the movie. After hovering over the kennel all day long, toward evening I detected definite signs of progress.

With raw terror on my part, and bored complacency on Topsy's, I at length succeeded in delivering seven ebony puppies, the last of which was an undersized black butterball that I immediately baptized *Cinder*, or for short, *Cindy*.

Something of a midget myself, I've always identified with the runt of the litter. Cindy was mine because she needed me, not only at birth, but throughout the rest of an extended canine career.

As a hunter, she was a bust, since she hated the very sight of guns, was terrified of the noise that they made, and fled from any sylvan creature larger than a sparrow. Fortunately she and I indulged similar tastes in hunting for arrowheads, digging for artifacts, and nosing for seashells.

Evenings, while I read or did needlepoint, Cindy lay before the fire, with forepaws daintily crossed, looking in

profile a bit like Cleopatra. When, as all too frequently occurred, I fell prey to respiratory illnesses, she perched atop my bed, defending it with her life against marauding physicians, children, or husbands.

Throughout our time together, my little dog brought me continual delight, with no attendant pain, and I grieved, as for a person, when her shorter life span deprived me forever of the pleasure of her company.

Bing delayed our departure for Las Cruces until May 11th, a tactical blunder which afforded me the opportunity to select my play for the summer.

While I sat in our isolated Mexican retreat, waiting for the script of *Mary, Mary* to arrive, I amused myself with equally futile attempts to vaccinate the population against smallpox, and to interest Harry and Nathaniel in the world of academe.

But my enemies are everywhere, and they do not sleep. A serious leak in my security had delivered said script to Bing's right-hand man in Los Angeles, who, in turn, had packed it in with a load of artichokes, which he then warehoused in strict obedience to my husband's injunction to hold them until they fully ripened.

Before the script could make its way overland by vegetable truck to Las Cruces, it was June 11th, and high time for me to hit the road north.

Arriving in Hillsborough, I had only brief hours to assemble a contemporary wardrobe for the play.

I found myself cast in the role of Indian giver. As Bridget Brennan deposited my parents and me at the plane, I snatched from her back a coat that I had presented to her the preceding Christmas.

Jim Kirkwood, my leading man in *Mary, Mary*

While Bing gave me a taste of what I was missing by whisking Harry off for a romantic tour of Hawaii, I arrived all-unprepared in Vineland, Canada.

It transpired that I was in good company. Our director had rented his home from a beekeeper, who refused to vacate until his pets swarmed. Meanwhile our brave leader was camping out in the auditorium, and experiencing a level of stress which occasioned a heart attack two days into rehearsal.

Like me, my leading man was writing a book, which occupied most of his time and energy, and all of his interest. At his insistence, I actually changed several of my lines to include the title of his masterpiece, and then, while I was in the area, tossed in references to *Bing and Other Things.*

The supporting actor, who played the role of "the mature movie star," threw a monumental fit when asked to share a dressing room with his colleague who played Oscar, so terrifying the latter, that he swallowed his dialogue, even in rehearsal.

Somehow all this reminded me of home, so I sprang into the breach, and settled the matter of dressing rooms then and there. However, between dealing with everyone else's problems, and seeking out places for my mother to visit, and my father to fish, I managed to arrive at opening night without the faintest notion of my role.

I was not alone. Our unprepared cast wandered through an undirected production without ever identifying with their parts.

The drama critic for the *Toronto Star* attended the opening night, and penned a scathing review of the entire shambles, in which of course I starred.

This was a new experience. I had closed theaters in my day, but they had all been well-nigh empty at the time. Never before had I been so thoroughly panned for a sellout.

Upon mature consideration, I concluded that the critic was justified, and wrote him, stating that I agreed wholeheartedly with his evaluation of my performance. In return, I received a bewildered note, in which he conceded that such an admission was unique in his experience.

Do-gooder that I am, I did salvage something from our disastrous weeks in Vineland. Franchot Tone's natural son, who had been a psychiatric resident at Queen of Angels Hospital when I was studying nursing there, visited me backstage, and asked if I could arrange for him to meet his father.

I contrived an interview when the latter guest-starred with Bing, and the son, who had spent his youth in foster homes, cared for the actor in his waning years.

Between Vineland and our play's next stop in Laconia, New Hampshire, I flew to New York, and auditioned for the role of Eliza in a company touring with *My Fair Lady.* To everyone's surprise, I landed the part, and immediately phoned Bing in Hawaii to announce my latest triumph.

"I'm going to sing in a great musical, and I'm going to be a star like you," I kept repeating.

"You are going to do no such thing," Bing announced firmly. "When you finish your run in *Mary, Mary,* you are rushing straight home to your neglected children."

I was ready with what I deemed to be a series of strong arguments, but

Stagecoach was released on June 15, while I toiled in *Mary, Mary*.

somehow Bing didn't seem to have left much room for them.

I sadly informed the producers of *My Fair Lady* that I was no longer available, and thus nipped my musical career in the bud. If I'd had any singing voice at all, I'd have been furious.

As it was, I licked my wounds for a matter of hours, before deciding that I'd return to my wifely chores all right, but when winter came, I'd make my bid to star in the new Broadway musical production of *Breakfast at Tiffany's*.

Unaccountably, I actually convinced producer David Merrick that I should have my chance, but the writer remained adamantly committed to Mary Tyler Moore.

As a consequence, I missed my opportunity to appear in one of the biggest busts in Broadway history, and Mary absconded with the nervous breakdown that I so richly deserved.

Meanwhile, let's return to *Mary, Mary,* where our little caravan is wending its weary way through successive week's stands in Laconia, Ivoryton, Fitchburg, and Falmouth, while gradually jelling into a halfway reasonable production, as a consequence of memorizing roles, patient experimentation, and utter exhaustion.

On the afternoon of our final day in Falmouth, I received a garbled telegram from the Canadian critic who had denounced us in Vineland. Sure enough, he appeared backstage after the performance, to recount his many adventures with plane, train, and bus, in a lengthy pilgrimage to determine whether we had in fact improved.

Amazingly, he was now ecstatic, avowing that never in his entire career had he seen such rapid progress made in a single summer. I could have

listened all night, but my father, who had a 3 AM fishing date, wandered up to announce, "Well, sugarpuddin', it's past your bedtime, so tell all the nice folks good night."

Undaunted by such apparent want of appreciation, the critic retraced his route by bus, train, and plane, to write a glowing review in the Sunday edition of the *Toronto Star*.

If he has yet to embark on the Stygian ferry, and chances to read these lines, it may be a consolation to him to learn that I still treasure it, and make a habit of reading it when feeling unappreciated, which is to say relatively frequently.

Between performances, I had found three occasions to visit Bing's brother, Everett, who had been hospitalized in Sharon, Connecticut. A diabetic, he had undergone successive amputations for the gangrene resulting from his poor circulation, losing first his right toe, next the foot, then the entire leg, and finally the left leg.

Weary of the torment, he had flatly refused further operations for his rapidly spreading tumors. Since fresh bruises would lead to more gangrene, there was no hope of prosthesis, so Bing had presented him with the world's most luxurious electric golf cart, which permitted him to remain self-sufficient to the very end.

Just as I was finishing the tour, word came of Everett's sudden death. My parents and I rushed down to Connecticut to help his wife Florence with the funeral arrangements, and to try to console her for her loss.

Florence wanted Bing by her side, but I knew that there was no hope of his returning from Hawaii. Everett had been his agent and manager, and the

Bing and Remus at Rising River

Sister Damian Marie with John Scott Trotter and Harry at Las Cruces

two had been very close throughout their lives. But Bing had a need to remember his friends and relatives at their best; he had never been able to stand the thought of his big, strong, athletic brother as a dying cripple.

Bing had also reached the age when it's funeral-of-the-week time, and his lifelong horror of death led him to send help whenever possible, but to avoid the final hours. He especially loathed lingering illnesses, and was determined to bow out swiftly and gracefully when his own time came.

On July 31st, I finally arrived home. Bing was in Los Angeles, taping shows for the *Hollywood Palace*, and spending time with his first four boys, so I devoted myself to dictating the final version of *Bing and Other Things*, and to exposing the children to Dr. Sullivan's latest programmed textbooks.

Mary Frances was now almost as fast at math as at reading, and of course she delighted in showcasing her talents, but the boys continued to resist anything that didn't involve vigorous outdoor exercise.

When Bing arrived home, he spelled me with the children, and suggested inserts for my book, reminding me that, although we had four houses, all were in constant use. Our Rising River Ranch was managed by my sister and her husband, who raised cattle and quarter horses, as well as opening it up to friends for hunting and fishing.

The house in Palm Desert was used constantly by other members of our family, as well as by the Immaculate Heart Nuns, whose graduate school had also taken over La Casa Crosby in Las Cruces, which they in turn shared with the National Science Foundation for research in biology.

Bing loved to buy houses, but he never felt comfortable as a rich man, because he couldn't stand the thought of enjoying things that others didn't have. He therefore tried to assuage his guilt by sharing his possessions. I, who had never had a farthing to my name, was happily prepared to enjoy them to the utmost, all by myself if necessary.

The month of August was an interlude that finally permitted us time to appreciate our new home. For Bing, the entire surrounding area was, of course, filled with memories of Seabiscuit racing around his training track, of the huge formal gardens, and the many greenhouses.

With the property reduced to five acres, it was now Bing's family that lived in the big house. The attic theater, where his goddaughter had produced her childish dramas, had become the schoolroom, where his second wife applied her teaching certificate to inculcating reading and writing skills in their three children.

Indeed, Bing's tale of the huge emerald ring, which a furious Anita Howard had thrown down a heating duct in that self-same attic, has had said wife thoughtfully examining the registers, and probing tentatively at the walls and ceiling, ever since.

On August 27th, Bing and I flew to England, where he was scheduled to catch a salmon for the TV show *The American Sportsman*, before filming another television special in Ireland.

We stayed at the Trout Hotel in the Cumbrian Lake District, while Bing fished in what looked like a small river to me, but was locally denominated the Derwent Water. I was permitted to stand by the bank, so long as I neither moved nor uttered a sound.

The gilly of Derwent Water

Bing and Lord Egremont

I watched solemnly, as my husband flailed away all day every day for a week, without getting so much as a nibble, while his gilly (fishing guide) invented ever more exotic excuses for the dour (wily) ways of the salmon.

Eventually even I detected a certain monotony in the routine, wherefore I abandoned the watercourse for a stroll about the picture-book village. In the course of my rambles, I met Lord Egremont, who owned Cockermouth Castle and the lands where Bing was trying to fish.

That evening, he showed us his thirty-foot-deep dungeon, and remarked dryly, "That's where we've always put the poachers."

From my own experience with the paucity of prey in his stream, I suspected that the local pilferers would perish of inanition long before any such punitive measures became necessary.

Nonetheless, Lord Egremont was a true lifesaver, because the angling really was beginning to pale, as Bing grimly embarked on his second salmonless week.

I therefore chose to accompany his lordship on his daily rounds, descending into a hematite mine, awarding the blue ribbons when he judged a county fair, attending the races at Doncaster, and meeting Sir Stafford Howard of Greystoke Castle, a relative of sorts of the fictional Tarzan, whose real-life ancestor had escaped the Tower by following Henry VIII's admonition to mind his lands in the North, when Catherine Howard's adulteries were at length discovered.

The present Lady Howard was a fellow Texan, who was refurbishing her castle with odds and ends, disinterred from barns or spotted at auctions, since all the ancestral heirlooms had served as firewood for the soldiers billeted there during World War II.

We dined at Lowther Castle with Lord Lonsdale, who had also married an American.

The titled couple had survived confiscatory British taxes by taking advantage of a loophole in the law, which stated that a roofless dwelling couldn't be assessed. We ate in the only part of the building without a direct view of the stars.

After two weeks of fruitless fly-casting, even Bing decided that he had earned a furlough, so we left for Sussex, to visit Lord Egremont's wife Pamela at Petworth, their southern residence, and one of the celebrated stately homes of England.

Petworth was immense. All four of the Crosby dwellings would have fitted neatly into a corner of the drawing room. So I shuddered as I watched Bing eying it narrowly.

As the evening wore on, his appraising glances, at the Grinling Gibbons carvings and the Holbein portraits, warned me that he coveted this monument to feudalism and fiscal insanity. Unless I distracted him forthwith, he would have to have it.

"Just how long would it take to build a place like this?" he inquired thoughtfully of our hostess.

"Well," she reflected dubiously, "the chapel dates from 1160, and the owners have been adding bits and pieces ever since."

Bing's eyes fixed upon eternity, and I hastily introduced the subject of the tennis courts, which it seemed had hosted the sport for royalty since the 16th century. Somehow my spouse didn't seem to be paying full attention,

At Howth Castle

With two members of the cast of *A Little Bit of Irish*

but fortunately it was at this moment that Pamela took it upon herself to bedazzle him.

She insisted that Bing sing her favorite songs, while she accompanied him on the piano. When he acceded, it was clear that he wasn't quite himself, because he invariably refused to perform at social gatherings. Nevertheless, I busily heaped coals on Pamela's fire, prepared to risk anything to get his mind off her forbidding hulk of a house.

On the following day, Pamela insisted that she and I enter two of her enormous hunters in a local gymkhana. Since I can't ride worth a lick, of course I won nothing, but my hair-breadth escapes from disaster finally did attract Bing's attention, and I was relieved to hear him talking horses with our host for the rest of the day.

Back we traipsed across England, so that I could stay with the Howards, while Bing commuted from Greystoke Castle to Cockermouth, where he was still trying to hook that wily salmon.

After another week of medieval living, he actually managed the feat. At long last, the patient producers of *The American Sportsman* could acquaint their stateside audience with the wonders of fishing in the North Country, and we could hie us off to Dublin.

And none too soon. As I packed our bags, I saw that my spouse, his mission temporarily accomplished, was finding time to attend to the surrounding architecture. Given another day, he'd have been taking the measure of towers and moats.

In Dublin, I learned to my horror that we had somehow acquired Cotton Bay and Harrigan, two untried race horses, who were to play leading roles in hundreds of transatlantic letters over the next years, but to display a positive aversion for competition when the chips were down.

Between scenes shot in the Guiness Brewery, Howth Castle, and the Abbey Theatre, we shopped for antiques, and even visited my first pub, where I boldly downed half a glass of stout, and was promptly deathly ill for two days. Whatever my faults, alcoholism is not among them.

We returned home by way of Scotland, where Bing practiced for an upcoming Canadian golf tournament, and then Vancouver, where he competed in the event itself.

Hardly had we settled in, when our butler Alan Fisher and his wife Norma departed for England, leaving me to manage the household. Bing stolidly observed my two-and-seventy daily catastrophes until October 7th, when he deserted for the safety of his club at Cypress Point.

He returned, calm and rested, to discuss the problems posed by our Palm Desert home: All its rooms had easily-opened sliding doors, facing the pool. Our children swam well, but they nevertheless still thought on their own age levels.

Bing had an all-too-clear memory of the day that he had chanced to stroll past his brother Bob's pool, to find three of his nephews sitting on the bottom of it, with their noses barely protruding, snorkel-like, from the water. He had fished them out unhurt, and pieced their story together.

It seems that they had been wrestling on the edge of the pool, and had fallen, fully-dressed, into the water. Competent swimmers, but mindful of a parental injunction to do so only in their bathing suits, they had dutifully settled

21

Our Las Cruces home

The brant adventure with Charlie Jones

down to await further orders. "Could any kids really be that dumb?" Bing had inquired indignantly.

After a long, contemplative look at our brood, he had then issued orders to fill in the pool of their Hillsborough home, an expedient which made sense on five acres, but was inappropriate at Palm Desert, where the much smaller house was built around the water, and there were three neighbors' pools within a hundred yards. With regret, we decided to part with our beloved honeymoon home.

It sold immediately, but the furnishings which it had contained rained down on staffless me in Hillsborough. I comforted myself with the reflection that, given Bing's propensity for buying and selling homes, we had been playing musical furniture from the start.

As a result, I had evolved a unique decorating style, which my friends had long since denominated "Old Leftovers." Resourcefully, I tucked everything somewhere.

Typically, Bing fled to Las Cruces, whence he mailed me a description of a twenty-year goose hunt, which made our participation in World War II look like a minor punitive expedition. I append an abbreviated version:

"Kathryn, as you well know, our Las Cruces neighbor, Charlie Jones, has always combined insatiable intellectual curiosity with high purpose and relentless determination.

Two decades ago, he first heard of flocks of strange ducks, said to be wintering in remote Magdalena Bay, whose estuaries run twenty miles southeast from the tiny cannery at Soledad.

More recently, the few natives who had explored those waters in their dugouts declared that they had indeed seen some odd migratory birds, which arrived in November, and departed in March.

His curiosity now fully aroused, Charlie summoned his pilot to fly him to Soledad. But the manager of the cannery had borrowed Jones' plane to check on a beached fishing boat.

Poor Charlie had to make do with a waterlogged skiff, on which he mounted a venerable outboard, only to spend hours in fruitless exploration.

With the afternoon wearing on, and the tide receding to a point where it was prudent to steer well out into the channel, Charlie finally spied his plane, skimming back over the mangroves.

It spooked a flock of dark birds, all but one of which winged off into the gathering dusk.

That luckless fowl flew full-tilt into the plane's right wing, and dropped three-hundred feet, to splash down directly in front of the skiff.

Jones retrieved it, and found that he was holding not a duck, but a cousin of the snow goose called the black brant, a wily game bird which breeds in the arctic and summers there, before flying down along the Pacific Coast to winter in California, and in a stretch of northern Mexico, but never, so far as anyone knew, this far south. Charlie began to scent a real challenge.

When the tide ebbs, the inaccessible east side of Magdalena Bay is lush with eel grass, the sole diet of the black brant, presenting our hero with a logistics problem which would have baffled Nimrod himself.

But after ten years of frustrating trial and error, Charlie finally succeeded in outmaneuvering wind, fog, reef, and tide, to shoot his first representative of the species.

Success at last

Since that day, ten more years had past, and I found myself setting out from Las Cruces in Charlie's DC-3 for the hour-long flight to Soledad.

A two-ton truck preceded us by three days, laden with a couple of sixteen-foot Bear River flatboats, shallow of draft and ample of beam, powered by 45-horse Johnson water-propulsion engines (no propellers, of course), life preservers, four dozen decoys, waders, shotguns, shells, camouflage clothing, wind-breakers, collapsible rafts, camp stools, shovels, hundreds of gallons of fresh water, and countless other impedimenta.

Charlie had timed our trip so that we arrived at high tide, and the flatboats made good speed along the main estuary.

After a two-hour's run, we beached them under some mangroves, unloaded our gear, and set out decoys, while the subsiding waters gradually exposed long stretches of eel grass.

In lieu of a blind, we sat on stools under a mangrove tree, camouflaged by leafy branches in our hatbands. After forty minutes of sheer boredom, Charlie called out, "Brant coming in low at 3 o'clock!"

From about two miles to the north, innumerable tiny black dots were headed our way. Their pace was leisurely, and unlike the more familiar honkers, they made no sound.

I watched in awe as these rare creatures, all the way from the Bering Sea, advanced on whispering wings. While still half a mile out, the flock suddenly wheeled, and after describing several slow circles, landed smartly on the water.

"Somebody must have moved," muttered Charlie hoarsely, "or they caught a flash of reflected sunlight off the motor of one of the boats."

Personally, I couldn't believe that the brant had spotted us, since we'd been skulking like so many commandos prior to a raid. But now all they had to do was sit comfortably out there, until the ebbing tide forced us to pull up and leave.

Indeed, that seemed to be the script, but a dozen birds foolishly abandoned it. Suddenly they rose from the bay, flew due south for a quarter of a mile, abruptly wheeled, and headed straight for our shoreline.

"Brant at 9 o'clock," Charlie rasped. "Keep down."

Then, after a few breathless seconds, he roared, "Now!"

Until that solemn moment, I hadn't dared to peek, but I instantly jumped out from under my mango tree, and sure enough, there they were, setting their wings right over our decoys, not thirty yards away.

Charlie fired, waited politely for me, and then fired again, while I just stood and gaped. I had never suffered from buck fever when shooting big game, so I hadn't even considered freezing at the sight of a few birds.

But somehow the combination of our meticulous preparations, the rarity of the birds, and their long pilgrimage, had got to me. I hadn't so much as raised my gun.

Two brant floated in the water, and the rest of the gaggle was well out of range, in pursuit of the flock on the bay, who had risen at the sound of shots and sailed off into the far distance, clearly vowing never to return.

Appalled at the thought that twenty years of strategic brilliance and tactical perfection should have ended in

Magdalena Bay

Charlie Jones and Harry

me, I gasped out apologies. I seemed to have forfeited my once-in-a-lifetime occasion to bag a brant.

Meanwhile Jones was philosophically retrieving his birds, and moving the decoys out a few yards, lest they be stranded by the ebb tide.

Hoping against hope, I asked him, "Is there any chance that they'll be coming back?"

Charlie disillusioned me quickly. "Not the ones I fired on," he admitted, "or their cousins out on the bay, but there's always a remote possibility that they may have associates who have yet to arrive."

In spite of his words, my spirits revived. If fate accorded me another opportunity, however slim, I wouldn't muff it. Hit or miss, I resolved to throw some lead into the air.

We floundered back out of the muddy water, and sat for a long, silent hour, staring up at the branches of the mangrove trees, while the tide slid out from under our decoys.

Just as we were about to move them for the last time, Jones shrilled, "Brant at 12 o'clock."

Peering between the branches, I saw a flock sweeping straight toward our shore, with no pause for surveillance. Like so many homing pigeons, they were heading directly for the nearest decoys.

Moreover, this group wasn't silent. It was emitting a low, clucking sound, reminiscent of the ladies' lounge at a country club.

The geese swung in a wide circle about the decoys, their ebony bodies glistening in the bright sunlight, and their white collars standing up like dickeys on a clutch of aldermen.

Once again, I was simply standing there mesmerized, but Charlie was now aware of my problem.

He shouted, "Shoot, Bing," and gave me a sporting chance before banging away himself.

Without even pausing to aim, I loosed two shots directly into the flock, reloaded, and fired again. The brant disappeared downwind, but I seemed to have downed a pair of them.

Thereafter new groups of birds came wheeling in over the decoys in such rapid succession that I lost all track of time. At last there was a lull, during which I noticed a long-billed grey bird, about the size of a quail, paralleling the shoreline.

"That's a godwit," Charlie grunted.

"Fine, what's a godwit?"

"A species of snipe, a shore bird that travels and nests with the brant."

"Sort of a camp follower?"

"You might say so. I prefer to think of it as a mascot."

"Is it a game bird?"

"A delicious one."

So the interludes between arrivals of the brant were enlivened by spectacular exhibitions of flying from a leggy bird which dives and ducks like a white-winged dove.

For two more hours, we forgot about our boats, lunch, and welfare. When the brant and godwit finally abandoned us, we had to collect our trophies and decoys in desperate haste, because a successful exit had become marginal.

In effect, the tide was so low that we scraped bottom continuously, and made a number of wrong turns, but by dint of poling, pushing, and pulling, we finally reached the dwindling main channel back to Soledad.

Merry Christmas 1966

When we arrived there, we found that we had taken enough brant for dinner and godwit for breakfast, a result which Charlie pronounced to be his best ever.

The whole excursion had been a tribute to his patience, dedication, and organizational skills. Back home in Las Cruces, he showcased his cooking by offering a menu of bland turtle soup, charcoal-grilled brant, Waldorf salad, and wild rice.

You and the kids may have to perform in the Christmas show without me. Charlie says that he's planning to stay on forever, and I am not one to let him suffer alone."

Not for the first time, I marveled at Bing's schizophrenic doublethink. Even as he gently mocked humanity's foibles, he enthusiastically participated in them. No man ever had a keener eye for the absurdities of life, or took a greater delight in playing his part.

Though I remember Charlie Jones primarily as the close friend of Dwight Eisenhower and Richard Nixon, whose presidential flags we often saw flying over his neighboring home, for Bing he would always remain the doughty campaigner against the artful brant.

Oh yes, in spite of his threats, my hunter did return in time to prepare what was to be the prototype of all the Crosby family specials to come. The children reveled in the elaborate production numbers, and a very merry Christmas was had by all.

Singing *Teamwork* before an ancient Egyptian

1967

The first weeks of January passed in a blur, with Bing in Tinseltown, churning out episodes of the Hollywood Palace, and me at home with the children, pruning the rose trees to a fair-thee-well, and practicing piano for reasons that I dared not entrust to the vagrant breeze.

On January 19th, we went down to Pebble Beach for Bing's tournament. After two days of hard work, he relaxed at dinner with friends on Saturday night. Toward the end of the evening, he waxed contemplative, and took to staring hypnotically at the pear in his brandy bottle, and asking himself how it got there.

After indignantly rejecting my practical suggestion that the distillers had simply blown the bottle around it, he resolved the problem of its exit, if not its entry, by draining the receptacle, dashing it into the fireplace with a chivalric cry of "To the Queen," and solemnly ingesting the entire pear with a right good appetite.

We bade our bemused hosts farewell, and were making a beeline for the waiting car when a four-foot hedge had the temerity to intervene. Bing eyed his adversary warily, feinted once, and launched himself into the air. Since he cleared the top of the hedge with inches to spare, I was surprised at the crashing and thrashing that ensued.

Taking the coward's way out, I exited by the adjacent gate, and strode full into a clear understanding of the difficulty: While Bing had accurately estimated the height of the hedge, he had reckoned without its five-foot width. As a consequence, he had sailed

At Palm Beach

triumphantly over the former, only to plunge vaingloriously into the midst of the latter. I extricated him, and pointed him toward our vehicle.

But now it was I who had miscalculated. My saturated husband was not one to admit defeat so easily. At the door of his car, he turned for another view of his adversary.

Sure enough, it was still only four feet high. This time he showed the respect due to a worthy antagonist, taking a longer run, and windmilling his legs in a version of the scissors jump which had been in vogue in his far-off school days.

Once more my champion cleared the barrier with contemptuous ease, and again there was a sound of snapping twigs and thrashing limbs.

Bing was apparently acquainting himself with that basic principal of Newtonian physics which states, in part, that a hedge is precisely as wide from south to north as it was from north to south.

At this point, even I fully expected to see whatever was left of Bing exiting sedately through the gate. I came face to face with my mistake when a dark silhouette suddenly appeared above the barrier, poised there for one glorious moonlit moment, and then, in obedience to another of those Newtonian constructs, disappeared into the bowels of the hedge.

This time I actually succeeded in maneuvering my disgruntled spouse into the car, and drove hastily away to the tune of, "It tricked me the first time by concealing most of the jump, and it was the same going back. By the third time, I'd taken its measure, and I'd have cleared it too, if my foot hadn't slipped on the takeoff.

Let's go back. I'll shed my shoes, and time my approach for an earlier jump, combined with a western roll."

The following morning, I was still in the doghouse for my flat refusal to return to the scene of Bing's moonlight Olympics. As their erstwhile star interrupted his checking of the final tournament pairings to shoot the occasional accusing glance at me over his Ben Franklin glasses, I failed to recognize, in daylight's Dickensian curmudgeon, the figure of my erstwhile airborne nocturnal sprite.

After an interlude in the snow at Rising River Ranch, I accompanied my sister to Florida, to present a style show for Jean Louis. The miracle of jet travel presented us with a number of sharp contrasts, separated by our few hours in a plane.

White snow geese yielded to pink flamingos, the stormy summits of Shasta and Lassen to serene, golden beaches, the contemplative gaze of our cattle to the appraising stares of society matrons, rugged simplicity to sybaritic luxury.

To the charity luncheons, Rose Kennedy and her set wore their "barbecue jewelry," consisting of the colored stones, such as emeralds, rubies, and sapphires. Diamonds were reserved for formal evening functions.

The largest I ever saw was worn by Walter Annenburg's sister, and was later to be purchased by Richard Burton for Liz Taylor.

When I admired it, the proud though plain possessor smiled with smug satisfaction and confided, "I just call it the equalizer."

Frances Ruth and I were being properly spoiled by breakfast in bed and frozen daiquiris in the pool. So of

In the palmettos

Dr. Denton Cooley and visiting mendicant

course Bing chose that moment to arrive, and to take his protesting hedonists hunting.

In and out among the palmettos we dodged, collecting chiggers, and ostensibly pursuing quail. Bing, however, was more quarry than stalker in the eyes of several of the attending social lionesses.

Apparently laboring under the misapprehension that their cameras rendered them invulnerable, they sprang out from behind thickets at odd moments, and snapped their shutters in a manner ill-calculated to improve our crooner's aim.

Just as he was flushing his first large covey of quail, a corpulent matron bounced up from among the bushes to snap a superb picture of the muzzle of Bing's shotgun, aiming directly down her throat, and of the horrified visage behind it.

"Gotcha!" she shrilled delightedly.

"And very nearly vice versa," Bing sighed grimly, breaking his weapon and removing the shells, as a prelude to abandoning the chase. We flew straight home, where I received a surprise.

After my failure to design a new habit for the Immaculate Heart Nuns, I hadn't awaited a second appointment as wardrobe consultant, but greatness was suddenly thrust upon me.

The precarious financial position of their college had forced every board member and administrator to go begging again, and all wished to be appropriately attired.

In retrospect, I surmise that I had been sought out more for my social contacts than for my aesthetic judgment, but I was absurdly gratified at the time. I first flew my little group of academics to Houston, where I shepherded them through the aisles of the city's leading department stores, introducing my aging charges to the wonders of twentieth-century female apparel.

Touching indeed were their responses to brassieres, panties, girdles, slips, and nylon stockings; and then came the rainbow colors of dresses and suits.

I was only sorry that Bing couldn't join us. After all, he was financing the entire purchasing spree, and I was confident that he'd have considered his money well spent.

Mindful of my previous abortive fund-raising sortie into Texas, this time I had planned with care, and I was sure that I could get within hailing distance of a few tycoons.

To be sure, my first billionaire smoothly parried my clumsy efforts to get his name on the dotted line, but he did agree to introduce me into the prestigious Houston Country Club, where I could unveil my acolytes in all their new-found loveliness.

Into the dinner dance they teetered precariously on their high heels, while I kept a wary eye out for potential victims. My first would-be conquest was the President of Sinclair Oil, but I was soon disillusioned by my resident guide.

"He don't have no money," I was informed succinctly.

"But Sinclair Oil must be a very wealthy corporation."

"The company's rich enough, but he's just a poor salaried man. Y'all keep right on lookin', an' I'll tell ya when to move in and strike."

Denton Cooley, of heart transplant fame, had played in The Crosby a month earlier. He now appeared on the scene, and recognized me.

Sister Anita Caspari out of uniform

"You're really choppin' tall cotton tonight," he observed. "I've just picked up five million for my just cause. It'll be interesting to see how you make out"

He looked on sardonically as I, in spite of the most earnest efforts, met with nothing but failure all evening. But speaking of "making out," I felt that the lion's share of the blame fell squarely upon the pudgy shoulders of Reverend Mother, who consistently rejected a flattering number of invitations to dance from increasingly well-lubricated leading citizens.

When she finally explained to one of her more steadfast swains that she was a nun in civilian dress, he agreeably threw an arm about her waist and trumpeted, "Ok, sister baby, let's you and me cut a rug."

I said it then, and I'll say it now: Reverend Mother's failure to oblige in this one particular could easily have cost the order a million dollars, so I ask you, was hers a true vocation for martyrdom?

As a direct consequence of her uncooperative attitude, we departed with empty purses for our principal target, the Dallas-Fort Worth poverty pocket.

Once there, we first visited billionaire H. L. Hunt in his office. While we shifted uneasily against the palpable springs in his cracked leather chairs, he crossed his legs man-fashion to reveal unmatched socks, depending from exhausted elastic about shoes that had outlived their soles.

"I sure am glad to talk to you about raising money," H. L. smiled broadly. "I never can get enough of it for my own righteous causes. If we're going to save this republic, we'll all have to pitch in and elect us a real president like good old Calvin Coolidge. Now there

was a man who knew how to leave all our problems alone.

'He governs best who governs least. The real business of this country is business.' If you can just get the power of the Catholic Church behind my radio crusade, we'll finally have the funds we need to rid ourselves of the bureaucracy that's strangling our society."

The kindly, grandfatherly eyes twinkled behind the rimless spectacles, and my nuns commiserated with their host on his financial difficulties. At long last, I broke into their explanations of just what the Church could do to help, thanked good Mr. Hunt for his time and counsel, and guided my troops through the door, while they still had the shirts on their backs.

Our advisor's last words were, "You girls are great little old fundraisers, and I know you'll have no trouble finding your money. Y'all come back, and I'll tell you some more about the problems I have getting mine."

The Hunt interview had been straightforward enough, though 180 degrees out of phase. The next was a masterpiece of counter-espionage.

My spies had advised me that Mattie Caruth Bird had just donated two million dollars to the city of Dallas, an act which seemed to place her in the ideal tax bracket and frame of mind for our purpose. It was not until we visited her, that I discovered how seriously I'd been misinformed.

Although some of the facts remain hazy to this day, there is no doubt that she had erected a building to house the world's largest mural, a truly Texas-sized version of the last supper.

A dove, sent as a heavenly messenger, had convinced its creator that he should paint said masterpiece as a

My so-called aesthetic advisors, Sister Helen Kelly and Sister Anita Caspari

permanent memorial to Mrs. Bird's sainted mother.

Mattie had enlisted the aid of some twenty lawyers, accountants, and business managers, to convince me that Bing should purchase it, and donate it to Dallas, for the greater glory of God and a two-million-dollar tax loss.

From the first moment in Mattie's living room, there was no doubt that we were at cross purposes. My vacant gaze strayed to the French windows behind the sofa.

A quick leap, a bounce off the springs, and I would sail Peter-Pan-like into the world of sunlight, with barely a tinkle of broken glass to mark my egress. But my retinue, still scarcely able to maneuver on their high heels, would be left in the lurch.

I turned back to face the music, certain that there was no longer any way to keep me from purchasing a mural the size of a football field, or to hide my crime from Bing, or to pay him back in the next five-hundred years, even assuming that I'd survive for the minutest fraction of that time, after he'd discovered what I'd done.

Oddly enough, it was my innocent associates who rescued me. Mattie had evidently planned to trap and pluck her little pigeon in isolation.

When she saw that I too had a team of counselors, she gazed upon them with the rampant paranoia of the truly deaf, and hissed at her crew, "Who are those other women?"

As soon as I understood how the land lay, I'd scuttled all thought of a plea for funds in favor of bargaining for my life. Now I detected a faint ray of hope, which I promptly pursued to its inexorable conclusion.

"These," I announced firmly, "are my aesthetic advisors. I never purchase a work of art without their approval. Would you mind showing them your masterpiece?"

Glory be to God, it worked. Under cover of my pretext, we beat a hasty retreat out the front door.

To be sure, we were then bundled into the waiting Rolls, but there our surprised hostess found that we outnumbered her.

The Bird retainers were constrained to follow at a respectful distance, while we had her all to ourselves for a lively discussion of religious art, in which the sisters, bless their larcenous little souls, played their assigned roles to perfection.

We arrived at the mural, whose primitive style might best be described as Early Baltimore Catechism.

I oohed and aahed during the entire fifteen minutes that it took me to promenade the length of it, my solemnity disturbed only by the irrepressible giggles from my newly-consecrated artistic authorities.

Fortunately their hilarity failed to disturb Mattie, who delivered her entire harangue with such polished assurance that I was almost persuaded that I was not the first to be offered this golden opportunity to serve God and mammon at one fell stroke.

As the Rolls wound its stately way back to our car and freedom, I conferred gravely with my advisors, who were making heroic efforts to swallow their mirth. "It's your skins too, you know," my stern glance said.

The whole matter of our escape was still uncertain, when we found ourselves once more in the garden with the

Off to Las Cruces

With Monica Yamamoto and Dierdre Buckley

plastic daffodils beside the Bird residence. It seemed that the wheel had come full circle, but this time, thanks be to God, or to Quetzalcoatl, we were not alone.

To our hostess's mild annoyance, we almost trod on her pet boa constrictor, surprised in his version of *flagrante delicto,* with the nether half of a neighbor's pet cat, playfully dangling from his smiling jaws.

We seized upon this fortuitous interruption and fled, reciting a brace of Hail Marys for the cat's departed or departing soul, and suppressing the doubtless sinful reflection, "Better him than us."

During our protracted stay in the Dallas area, I gained access to four charitable organizations and thirty-one millionaires. Most were hospitable, and several expressed what seemed to be genuine interest in the plight of Immaculate Heart College.

Some told amusing stories, while others offered fatherly advice, and promised to keep in touch, but the result was always the same: Nary a penny did we collect.

Indeed, we were beginning to reflect that academic solicitation just wasn't what it was cracked up to be when, passing through Oklahoma on our return trip, we caught sight of the lofty Prayer Tower at Oral Roberts University, and watched in awe as the mail trucks poured in with their cargo of letters, stuffed with crumpled, dirty dollar bills.

"Perhaps," mused Sister Helen, our President, "we could launch some sort of charitable effort from the top of the library. The matter will bear thought. It's obvious that we don't as yet have the knack of campaigning."

Here it was only April, and I'd already seen to most of the needs of God and man. Musing that, as a fund raiser, I seemed cut out to make a splendid wife and mother, I whisked my brood off to Las Cruces, with Bing protesting that if I begged money from any more of his friends, he'd divorce both me and the Church.

I'm not sure whether this last threat stemmed more from the reports of my trip to Texas, or from the fact that the preceding evening between entree and dessert, I had, apropos of nothing at all, asked Dr. Sullivan for ten-million dollars.

"I will not have a friend, who is a guest in my house, treated that way," Bing had stormed.

"But you said that he has lots of money which he has no use for, so what better charity could he choose?"

"Suppose we let him decide that."

I assented glumly, knowing what the decision would be. I was becoming an old hand at this failure business.

Speaking of which, I was recruiting reinforcements for our Mexican pilgrimage, in spite of Bing's dim view of their prospects for survival. Since I well knew that I couldn't endure another spring of his children without considerable assistance, I turned a deaf ear to his warnings, and insisted on enlisting two trusty lieutenants.

Since Bridget Brennan, still exhausted from her previous tour in Las Cruces, had begged to be furloughed to the lighter task of spring cleaning in Hillsborough, I had chosen my brace of stalwarts to fill the hole which her desertion had left in my defensive armor.

Dierdre Buckley, a countrywoman of hers, was to replace her as governess, while Monica Yamamoto, a sturdy

A bird's-eye view of Rancho Las Cruces

Japanese nutritionist from my adopted Immaculate Heart College, was to serve the dual functions of supplanting the redoubtable Brunhilde, and of spelling Dierdre in her inevitable moments of dark defeat.

Brunhilde had left our employ after narrowly losing a heroic, single-handed struggle to subjugate all other members of the staff. Rumor had it that this failure of The Third Reich had been only temporary, and that she now ruled a new household with her customary persuasive force.

Bing's misgivings had derived from the fact that I was importing two attractive young ladies into a setting where they would have absolutely nothing to do in their leisure hours. Of course I saw no impediment there, since I counted on our children to prevent them from having any.

Monica, in particular, was initially overwhelmed by the exuberant disorder of our kitchen, and the wholesale want of direction from me.

Our first few days were another of those Mexican standoffs, in the course of which I looked forward to being surprised by her menus, while she waited patiently for me to tell her what to prepare.

Monica had a personality so authoritarian that it made even Brunhilde's look like a monument to free will. When I invited her to replace Dierdre temporarily, on a drive up the arroyo to collect cacti with the children, she packed neither food nor water, a fact which we discovered only at our noon stop, when we were already famished and perishing of thirst in a rocky desert. Her only excuse was to insist self-righteously that she "had had no orders."

True to Bing's prediction, if not his reasoning, Monica slipped into a deepening depression, which turned suicidal when I tried to distract her by assigning more hours with the children.

In an effort to vary her routine, I then invited her to accompany me on my expeditions to inoculate the locals and to collect shells, but somehow stabbing natives and washing murexes didn't quite cut it either.

Finally I flew her to La Paz, for an appointment with a physician who had previously proved more than helpful to my menage.

The results were electrifying. That very evening, the banging of pots in the kitchen would have done credit to Brunhilde in her heyday. In an orgy of creative cooking, tasty oriental delicacies poured from an apparently bottomless cornucopia.

The following morning, Monica tore the children from their beds, fed them a series of unrecognizable but obviously palatable dishes, and raced them off to the beach, to return well after noon, dragging her reeling and exhausted charges behind her.

Now this was something like it. Had our murderous little perpetual-motion machines finally met their match? Could I at last rest in peace?

No, Monica had simply discovered the charms of pep pills. Sadly she was soon to learn of their limitations, as the children delightedly spent the next days testing the endurance of the only adult who had ever shown the slightest inclination to keep up with them.

Something had to give, and finally it was a thin, pale, and desperate Monica who begged me for a one-way passage back to San Francisco.

With Rosemary Clooney and my progeny

When last reported, the coward had escaped to the Philippines, where as a missionary social worker, she reported that, compared to dealing with our cheerful little psychopaths, running an orphanage full of Tagalog tykes was an endless, blissful vacation.

It is indeed an ill wind that blows no good. Dierdre had availed herself of the temporary respite from the children, provided by Monica's euphoria, to fall desperately in love.

Given the lack of eligible males in the immediate vicinity, this in itself was evidence of both ingenuity and determination.

The object of her affections was a pint-sized Mexican entrepreneur, upon whom our Celtic Amazon had cast her wandering eye while he was fulfilling a contract at our hotel.

Nothing would do but that she must meet her cavalier for a big night in the city, and this involved persuading me to convince Bing that we could somehow manage the children without her, while our driver bounced the truck for three hours over the trackless waste that separated us from La Paz, awaited the lady's pleasure, and reversed the procedure to carry her home.

I lent Dierdre my only available evening dress, and well nigh fitted her into it by dint of ignoring all but the most essential fasteners. "You'll just have to give up eating and breathing," I warned her practically.

In an effort to forget her hunger pains, Dierdre devoted the morning of her great day to playing catch with Nathaniel. It was almost noon when I heard the first fateful shriek from the direction of the beach.

Looking out, I saw that our governess had abandoned her charges, and

was racing headlong toward me. When Dierdre fell sobbing through the door, her problem was immediately apparent. One of Nathaniel's "high, hard ones" had struck her in the mouth, leaving her lips swollen and beginning to bleed.

Moreover it had also broken off the stumps which formerly supported her capped incisors. She had only an unsightly, blackened hole where her two front teeth should have been.

Desperately I sought for words of comfort, as I applied an ice pack: "Carlos wears dark glasses night and day," I ventured. "I doubt that he'll see more than vague outlines in the dim light of a nightclub."

"Do you really think so? Would you go anyway?"

"Of course," I lied gamely.

Thus it was with mixed feelings that I watched our truck drive off into the blazing desert sunlight, with Dierdre installed to the right of the driver, half into my Jean Louis gown, which the heat had already transformed into a sodden mess.

It was long after bedtime when our voyager returned, and I didn't dare wake Bing by sneaking out to greet her, so I had to contain my curiosity until the following morning.

While the children swam, I found Dierdre seated on the beach, gazing dreamily out to sea. Since she seemed unaware of my approach, it was incumbent upon me to break the silence.

"Well, how did it go?" I inquired apprehensively.

Dierdre returned from a great distance, slowly focusing her violet orbs until she finally gave some sign of recognizing me.

Harry, Maria Ferrar, Juan Geraldo, Mary Frances, and Nathaniel

"It was wonderful," she then breathed. "Just wonderful."

"Really?" I gasped with mixed relief and bewilderment. "Would you care to tell me all about it?"

"Well, I met Carlos at Los Cocos, and sure enough he had his dark glasses on. It was still so light that I was afraid to open my mouth, so I just talked out of the side of it like this."

Whereupon, with the long purplish bruise from Nathaniel's pitch stretched tight over her upper jaw, she gave a creditable imitation of one of my patients with an uncorrected hare lip and cleft palate.

"Good thinking," I applauded.

She rewarded me with a wide, black grin, for now my voice rang with sincerity. Given the alternative, the hare lip was certainly my choice.

Dierdre resumed her narrative: "He invited me for a drink, so I asked if we could sit on the terrace and watch the beautiful sunset. I thought that would dazzle his eyes, and keep him from seeing me clearly. After that, we went in to dinner."

"Dinner?" I gasped. "How did you manage it?"

"I just chewed with my back teeth."

"Why didn't I think of that?"

"Then we went to the hotel's night-club, where it was so dark that I couldn't see his face. I knew that he hadn't taken off his glasses, so I was sure that I was safe."

"Didn't they turn up the lights from time to time?"'

"Yes, but he always seemed to be applying chapstick or combing his hair. At first I was worried about the dancing, but the music was so great that I really got into it, broke a heel, and had to kick my shoes off. After

that it went even better, since I'm so much taller than he is.

I did have a bad moment when someone blew smoke in my face, making me cough until I broke that last hook on your dress. But I didn't say a word to Carlos. I just ran back into the kitchen, and borrowed a safety pin.

When I came back, he hadn't even missed me. He was still dancing in the dark all by himself. I'm in love. He's just beautiful."

"Did you tell him so?"

"Oh yes, again and again."

"Then I guess that was all that was necessary. You did your part."

I reflected that the truly self-sufficient Latin Don Juan, wrapped in his protective blanket of narcissism, had no real need of a girl. A mirror would satisfy all his ego needs, and cause far fewer problems.

Dierdre would never marry her prince from La Paz, but she would make some lucky Irishman a noble wife. In the interim, she alone of all the past and present candidates for governess, was equipped to take on our little terrors, and fight them to a draw. This girl was a trump.

With her help, I gradually evolved the Crosby version of an academic schedule.

It was comprised of breakfast, two hours of recess, consisting largely of racing across the beach with Dierdre, one hour of the Sullivan Spanish program for all hands, including her, Bing, and myself, lunch, two more hours of baseball and bashing around with Dierdre, designed, like the morning session, to tire pupils to the point where they would sit still, and to permit teacher and spouse to escape for recess periods of their own, and finally

With neighbor Thea Bacon

basics such as English, history, and math, until dinner time.

We had some excitement the third week, when the propeller of our new fishing boat broke off, and we found ourselves playing games with some very rocky cliffs. After repairs were made, I caught a palometa, a very rare fish which even the Mexicans were hard put to identify, because they had never before boated one.

Bing beamed with pride, and devoted weeks of research to determining whether the proper English name was *yellow jack, Pacific permit,* or *California permit.* He sent pictures to the International Women's Game Fishing Association, and I received in return a pin, which reminded me of those that I used to earn in Sunday school for memorizing verses from the Bible.

Meanwhile I had focused on the fact that the fish was delicious. In truth, we had always enjoyed all the sea food we could eat in Las Cruces, including superb shell fish of every variety, but we lacked such nonessentials as meat, eggs, dairy products, fresh fruit, and vegetables, all of which were practically unknown on our arid peninsula.

Since the children indignantly refused to drink powdered milk, for several years I'd been nagging Bing to buy a cow. He was businesslike enough to realize that we'd have nothing but cactus to feed it, so I finally settled for improving our level of nutrition by planting a vegetable garden.

To care for it, Bing imported a plump, engaging, old farmer, who was overjoyed to find that, for the first time in his life, he had ample water available for irrigation.

In no time, with the aid of our desert sun, we had a magnificent spread of carrots, melons, radishes, onions, tomatoes, and zucchini, which sufficed both to feed our little household, and to supply all the guests at the hotel.

The children considered our farmer to be the greatest thing since popcorn. His only English consisted of a grinning, "Hokey dokey, madám," and it amused them to hear him apply the expression indiscriminately to them, to Bing, or to me, as the occasion demanded.

Sadly, they were destined to lose their new-found friend. Lack of water had made the tourist business in our area precarious at best.

By some miracle, the hotel suddenly had a full house, but nary a drop of water to mix with a fisherman's bourbon, not to mention cook his food, or wash the soap out of his long-suffering wife's hair.

Like an avenging fury, the manager rushed forth to ferret out our irrigation system, which just happened to utilize all the water hitherto destined for his establishment.

Thus was our hero expelled from the very Garden of Eden that he had newly created. The children had no time to mourn his passing, because they were promptly drafted into a race to eat as many vegetables as possible, before the latter expired for want of the *agua* which had been diverted back to the needs of the hotel.

For years thereafter, Bing and I found it hard to look a vegetable in the face, and our offspring have yet to make the slightest effort to do so.

A new partner in the hotel was Desi Arnaz, who had loaned substantial funds to our local developer, and had thus received permission to construct, for his latest wife, a lovely home with a Moorish tower, a guitar-shaped swim-

Bing and Desi

ming pool, and a gazebo overlooking the blue waters of the Sea of Cortés.

Bing viewed Desi as an ideal neighbor, who never tired of taking the children fishing, showing them how to prepare delicious Cuban dishes, and teaching them to sing naughty Spanish songs. Desi became a fixture at the club, where he loved to entertain the guests, who without exception found his ebullient Latin charm irresistible.

Unfortunately, after a certain number of drinks, Desi couldn't resist himself either. With inexhaustible energy and a voice that shook the most remote residences, he would accompany himself on the guitar until dawn, refusing to let anyone leave the party.

It was an act that would have cost our fishermen dearly at a leading nightclub, but for serious sportsmen, who customarily breakfasted at 5 AM, an evening or two of such entertainment was quite enough.

No one realized this more clearly than Desi, who was always contrite when he awoke the following afternoon, and back at the bar with his guitar that same evening.

"Desi's not drinking any more," his wife Edie informed Bing one morning.

"No," agreed Bing solemnly, "nor any less either."

At the end of April, I flew to La Paz, to visit my former pupils and their disgruntled mothers, who constituted the remains of my political action unit, now that their male counterparts had reverted to scab labor.

At the request of the group's leader, I received at the airport an innocuous-looking package, which had apparently just been smuggled in from Los Angeles by an Aero-Naves stewardess.

After delivering it, and inspecting the children, who regrettably seemed to be thriving without the benefit of my inestimable assistance, I discussed the adoption of my former star reader by a stateside couple, before retreating disconsolately to interfere elsewhere.

A week later, Bing returned from La Paz with a brow of thunder. "You've really torn it this time," he began. "How could even you ever imagine doing such a thing? You, a wife, a mother, and a devout Catholic."

My more recent transgressions were far too numerous to permit of an immediate reaction. Lest I confess to any hitherto perfect crimes, I requested that my spouse try to be a trifle more specific.

"You smuggled all those coil things in from Los Angeles. Was that really the best use you could find for your medical contacts?"

Zounds, this was poetic justice at its worst. I was being accused of a crime that I hadn't got around to committing yet. "What coil things?" I demanded, all outraged innocence, and preparing to counterattack.

"You know perfectly well. Don't play the simpleton with me. The quack has confessed, and his only excuse was that it had to be all right if Mrs. Crosby was in on it."

Curiouser and curiouser. "Which quack is that?" I next inquired in genuine bewilderment.

"The one who puts those things wherever they go. Installs them, if that's the word for it."

Half an hour of patient questioning elicited the following information: The package that I had received from the stewardess had contained two-hundred intrauterine devices, which were of

With Nathaniel and Cindy

course prohibited in Mexico. A physician, sympathetic to the plight of young and often single women, unable to support their herds of children, had agreed to insert the coils if they were delivered into his hands.

To circumvent customs, I had been chosen as the unwitting bagman. As a result, with their finely developed sense of justice, the local ecclesiastics were voting to excommunicate Bing.

The fact that we both sympathized with the plight of the poor women who had victimized me, simply made matters worse. Caught in the middle, we could find no plot of ground on which to make a stand.

Unable to concoct a plausible story, Bing finally settled for the truth. He informed all the authorities, civil and ecclesiastic, that his wife was *muy obstinada,* and therefore not to be held responsible for her actions.

As a dialectical consequence, her husband could hardly be called to account either. This was doubtless the only explanation that would have satisfied Mexican males, who shook their heads, and admitted sadly that they had wives of their own.

Not for the first time, Bing had come to the conclusion that I badly needed a keeper, so he included me in his fishing expeditions throughout the month of May.

Since this activity conflicted with certain clandestine plans of my own, I feigned seasickness so impressively that I even now become giddy at the mere sight of a boat.

This led to a compromise. I still had to be isolated from worldly temptations, so instead of leaving me at home, Bing accepted me as a passenger until we reached choppy water, or I turned a becoming shade of chartreuse, whichever came first.

He then abandoned me, Robinson Crusoe fashion, with my beach bag and my dog Cindy, on the nearest tropic isle. There I was to read, sun myself, and comb the beach for gastropods until his return at day's end.

But alack my trusting jailer had never thought to examine the contents of my beach bag.

Tucked away, under a novel or two and a manual of marine life, lay my script of *The Guardsman,* the Molnar play which Alfred Lunt and Lynne Fontaine had made famous.

Throughout it, the heroine plays a Chopin nocturne, a fact which, as I had hitherto confided only to Cindy, had led to all that practice on the piano earlier in the year.

Now I was faced with the serious task of learning my role, so up and down the strand I strode, declaiming to the sun, the sand, the cacti, the gastropods, and Cindy, all of whom had suddenly become the occupants and furnishings of a Viennese drawing room, and one of whom barked enthusiastic applause whenever I outdid myself.

On May 29th, Bing and I flew in a friend's plane from Las Cruces to San Francisco. On the way, he discussed his plans for a summer vacation in Europe so enthusiastically that my poor heart grew cold.

As soon as we arrived home, I decided that I'd best face the music:

"Bing, I have something to tell you, if you'll promise not to be cross."

"OK, what is it?"

"Don't act so suspicious."

Those eyes of arctic blue continued to glare daggers at me. Could he be recalling certain similar scenes?

Jean-Louis' opera gown for *The Guardsman,*
which my daughter was later to wear for her wedding

"If you don't promise not to be angry, I won't tell you."

"All right, all right, tell me for God's sake. I promise not to fly off the handle."

So I told him that I had contracted for eight weeks of *The Guardsman* at the Drury Lane Theater in Chicago, and he was furious! All of which just goes to show that you never can trust a man.

Bing left on June 3rd for a month in Europe, and I straightway fell into bed with pneumonia. In a pinch, I could play the liberated woman, but only at grave hazard to my health. Now mine was a soul in conflict.

To be sure, after my two-and-seventy catastrophes in Europe the previous year, I had no further desire to discover Molly MacNeal awaiting me at the airport in London. "Let her keep to her side of the Atlantic," I fumed chauvinistically, "and I will stick to mine."

On the other hand, I would miss my husband mightily, and I had yet to score what might be termed a definitive triumph in the theatrical world. Enmeshed between the Persian spears and the sea-wet rock, this apprentice Spartan took to her trundle bed, and gasped her lungs out.

Bing's first letter was dated June 3rd, from in flight aboard Lufthansa:

"I always seem to be leaving home with deep misgivings, mostly about you. Please stop agreeing to do everything that others demand.

Never say *yes* until you've decided that the commitment is appropriate for you. And for God's sake leave yourself time for rest.

Now please find my air-travel credit card, which is somewhere in my desk. You'd best send it to the Connaught Hotel, because I don't know where I'm going from there.

Before I sign off, let me reiterate my plea: Don't let the charlatans and phonies use you. It's degrading!

PS. If you're still experiencing difficulty with that piano solo, why don't you just play *Claire de Lune*. It's similar in type, and at least you know it.

June 7th: Sorry to hear that your pulmonary malaise lingers on. Check out all possibilities of infection. Some of the women you treated in Mexico could have been carrying almost anything.

I taped the Evan Andrews TV show Sunday with Bob Hope. The big race is today, and Paddy is wildly optimistic, but the favorite looks unbeatable.

Our horse has lots of personality, but he's just too small. I hope he runs creditably, because he's been made second favorite, and we'll have to slink out of town if he doesn't finish in the money.

June 11th: Arrived in Marbella from London yesterday. Circled the Rock of Gibraltar as we approached the airstrip. The whole area is quiet, with tiny houses, poor roads, and no industry, but the hotel and golf course are simply magnificent.

I had four birdies, and beat a pleasant Englishman out of lunch. I'll drive to Algeciras for mass tonight. It seems odd to attend church at 8 PM, but no one dines here before 11.

June 14th: I hear that, back in London, Dominion Day's race was a mystery. He was listless in the saddling ring, ran the same way, and wasn't even breathing hard upon his return to the paddock.

Unfortunately, huge sums had been bet on him. After what happened in France, Paddy was loath to mention it,

Sinbad remembered

but he believes that the horse had been administered a sedative. I mention this only because you're not here to shout it to the press.

By the way, your last letter speaks of *pressure* and of *punishment.* As you must recall, I informed you months ago that I was planning to spend the summer in Europe.

You elected to perform in *The Guardsman,* instead of coming with me. Please explain how that makes me the author of any pressure that you may choose to feel.

You also asked me what I want you to do. I believe I've made that clear from the outset. Obviously I refuse to play the boss, and forbid you to go where you will and do what you wish. But I had hoped that you might occasionally consider my advice, if only because I've been around this planet somewhat longer.

It does gall me when you speak of my trying to break you, as if anyone could. Am I really such a heavy? Do I deserve such treatment?"

Yes, on all counts. Was this reasonable and considerate creature the same man who had stormed out of the house hell-bent for Europe, a month early, without clothes, money, travel card, or anything to do when he arrived?

Yet it's certainly true that he saw clearly the defects in my character to which I was oblivious at the time, while I'd developed into something of an expert on the subject of his personality quirks. We are all so quick to sense another's flaws, and so stubbornly blind to our own.

"June 17th: I have no clue to your whereabouts, so I trust that this will be forwarded to you. I pulled a muscle in my neck while playing golf with Alex

Hohenlowe (the prince who had married Honeychile Wilder). A couple of martinis, three pain pills, and a jar of magic liniment got me home.

I won't, however, be able to stay to see el Cordobés fight, because I'm scheduled to visit a neurologist in London on Monday. It's sad to abandon the quaint little Moorish towns of Andalucía, where everyone remembers you and your delightful role in *The Seventh Voyage of Sinbad.* When they ask for you, I have to tell them that you are off fulfilling yourself."

Ouch! At that very moment, I was hauling myself up out of a sickbed to cohost the Mike Douglas Show. Fully determined that it and I must go on, I appeared in Philadelphia that Monday, and stayed with it all week, thin, pale, haggard, and hoarse, but nonetheless demonstrably there.

I interviewed Rosemary Clooney, and we sang a duet. I then wrote Bing to ask if he would put her on one of his forthcoming specials.

"She needs the kind of presentation that you can offer her," I insisted. "Showcase her once, and she'll be off like a skyrocket. By the way, she adores you so that I can't for the life of me understand why I haven't plunged a knife into her.

On another tack, Bridget is still saying novenas for Dominion Day's Irish Derby performance."

"June 19th: I was happy to hear from you, and to be reassured that you're still among the living. Royal Ascot offers a splendid spectacle just before the first race, as the reigning family comes driving down the straight in six hansom coaches.

I had a drink with Princess Margaret in the royal box, and informed

Dominion Day winning the Blandford Stakes

her that you were off earning my betting money.

I've scratched Dominion Day from the Derby. Paddy says he's not himself, which leads me to wonder just who he thinks he is, but in any event he's too good a horse to run when he's not right. I'll cancel Ireland, play some golf in the Lake Country, and then head on back to Hillsborough."

On June 22nd, I flew to Chicago with my mother, Bridget, and Nathaniel. The producer had wanted me to bring all three children, and to write in a new opening scene in which they, in the roles of my little niece and nephews, played angelically about the drawing room, while I mercilessly banged out my étude on the piano.

Fortunately he accepted my admission that I was in no position to guarantee the desired behavior. I had conjured up visions of Nathaniel leaping into the laps of frightened first-row spectators, while Mary Frances captured center stage, determined to play all the roles in a tight little tragedy of her own devising, and Harry saved the day from backstage by shorting out the lights.

This year, an addition to my dressing room had indeed converted it into something almost worthy of being termed a star's apartment, albeit an extraordinarily small one. In it, our little group dwelt like so many sardines during the eight-week run.

Since ours was a dinner theater, the proprietor was in a position to spoil us by furnishing all the food we could eat, largely southern-fried, thanks to the origin of his chef.

This sat well enough with my mother and me, who had teethed on worse, and of course Nathaniel could digest old boots and nails. But in Bridget's case, the sudden excess of fats brought on a series of gall-bladder attacks, which added high drama to the off-stage aspects of my performance.

Bridget was in charge of my coiffure and wardrobe. In the course of the play, she had to redo my hair three times, and to help me through six rapid wardrobe changes. At first this routine occasioned considerable mutual distress, but in time we both familiarized ourselves with the drill.

Bridget let down my hair, while mumbling a Hail Mary in a cold sweat, ironed a dress, while propped up in a corner, and helped me on with it quickly, before doubling up in agony.

Three weeks into the run, this routine became less stressful, as she learned to forego our customary breakfasts of fried chicken, sausages, bacon and biscuits.

Otherwise rehearsals and performances proceeded surprisingly smoothly, with a strong cast and a competent director. I'd been worried about the leading lady, who was facing a challenging role while still weak from her recent illness. But as I got into the swing of things, my only real difficulty lay in the schizophrenic split between my roles as actress and pianist.

It took all my mental energy to play the Chopin étude passably, and this left nothing available for my histrionics. On the other hand, a sparkling performance seemed to drain the music right out of my fingers.

I can't say that I ever resolved this conflict, but toward the end I succeeded in effecting a more equitable apportionment of my all-too-scarce resources.

Meanwhile, having found his horse to be about as dependable as his

With Bridget Brennan, and Alan and Norma Fisher

woman (I told you he had a way of picking winners.), Bing arrived home from England on June 30th.

His first letter complained that I'd been ignoring him (I wrote only once a day.), and described the 4th of July celebration at the Burlingame Country Club: "Mary Frances took two thirds in the swimming races. Not bad considering that she was competing against boys twice her size. In sports, as in all things, she seems to have the poor louts mesmerized.

She really rubbed it into Harry, who couldn't compete because of all those stitches in his chin from falling off his bike." (My God, what stitches, and for that matter, what bike?)

These are the raw materials of a heart attack for a mother two thousand miles away. On the other hand, a complaint was hardly in order, lest it elicit awkward questions as to just why I wasn't at home with my eldest in his hour of need.

"I shot a 72 in the afternoon tournament," Bing continued, "and took the kids to a fireworks display in the evening. It commenced well enough, with about thirty children lined up to take regular turns setting off their cherry bombs and skyrockets.

However, in spite of frantic parental attempts to preserve order, the scene became increasingly chaotic. All too soon, we were reenacting the Battle of the Bulge.

Only the intervention of Divine Providence averted widespread mayhem and subsequent incineration, as the antagonists fired away at each other with Roman candle 'bazookas,' and hurled cherry bomb 'grenades.'

Diving into the thick of the fray, I retrieved our three recalcitrants, and dragged them off kicking, screaming, and protesting that they were giving better than they got.

July 10th: Harry was so excited over his forthcoming visit to the ranch that he rose at 4 AM to mess up his suitcases.

Air West precipitated a crisis by rejecting his stingray bicycle, but I resourcefully removed the wheels, and found a spot for it. He refused to let anyone touch his guitar, which he carried around his neck, or his bag, on which he sat.

I'm taping a TV show on the 24th, and the director arrived yesterday. Of course Mary Frances spotted a potential conquest, and had him convinced that she was just perfect for the daughter's role before I finally appeared to rescue him.

She has also decided that she is going to Hawaii. When I objected that I had planned to travel alone, she announced firmly that she had been packed for a week.

I seized upon the lack of a governess for her, but she rejected that lame excuse, informing me that she is a big girl now, who doesn't need a babysitter.

July 14th: On the flight to Hawaii, I had to entertain the stewardesses (much against his will, no doubt), while Mary Frances tripped up forward to regale the crew with endless riddles and one-liners such as the following:

'I have a goat that has no nose. How does it smell?

Terrible.

Did you take a bath last night?

No, is one missing?'

Your daughter also disclosed a surprising number of zealously guarded and hitherto unrevealed family secrets. We must henceforth bite our tongues in

With Pearl Bailey

the presence of that young lady, or consider removing hers.

She'll do anything to please an audience. Sounds familiar somehow. Must be something in the genes, or perhaps in the water.

My sore eyetooth kicked up on the plane, so upon landing we raced to Honakao, a plantation village of 500 people, where a genial product of the Northwestern School of Dentistry performed a root canal to relieve the pressure on an abscess.

I emerged from my ordeal to find Mary Frances garbed in a lavender mumu and a pair of Hawaiian slippers, gifts from some new friends to whom she was teaching the words and music to *Secret Agent Man*. She insisted that I be included in the ensuing photo session, with my jaw swollen like that of an inept pugilist after ten rounds with Rocky Graziano.

For dinner, Mary Frances wore her new mumu and a ginger lei, and did her own hair in a loose-flowing arrangement which she evidently conceived to be Polynesian. She effortlessly captured the maître d'hôtel, but somewhere between the hors-d'oeuvres and the soup, an overwhelming lassitude finally set in.

It was midnight at home, and it's easy to forget that our imperious woman of the world is still only seven years old. After her nose dipped into the rice pilaf for the third time, I carried her straight off to bed.

The following day, I played eighteen holes with Nelson Rockefeller and a couple of professionals, while Mary Frances bounced around in an outrigger with his daughter Melinda. The local pro tried to match our best ball, but we easily beat him for the drinks.

We also dined with the Rockefellers. Happy is doing a wonderful job of directing the activities of a clutch of offspring, aged seven to seventeen, some his, some hers, and the remainder jointly owned.

After dinner, the hotel sponsored a luau. I performed briefly, before Mary Frances stole the show with a series of outrageous jokes and a libelous song about her teacher.

The old order changeth, yielding place to new. You and I had best be prepared to cede our spot to this representative of the now generation.

(Indeed we had. Things had progressed to a point where even a poor dimwitted male noticed.)

"Mary Frances is always picking things up. She made a bad choice this morning when she seized upon a sea urchin, which of course stung her in the hand, whereupon she dropped it onto her bare foot, only to be stung again.

She is showing the marks to everyone in the dining room, retelling the story in graphic if exaggerated detail, dramatizing her every response, and coquettishly marveling at her miraculous survival.

July 17th: I'm happy to hear that your performance is garnering such rave reviews.

Mary Frances is inviting everyone she meets to lunch with us, and eating like a stevedore herself.

I anticipated jubilation when she heard that she had the part in my TV show, but she simply accepted it as her acknowledged right.

July 24th: We're back in Tinseltown, and 'Princess Papooli' is having a glorious time, with hairdressers, wardrobe ladies, and of course the director hovering over her.

With Governor Connally and friendly director

With Roone Arledge, Phil Harris, and Bill Holden

She's lapping it all up, and lunching and swimming with Maria Ferrer between rehearsals.

I, on the other hand, am having my troubles with the sponsor. He is a cigarette manufacturer, and I'm playing a victim of throat cancer. He wants me to settle for another malady, and of course I refuse.

The fault is mine for not inquiring at the outset where the funds came from. If I'd known that it was a tobacco company, I'd never have accepted the job.

July 29th: Last night Mary Frances demanded that we dine in a place where she could devour 'about forty snails loaded with garlic.' So I chose a French restaurant, where the little glutton almost made good her boast.

By the way, did you know that she had planned to inaugurate an apiary at Hillsborough? As we were climbing aboard the plane in Honolulu, I noticed a hollowed-out stick, which she had hitherto concealed amidst her luggage.

In my case, age may not have brought wisdom, but it has bred suspicion. 'What's that?' I asked.

'Just a stick.'

'Is there something in the stick?'

'Nothing important.'

'Would you mind telling me just what is so unimportant?'

'Yes.'

'Tell me anyway.'

'A queen bumblebee.'

'Well, you can't take it with you.'

'Why not?'

'Because the United States' health authorities won't allow it.'

'That's all right. They won't know.'

'The airline won't allow it either.'

'So I won't tell them.'

'But I will.'

'Why?'

'Because it might come out of that hollow branch, and buzz around the cabin until three or four elderly ladies die of shock.'

'The airlines are ridiculous, the health department is full of idiots, and even my own father is against me.'

Nevertheless I played the role of Roman father. (Surprise! I'd expected him to buy her the airlines.)

"When, in the face of screaming protests, I shook the queen out of the stick, she proved to be about the size of a field mouse, but lethargic, and apparently harmless.

Mary Frances insisted that she was going to carry her bee back onto the plane in her pocket. When I prevented that, she demanded that we take it twenty miles down the coast to leave it where she had found it. At this point, it was I who in bewilderment asked *why?*

'So she can be with her friends.'

'We don't have time for a drive. We'll have to release her here, where she can find new friends.'

There ensued a wild temper tantrum, with high-pitched wailing, rivers of tears, much stamping of small feet, and finally holding of breath, with consequent lavender cast of countenance.

Somehow my terror of bureaucratic authority made me stick to my guns, so unless the brat has tricked me again, the queen is still holding court at the airport in Hawaii.

This morning, I rehearsed with your daughter for a couple of hours, but it's rather rough sledding. She is letter perfect in her own part, but she devotes so much energy to correcting me on mine that she has little left for dramatic interpretation.

August 4th: I'm penning this from the St. Regis Hotel in New York City,

Roone and Phil à la Julia Childs

In the blinds

The Governor and the chef

Cheyenne's Clint Walker

whence Phil Harris, Clint Walker, Texas Governor John Connally, and I are on our way to Africa for *The American Sportsman*.

Sorry I couldn't find time to stop off on my way past Chicago."

Hah! So he thought *he* was sorry! I'd invited his relatives and friends to join him at the play, and I had the entire cast swooning at the thought of his attendance.

I therefore suggested that they write notes, expressing their disappointment, all of which I tucked in with the letter wherein I dropped my own bombshell:

"Mother Humiliata and I are leaving for Rome on August 26th. If you pass by Italy on your return from Africa, we can rendezvous there, vacation together for two glorious weeks, and still arrive in Montreal for Expo '67 by September 29th."

"August 7th: As a consequence of the 5,000 foot elevation here in Nairobi, it feels cooler than the actual fifty-degree temperature. Tomorrow we fly to Arusha in Tanzania, and then drive to our safari camp.

The camera men are planning to film Phil Harris, cooking grouse and making cornbread. He swears that he's finally going to hit the big time by replacing Julia Child.

August 12th: Shades of Ernest Hemingway. We are camping at the foot of Mount Kilimanjaro, rising at 5 AM, and driving for two hours in Land Rovers over roads that compare unfavorably with our La Paz to Las Cruces freeway.

Upon arrival, we sit in blinds, and try to pick off sand grouse as they fly into the water holes. The fun comes when, like children at recess, we abandon the cameras to snipe away at guinea fowl and francolin.

Governor Connally has shot his lion for the film, and a leopard to boot. Meanwhile *Cheyenne's* Clint Walker was scheduled to shoot a cape buffalo.

Day before yesterday, his keepers established Clint in a blind, shooed beast after beast in front of him, and watched him miss. Yesterday they repeated the experience.

But the first time that Walker fired today, two animals dropped, the only double in the history of buffalo hunting. The director had become convinced that Clint couldn't hit the broad side of a barn when standing inside it, and had therefore ordered one of the professional hunters to drop a bull for him. So of course the legendary Cheyenne Bodie picked that moment to pull off the shot of his lifetime.

For my part, if the situation doesn't improve, I'll have to ask Walker's friend to bag a few grouse for me. There has been so much rain that the birds aren't concentrating at the water holes, and the producer is worried sick.

I, however, am reveling in the abundance of other game, in a climate free from bugs and excessive heat. You might try convincing your father to import some of it into Texas."

Meanwhile, back in Chicago, I was nearing the end of a highly successful run. With a smooth production, favorable reviews, and standing-room only, things were going almost too well, and I was experiencing the growing feeling that this was not happening to me.

Sure enough, the widow of the play's translator swept in from New York like a *diabola ex machina*. Bursting into the producer's office, she accused him of swindling her dead husband.

With Ella Fitzgerald

As readers of **My Life With Bing** may have inferred from our producer's conduct during the summer of 1965, he was not the sort of man to bandy words with, or to exchange shots with for that matter, but shrieking women bewildered him.

"How did I swindle some jerk that I never even heard of?" he inquired, when he finally got a word in edgewise.

"You owe him royalties for every performance."

"I just looked. The creep's name ain't even on the program."

"And that's another thing. It was supposed to be, so just for starters you owe me triple damages."

The producer summoned the director, and addressed him as he would any other henchman: "Get this broad out of my office, and do something with her. I don't much care what."

The director, shy, sensitive, and still possessed of a mother of his own, never even considered strong-arm tactics. He diffidently suggested dinner, where he listened patiently all night long, while the aggrieved widow poured forth her outrage against an unfeeling world, and consumed two bottles of his employer's best Calvados. At the end of the evening, he dipped deep into the till, and paid her to depart forevermore.

This was not precisely the dénouement that the producer had contemplated. He fired the director on the spot, and was casting about for further culprits when I tripped in brightly to say good-bye, and to thank him for enlarging the star's apartment to accommodate my family.

"It was you that picked the play," he snarled. "You'll never work in Chicago again."

As we've already seen, I had closed a number of theaters in my day, but this was the first time that a theater had closed me.

I flew home to Hillsborough, and began trying to contact Bing by letter, phone, and wire, to see if he would meet me in Rome. On August 20th, I received this telegram: *Hollywood Palace rehearsal eliminates Rome possibility.*

For whom? For him, for me, or for both of us? Unable to establish further contact, I bought tickets for Mother Humiliata and myself, and flew to Rome on August 26th.

Since Bing was unwittingly financing the trip, I had determined to economize wherever possible, so we flew tourist class. At the airport in Rome, we deplaned with the first-class passengers. To my surprise, I saw among them Van Hefflin, my costar in *Gunman's Walk,* who had recently appeared with Bing in *Stagecoach.*

"Hi," I called out inventively, sweeping past his nose on the arm of a nun.

Politely Van reached out for a nonexistent pen to sign his autograph. Willy-nilly, I was traveling incognito.

I had yet to blow my cover when we registered in our hotel. Lee J. Cobb, with whom I had dined not a year since, was checking his mail at the desk.

"Hello, Mr. Cobb," I began, preparing to introduce him to my companion.

"Hello, sister," he replied to Mother Humiliata, as he marched off to the dining room. The lasting impression that I make on men never ceases to astound me.

I recurred to the problem that had brought us to Rome: Old nuns never die; they just fade into senile paranoia. The Immaculate Heart Sisters had

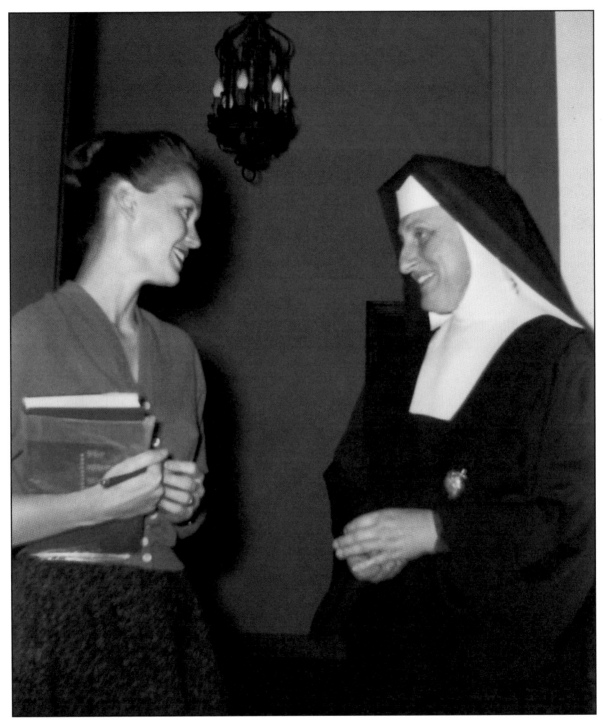

With Reverend Mother Humiliata

strict rules regarding dress, deportment, and every waking activity, but no one, least of all the rule-makers, ever seemed to follow them.

The matter had come to a head when a pair of rheumy old eyes had descried one of the younger sisters in tennis shorts. The mossback reported the incident to an equally decrepit colleague, who had just met two others in lounging pajamas.

Together the dotards stalked off to snitch to the Cardinal, who decreed that henceforth all nuns would be seen only in the uniform of the day.

A sister with a doctorate in theology had been invited to partake in a B'nai B'rith sponsored debate. As a matter of form, she had requested the Cardinal's permission. When it was refused, she protested that her participation had already been announced, and inquired respectfully what she should do.

"Take refuge in your vow of obedience," was the compassionate reply.

Like too many of her medical colleagues, a nun who hated her assignment as a nurse-midwife had become addicted to drugs. The Reverend Mother had requested permission to send her to a facility for rehabilitation.

The Cardinal, who had just refused a similar plea for therapy for alcoholic clergy, replied that, just as priests didn't drink, nuns didn't drug.

In more general terms, the order had surgical nurses, who had joined it to escape marriage and children, only to be assigned to teaching classrooms of some fifty first-graders, while skilled teachers, who couldn't stand the sight of blood, were relegated to gory duties in emergency wards.

Mother Humiliata and I had come to Rome to request a private audience with the Pope, wherein we might request that individual sisters be permitted to select their desired type of duty upon entering the order, and to modify their chosen careers whenever they deemed it appropriate.

Moreover, the Reverend Mother was prepared to request release from persecution by a Cardinal who ordered continual visitations, in the course of which each nun was subjected to a grueling private interrogation.

Pope Paul was a modernist, but even he found our nuns' problems too hot to handle.

He therefore delegated them to the Father General of the Jesuits, the Vatican's specialist in all no-win situations.

After a pleasant introductory chat, I waited in the anteroom, while Mother Humiliata joined the Father General in his private office for an ecclesiastical discussion.

When she emerged, her face was shining with an inner light.

"How was it?" I asked warily.

"Very inspiring."

"What did he have to say about the problems of your order?"

"He was most understanding."

"Did he promise to bring the matter to the Pope's attention?"

"Not exactly."

"Did he agree to take any sort of action at all?"

"Well, no."

"Fine," I reflected. "He's waiting for us to go home, and I for one am champing at the bit."

While attending mass at Santa Susana, the Paulist church in Rome,

A Hollywood Palace with Louis Armstrong

I made a last attempt to enlist the aid of a powerful member of that order. He listened gravely to my stories, and finally asked, "But why are the nuns discontented?"

"Because they have so many problems caused by the clergy. Don't your nuns here have difficulties?"

"No," replied his Eminence with a perplexed stare. "They live under the church, and they seem to like it there."

"What do they do?"

"Oh they clean the aisles, iron the vestments, sew altar cloths, polish the chalices, and make the hosts—that sort of thing."

"Does it keep them happy?"

"I don't see why not."

I'd been right the first time. It was definitely the moment to leave. "Mission accomplished," I glumly informed Mother Humiliata. "Let's head back to the hotel, and pack our bags."

"No," she decided, "there is still one liberal cardinal who I think will see us."

To my amazement, he did, vowed to carry our message to the Pope, phoned us to announce that he had done so, while also revealing that he strongly favored birth control, and was instantly rewarded by assignment to a leper colony in Africa, where, when last reported, he was still busily earning a martyr's crown.

It was just then that I received a letter from Bing, which suggested in the strongest terms that I abandon my role of religious agitator for the more pedestrian one of wife, mother, and perhaps even homemaker.

I immediately tried to phone Hollywood. After an hour of hanging on the line, I finally spoke to an Italian overseas operator, who affirmed that he had informed Bing that Mrs. Crosby was calling from Rome. "One moment please," he had continued, whereupon the connection had been broken, almost as if someone had hung up.

I insisted that my husband must have been called to the stage, and held the phone while the operator flirted with the girl at the ABC switchboard, who finally rang Bing's dressing room.

The transatlantic lovebirds had a wonderful time ascertaining that he didn't answer there, backstage, downstairs, or anywhere else in the Western Hemisphere.

Meanwhile I was cut off several times, but my operator always rang back with apologies and assurances that I shouldn't worry:

"I have seven more hours to reach your husband," he revealed, "before I must go home."

At long last, the girl at the ABC switchboard stated flatly, "Mr. Crosby has left for the day."

My Italian tried to carry things off in the grand style by admitting in mock tragic tones, "I have failed. Now what must I do, madam? Shall I throw myself into the Tiber?"

"Yes," I snarled. "You do that."

Could it be that I had stayed away too long? Abandoning Rome, the Reverend Mother, and all thought of Church reform, I boarded the first plane back to San Francisco, only to be rewarded by four days of utter silence, which might never have been broken, had it not been for Expo '67.

While my little allies packed their bags for Canada, I waited with feigned indifference for Bing's terror of managing them all by himself to reach the breaking point

I was almost beginning to question my strategy, when he finally hissed,

73

The Best There Is

"Are you planning to let your children travel to Canada and visit the Exposition all alone?"

"I understood that their father was accompanying them."

"He is, but why aren't you coming?"

"I wasn't invited."

"Well you are now, and you're limited to one medium-sized suitcase."

Overwhelmed by so generous an apology, I nonetheless pressed my advantage: "I'm not moving until you explain why you're not speaking to me."

"What do you call these noises that I'm making?"

"Why you weren't speaking to me then. I demand an answer."

"Just what is this, your latest form of blackmail?"

"Yes."

"If you must know, the Cardinal phoned while you were off on that crazy trip to Rome. He wanted to know why I was again financing a revolution in his Church, and why my wife was spearheading it.

I didn't have a rejoinder, because it was all news to me. Now I'd like an explanation too."

"Well if you're going to be so horrid about it, I've decided that I don't want to travel with you."

"Aargh!" Bing gurgled, offering a convincing portrayal of a beleaguered male succumbing to apoplexy. "We'll discuss it rationally en route."

"Lovely," I dimpled, and extracted my four already-packed bags from the recesses of my closet.

I returned from Canada to attend a meeting of the Regents of Immaculate Heart College. Before accepting an appointment as chairman of the newly-formed architectural committee, I finally had the good sense to consult

with my husband. "Just so long as you stay away from dogma," Bing sighed.

In the light of the massive violations of building and safety codes in the rickety structures on the college's tiny Hollywood campus, I embarked upon a megalomaniac scheme to translate the entire institution to a broad expanse of acreage in Claremont.

Disregarding, for the moment, the trifling matter of how Bing was to finance this move, I decided that, since the Immaculate Heart Order had originated in Spain, a Mexican architect was in order.

I therefore phoned my own architectural consultant, Merle Oberon, who recommended Juan Sordo, the designer of her magnificent home in Acapulco.

When I in turn suggested him to the regents, the whole matter was unaccountably tabled for the nonce.

In November, Bing and I flew to Las Cruces, to spend three weeks in paradise, hunting doves, attending church in our own tiny chapel, walking on the beach, fishing in the lovely Sea of Cortés, and shedding the cares of a turbulent world. For once, reality followed my script to the letter.

When we returned to Tinseltown on December 12th, to participate in a *Hollywood Palace* and a Minute Maid commercial, I began, with renewed energy, to schedule all the family's activities. For several days, Bing somberly observed the chaos which ensued.

Then he decreed, "It's time to give it up, Kathryn. We both know that you couldn't arrange a handshake."

"True, all too true," I agreed ruefully, recognizing the sad fact that we had indeed returned to civilization, an environment in which I had never proved exceptionally functional.

In this Christmas Show we "talked to the animals."

In spite of my inestimable assistance, we did manage to finish both the commercial and the *Hollywood Palace.* It was our first stab at the former, but our second at a Christmas Show in which the entire family took part.

(Yea, even unto the wife, since this was not a Bing Crosby production.)

The previous year, Dierdre had calmed the children's rambunctious spirits by encouraging them to play tag all morning, before finally shooting their scenes in the afternoon. We had then found ways to work three small zombies into the script.

This year, we shot in the morning, and only Nathaniel kept slipping off his stool into slumberland during the takes. His brother might have benefited from a dose of his lassitude. Harry kept leaving the set "to help the electricians and camera men," behavior which occasioned loud explosions accompanied by miniature lightning bolts, and elicited colorful language from his new-found friends.

There was no danger of his sister's leaving the scene. Her sole interest lay in stealing it. She had learned that the cameras tended to be focused on her father, so she set out to upstage him with every trick in her inventory, and some novel ones invented on the spot.

Regretfully, Mary Frances had to concede that her best theatrical ruses were wasted on this new medium.

If the cameras remained trained on Bing, the vast audience out there in televisionland would never know how cute she was being at the other end of the huge stage.

After serious thought, she at length adopted the simple but effective stratagem of draping herself about her father's neck, and eying him adoringly. Sure enough, an alert camera man, in search of a novel angle or an attentive face, would find her first.

Pictures of Mary Frances, idolizing her revered daddy, graced the theatrical pages of every major newspaper that Christmas.

So successful were the old pro and the little scene stealer that the camera strayed only once reluctantly over to me, and caught me trying to divide my cross-eyed stare between Bing and two gnomes, dancing off in opposite directions. A mother's lot is not a happy one.

After shooting the final scenes, I returned to Hillsborough with the kids, while Bing flew off to Ensenada to hunt blue quail with Phil Harris.

He returned home on December 24th. My father had decorated the tree, while my mother helped her exhausted daughter to prepare the annual Christmas Eve party for our staff and forty-five guests.

Bing wandered in just as we were about to serve, picked up the turkey, and carried it into the dining room. So it was he who received the huge round of applause from the assembled company, almost disabusing me of the notion that I inhabited a just universe.

All dressed up with Ben Hogan, Frank Stranahan, and Byron Nelson

1968

On January 7th, in our nation's capital, Westinghouse sponsored the showing of a film and an exhibit of art work, both produced by Sister Corita, the head of the art department at Immaculate Heart College. I read the poems which accompanied the serigraphs, and Art Buchwald of the Washington Post, an old friend to whom Bing had smuggled many a bottle of Scotch in post-war Paris, gave one of his inimitable speeches.

Of course any war has its darker side, and all this was simply a cover for our attempts to drum up sympathy for the nuns' campaign against their long-suffering Cardinal.

While still in Washington, I introduced Sister Corita to a number of eminent Catholics, with results which varied from a scandalized rejection of anything smacking of a woman's movement in the Church, to a promise from Sargent and Eunice Kennedy Shriver to use their influence with the Pope.

Having learned my lesson, I had the good sense to acquaint the hither-to-unwitting sponsor of our trip with such aspects of the plot as he was old and wise enough to understand. I anticipated some sort of explosion, but he simply shook his head slowly from side to side and decided, "I think it's time to hie me off to Pebble Beach for a few rounds of golf."

Bing stayed in Monterey through the end of the Crosby National Golf Tournament on January 14th, when Johnny Pott sank a 26-foot chip shot to beat Billy Casper and Bruce Devlin in the second sudden-death playoff in the history of the Clambake.

"I had hoped that the pros would score better," Bing observed, "but Spyglass defeated them all. After a month's frost, the greens were dormant, barren, slick, and well nigh impossible to putt on."

The day before the tournament, Billy Casper decided that he was going

With Juan and Malena Sordo

A picnic on Sheep Island in the middle of San Francisco Bay

to run over to Spyglass to get in a practice round.

"You can't," Johnny Pott informed him. "The course is closed."

Don Cherry looked up and asked hopefully, "You mean for good?"

Johnny Pott also teamed with Wall Street broker Virgil Sherrill to win the Pro-Am. In a subsequent letter to the latter, Bing suggested that victory might exact its price:

"Much as I hate to mention it, there's an unpleasant aspect to your triumph. It may be a mite harder to make money on the Florida circuit from now on.

After all, the winner of a prestigious event earns a certain respect from his potential victims. It will cost you a score of bad rounds to convince them that you are back in the groove, and even then you may have to offer this wary crooner a stroke or two."

The Board of Regents of Immaculate Heart College had rejected my recommendation that Merle Oberon's Juan Sordo design all the buildings for their new campus, in favor of a concerted team effort.

I replied with a number of choice remarks about camels, platypuses, and other creatures designed by committees, concluding with the stern reminder that God so loved the world that he didn't send a team, but all in vain. Reluctantly, I agreed to invite to my home representatives of the three firms that the board had selected.

They arrived on January 18th, and my Mexican immediately declared open war on an architect from San Francisco. Only the language barrier and the quiet tact of their colleague prevented a duel.

They were still shouting mutually unintelligible insults as I pushed them out the front door, and firmly locked it behind them.

Then I climbed up to bed, crawled in, and prepared to sob myself to sleep. Bing poked his head in just before the onset of the inevitable snores, to ask me just what it was that I had hoped to accomplish.

"To build a new school," I sniffed.

"Where?"

"In Claremont."

"Does any such campus exist?"

"Well, no."

Do you have the funds for any such buildings, if you did have the land to put them on?"

"Well, no."

"Let me see if I can get this straight: You are presently crying your heart out because you can't get the putative architects to agree on the hypothetical design of imaginary buildings for a non-existent campus. Under those circumstances, don't you find your grief, if not excessive, at least a trifle premature?"

Regarding the matter from Bing's perspective, I almost did. It has always proven difficult for me to assume another person's point of view.

For the moment, I was so enchanted by the novelty of it that I fell straightway into a dreamless sleep, whereas Bing, as I was to learn much later, sat down to write a letter to the president of the college, sternly insisting that I be relieved of my "overinvolvement in their plans, programs, and problems."

Bing then initiated a project of his own to distract me with a picnic. Thus it was that we spent the next day

Trader Vic and Helen Bergeron

The skipper himself

tramping behind children and dogs along Sheep Island, watching flocks of birds soar up into the scudding clouds, and ships glide past the skyline of San Francisco, toward the Golden Gate Bridge and the broad Pacific.

Bing had his way. Framed against the vast backdrop of sea and sky, my petty preoccupations of the previous day paled into insignificance. Try as I would, I couldn't work up much concern for them.

In furtherance of his campaign to take my mind off architecture, Bing invited me to join Trader Vic Bergeron and his wife Helen on a hunting and fishing expedition in Baja California.

The fishing part of the trip turned out reasonably well. The men deposited Helen and me on sandy points along the coast, where we could prospect for shells washed up by recent storms, while they pursued what Bing termed "funny fish," such as the huachinango, dorado, cabrilla, and pargo, which were good to eat, as opposed to game fish such as the big marlin, which simply flatter the angler's ego.

I think Bing would have been delighted to maroon me more or less permanently where he was sure that I was out of harm's way, but Vic insisted on devoting the second half of the trip to hunting. Since dogs couldn't venture into the cactus, the doves which we shot were retrieved by "bird boys," small truants who needed hawk-like vision to descry their prey amid the spiny growths.

But the first thing that I noticed was that their sight was impaired. As I pointed out to Vic, they seemed to be suffering from some form of pinkeye.

A do-gooder after my own heart, he returned to our boat to radio for his plane to fly a load of antibiotics down from San Diego. Proudly we delivered them to a tiny clinic in Todos Santos, where three overworked nuns constituted the district's entire medical staff.

The sisters beamed with delight as they accepted our present. Then, speaking slowly and employing simple words, as if dealing with small, none-too-bright children, they explained that we had hauled up a battery of artillery to kill a flea:

"The boys handle birds which are covered with lice and feces, but they never wash their hands and faces. When they rub the desert dust out of their eyes, the filth on their hands causes infections. What they need is a few bars of soap."

Bing and Helen, who had stood by in acute embarrassment throughout the entire proceeding, silently dragged the good Samaritans home.

The Bergerons had brought along a luxurious scrabble board to introduce the Crosbys to the game, thus initiating a savage rivalry, which was to endure for the rest of Bing's life. It was certainly uncharacteristic of him, for he had never played board games of any kind and, as Bob Hope frequently noted, "With his luck with the horses, he couldn't have anything left to wager on indoor sports."

Nevertheless, he became passionately fond of scrabble contests with his archenemy from Texas. His interest never flagged because the opponents were surprisingly well-matched. Of course Bing had twice my vocabulary, but I cheated like an Arab, constantly coining neologisms which occasioned endless morphological disputes.

On February 8th, we flew to New York, where Bing performed in Madison

With Phil Harris and friends in South Carolina

Another plantation, another hunt

Square Garden for the benefit of the Boy Scouts. Since we were already in the East, we then decided to join Phil Harris for a plantation hunt in South Carolina.

I had long since learned to enjoy the Southern routine of breakfast in bed and black-tie dinners, But Bing could stand only so much of it, and after a few days Phil became frankly and vocally restive.

Even the hunt was a pageant of sorts, and "the Indian" complained that he had come to shoot birds, not to crown the Queen. After walking behind a very British chief dog handler for most of the morning, and being permitted only the occasional token shot, Phil finally rebelled against the ritual, and charged a forbidden thicket.

"Steady, Mr. Harris, you've already taken a bird from that covey," the handler cried in alarm.

"But there must be forty of them left in those bushes."

"There is always tomorrow, sir."

"For me definitely, and maybe even for you, if you don't push me too far, but not for those sneaky birds. Run for your life. With a little luck, automatic weapons, a couple of loaders, and a few more packs of dogs, I figure I can just about wipe out the entire species before sundown."

Phil was still loudly protesting that "limeys lack a sense of humor," as Bing hauled him off to lunch, where the two cronies decided that the weather was doubtless better in Mexico, and departed for Las Cruces that afternoon.

I, on the other hand, seized the opportunity to return to Hillsborough, and raise funds for the new college campus that I was still determined to build. Having failed elsewhere, I decided

that the Grail might lie at my own castle gate, so I arranged a dinner at which to present my favorite nuns to the many millionaires of the San Francisco Peninsula.

The dinner itself was a great success, but it seemed that I had overlooked a minor detail. Most of the guests were Jewish, and ideologically disinclined to become major supporters of the Catholic Church.

Tactfully, I switched horses in midstream, presented the good sisters as a persecuted minority, and thus achieved immediate identification with about a third of my Zionists. Oppression was something that they understood.

Cyril Magnin not only contributed, but joined with Bob Hope's lawyer, Martin Gang, to form the duo of Sabra shock troops on the Board of Regents.

Since I couldn't ask my guests to do anything that I wouldn't do myself, as the high point of the evening I pledged an immediate contribution of a million dollars of Bing's money. It was a good round sacrificial number that made me feel warm inside.

Bing's reaction was somewhat less positive, so it was fortunate that I was in Palm Beach, preparing for a two-weeks' run of *The Guardsman,* when he arrived from Mexico on March 5th, discovered a grateful letter of acceptance from the sisters, and was on the phone immediately.

"What's this about my contributing a million dollars to the Immaculate Heart building fund by April 1st?"

"Isn't it a convenient time?"

"It's a well-chosen date, if that's what you mean. Just how do you expect this April fool to do it?"

"Well, you know that I don't try to pry into our finances, but I was reading

Heading for the mountains

Harry's record dorado

just the other day in *Photoplay* that you must be worth hundreds of millions. Surely we can spare a tiny fraction of that sum for the benefit of the Church."

"I do hope that's a royal or editorial *we*. You and your tapeworm may be in the chips, but there's no way that I can find that much cash on such short notice. I just phoned my business manager, and he says that the simplest solution will be for all of us to flee to Europe."

"It can't be that bad. Aren't you the one who explained that none of us owns this world's goods, that we are all just God's stewards."

"That's correct, but we don't keep all his property in ready cash. A man can have a hundred million dollars in prime real estate, and only $21.53 in the bank."

"Is any of that lovely acreage in Claremont, or anywhere else that might prove suitable for a campus?"

Bing had hung up in disgust. Never in his lifetime would I be sufficiently familiar with the financial world to appreciate the difference between the value of a man's financial statement and the amount of ready cash that he has about him at a given time. It would take years for Bing to work off the debt to heaven that I had so blithely contracted for him.

Feeling that I had made my contribution to the success of God and man in California, I traveled to Florida for a surprisingly successful run of *The Guardsman*, at the end of which Bing arrived to fly me off to Las Cruces.

It was now April 12th. Regretfully I packed away the play's Jean Louis wardrobe, which would serve henceforth only for costume balls, and flew off to Mexico and motherhood.

On the plane, I made my best pitch to convince Bing that he should costar with me in *I Do, I Do* the following summer in London.

Of course I was being used as the cat's paw. They wanted Bing, not me. But I still might have fished their chestnuts out of the fire, had it not been for that unlucky pledge to Immaculate Heart College.

As things stood, Bing was stoutly refusing to be associated with me publicly, since he might have to disown me if the nuns asserted their claim for the entire million dollars in the immediate future.

It was, alas, another debacle, which I charged off to bad timing, regretting only the fact that I couldn't follow my husband's irate advice to "bring the two-person musical out as a single, and just call it *I Do.*"

From Las Cruces, Bing took Harry out after game fish on our big boat *The Dorado*. At my request, they deposited Mary Frances, Nathaniel, my dog Cindy, and me, on a stretch of beach beneath the precipitous rock called Cerralvo Island.

After exhausting the beach's inventory of sea shells, I shooed the children ahead of me up the cliff. Cindy showed the way, Mary Frances followed like a sure-footed mountain goat, and only Nathaniel managed to get stuck on a narrow ledge.

Ever resourceful in moments of stress, I shrieked maternally, "Don't you dare fall, or I'll spank you."

Thus encouraged, Nathaniel scrambled to the top, while I tried to follow with a bucket of cold drinks and an embryonic shell collection. I was about three-quarters of the way to the

Patty Hearst, Ann Hearst, Trish Tobin and our brood preparing for
the Easter celebration

Dawn and George Coleman with our guests from Hollywood

summit, when I suddenly realized that the rotten rock was crumbling away beneath my feet faster than I could move them forward. A moment later, I was spread-eagled across the face of the cliff, and somewhat embarrassed as to what disposition to make of the bucket.

"Don't lose the drinks, mommy," Mary Frances howled helpfully from the crest, followed by an indignant, "Oh no," as I relinquished my hold on the pail to grasp spasmodically for any available handful of rock.

Only Cindy seemed genuinely concerned about my predicament. She worked her way gingerly back down the mountain until we were finally nose-to-nose.

"Help," I gasped hoarsely. "For God's sake, get me out of here."

Gravely Cindy placed her forepaws on my shoulders, and thoroughly licked my face.

All this, as the rock was slowly but inexorably crumbling away beneath me. So much for Lassie.

Turning my head, I caught a vertiginous glimpse of the upturned faces of Bing, Harry, and a Mexican boatman, racing for shore in our dinghy.

Somehow I supported the combined weight of woman and dog until Harry arrived, and Cindy joyously abandoned me for his more interesting company.

This eased my burden sufficiently to permit me to dig in until Bing, who must have broken all records scaling the face of the rock by a more difficult alternate route, was able to reach my hand, and to pull me to a less precipitous incline. There I lay flat, pressing my face and the full length of my body into mother earth, and shaking with a sudden and terrible chill.

It was a full half hour before Bing could finally disengage my fingers and toes, and carry me back to the boat.

He and the children were confirmed in their opinion that mother was just a poor party-pooper from South Texas, where the terrain is gloriously and ever-so-safely flat.

"You missed a great chance for a posthumous cancellation of my million-dollar pledge," I grunted to Bing, after I finally found my voice.

"It was almost worth the price to watch you practice open-pit mining on the face of that cliff."

The Hearst children visited us for Easter, and spent all day Friday and Saturday scrubbing the church. No one watching little Patty, industriously wielding her mop, or dyeing the eggs for the Easter hunt, could have guessed what fate the nightmare world of the 1970s held in store for her.

Sailing their own boat down from Los Angeles, came the producer and director of the *Hollywood Palace*. In a curious reversal of their customary roles, it was the director who captained the ship, and his landlubber boss who served as crew, shouted *Aye, aye, Captain Bligh,* stood the night watches, swabbed the decks, and ran futilely from starboard to port, hoisting and taking up sail, while his erstwhile subordinate lounged at the wheel.

"I suspect that a beautiful business relationship drowned somewhere off San Diego," Bing remarked, upon viewing their arrival.

The next to appear of our Hollywood guests were Cliff Robertson and his wife Dina Merrill, who landed their private plane unannounced, and found themselves abandoned on our tiny, isolated airstrip.

Felixa and Nick Vanoff

Bill and Faye Harbach

The girls from Hollywood

They might have been there yet, if Bing hadn't developed the habit of sweeping the bay with binoculars to search for schools of fish, or to count the marlin flags on the returning boats.

"How's the catch?" I inquired one sunny afternoon.

"So far it consists of Cliff and Dina, sitting on their luggage in the middle of our runway," Bing replied, smiling indulgently as I scooted off to pick them up in the jeep.

To my relief, it transpired that they'd been enjoying the vast panorama of sea and sky, and viewed my sudden arrival as something of an unwelcome interruption.

Their friends, who appeared that evening, included Dorothy McGuire, Henry Mancini, Helmut Dantine, Edgar Bergen, and of course his ward, Charlie McCarthy.

Dorothy's husband, John Swope, a noted professional photographer, left us with an exquisite pictorial record of the heroine of *Claudia* and *The Enchanted Cottage,* posed against our mountains, desert, sea, and sky.

Henry played his own *Moon River* for Bing to sing, and in spite of my best efforts, Helmut established himself as the local chess champion.

But it was Edgar Bergen whose impish sense of humor carried the day. First for the benefit of the children, and then for that of the child in all of us, he elicited outrageous remarks from walls, doors, windows, chairs, tables, dishes, glasses, empty boxes, and finally from our very lips.

Curiously, our preconceived notion of Bergen as the stolid straight man continued to reject the direct evidence of our eyes and ears. Charlie McCarthy might have been the source of such

offbeat remarks, but no such dark humor could issue from his ever-so-proper guardian.

For the first and last time, I saw Bing in the role of genial host. If he could ever have spared the energy, I reflected, he might have been a social director. I was reminded of the other dwarfs' comment on Dopey: "We think that he could talk; it's just that he's never tried."

On Sunday, I flew Padre Luis in from La Paz, and insisted that everyone come to mass. Never before had the good father faced so heterogeneous an assemblage.

Since no one knew when to sit, kneel, stand, or respond, the priest experienced difficulty in getting underway, but he finally reconciled himself to the fact that he was talking to himself up there, and went about God's business as best he could.

This approach yielded results beyond his wildest dreams, because the collection, at least, proved to be truly miraculous. In the intervening years, he has often spoken of it nostalgically, and he is still waiting for me to come up with another such congregation.

On Monday, all the ladies from Hollywood embarked on *The True Love* for a voyage to Punta Arena to hunt for shells.

We drove a Gila monster away from a tern's nest in the sand, and were rewarded by a superb histrionic performance from the mother bird, who tried to lure us away from her eggs by dragging her body piteously across the sand, while feigning a broken wing.

We pretended to be taken in, and followed at a respectful distance, but Nicky Dantine remarked, "She might just make it in Anaheim, but she'll

Rod Rodriguez meets the
Hollywood stars

Bill Harbach with the servers
of the hors-d'oeuvres

Nick Vanoff and a paso doble

never play the Huntington Hartford in good old Hollywood."

Meanwhile, Bing had taken the men out in our smaller boats, in pursuit of marlin for sport, and dorado for lunch. While they waited for a strike, they sat on deck and told stories.

Edgar Bergen got Bing started on early tales of their mutual friend W. C. Fields: "We were sitting under the umbrella on Bill's lawn at Toluca Lake, consuming a potable or two, or in his case seven or eight.

When he insisted that his faculties were unimpaired, I challenged him, as a former professional juggler, to keep four croquet balls in the air in his present inebriated state.

To my amazement, Bill did right well for a man who must have been dealing subjectively with at least eight spheroids, until three of his swans came floating up, and started hissing, as it seems is their wont when angry or affrighted.

Peering out indignantly through his alcoholic haze, Fields issued a pronunciamiento: 'I've been booed, jeered at, tarred and feathered, and stoned, but this is the first and last time I'll ever be hissed.'

Whereupon he pelted the swans with the croquet balls, missing them by a mile, but exciting their bellicose or amorous propensities. They charged up out of the lake, and Bill took off with his hands over his head shouting, 'Present your complaints to the manager. It's his job to refund all the money at the end of my act.'

Another time, we were playing a round with an aggravatingly meticulous golfer, who sized up a putt from all sides, discussed the grass, the wind, and the break with his caddy, and at

long last demanded, 'Was this green mowed today?'

After the lad had answered in the affirmative, the player repeated the entire routine, finally addressed his putt, missed it by a mile, and proceeded to bewail his fate.

Bill walked up to his own putt, went through a hilarious parody of our friend the fanatic's entire routine, settled his blade cautiously behind the ball, stopped once more, turned to his caddy and inquired, 'At precisely what hour was this sward cropped?'"

An ironically macabre note was to be added some months later. In Bing's boat, listening to his stories, was a guest who was himself to be the subject of a tale. The following August, just after we left our professional hunter in Africa, our friend was to hire him, and inadvertently shoot his right eye out.

In the midst of all our festivities, I discovered to my horror that Bing was negotiating with another guest for several properties in Ireland. When I complained that he might have first consulted me, he admitted that he hadn't because he suspected that I might object.

"You know that I've always wanted a medieval castle on the old sod," he protested.

"While you're in the area, see if you can turn up a medieval lass to inhabit it with you."

Fortunately Bing was diverted from his pursuit of foreign real estate by queries from a series of people who were putting him in books. He admitted to one author that it was his boyhood friend, Val Hobart, who had first employed the nickname *Bing*.

He told another that in his twelfth year, his favorite authors were Mark

Bing's birthday present

Harry's audition

Twain and Booth Tarkington, that he had generally preferred adventure stories and historical novels, and that his hobbies were all in the field of athletics, including baseball, basketball, football, handball, and swimming.

Bing agreed to write a forward to *Moonlight Serenade* at the request of Chummy MacGregor, but he insisted that the latter omit a description of the making of bathtub gin at the Leyenda Apartments so long ago.

"The statute of limitations probably precludes prosecution by federal authorities," Bing conceded, "but I'd prefer that these new children of mine remain ignorant of their father's former bootlegging activities."

Bing was further distracted by the performances of several of his more expensive race horses: Dominion Day had begun winning in Canada, while Society had triumphed over a strong field in England, and was to enter the Derby if he made a reasonable showing in the Dante Stakes on May 14th.

Meanwhile, back in Mexico, May 2nd and Bing's birthday were upon us. It began badly when a practical joke backfired, and we accumulated an ugly and very irascible donkey.

The animal belonged to a neighboring farmer, who kept it staked out near the mouth of an arroyo where Bing loved to hunt.

Our hero had come to fear its violent temper. On numerous occasions, he had narrowly escaped injury from its flying hoofs.

Mindful of this eventful history, George Coleman had rented the beast, draped a wreath of bougainvillea about its scrawny neck, dragged it across the cattle guard, and presented it to the startled Bing as his very own.

Oddly enough, there was a slight hitch. Innocent of the Spanish tongue, George had unwittingly given the owner to understand that he was purchasing the vicious animal. Happy to be rid of a useless and dangerous expense, the farmer refused to reclaim the beast.

We went through several painful weeks of reenacting *The Ransom of Red Chief*, before we induced the owner to take Diablo back by paying him a tidy fee, whereupon he professed himself willing to sell his donkey over and over again on the same terms, as long as the crazy Yankees remained willing and able to pay for him.

The Hollywood group arrived with presents, and sang a series of silly songs of their own invention, accompanied by the four mariachis who normally played for parties and dances at the hotel.

Harry, who had always watched the musicians spellbound, was now hiding well out of their sight, and trying to follow them on his guitar. I observed this until a mother's heart could stand it no longer.

Waiting until the end of a number, I advanced to center stage, and announced that my son was now going to audition to become a mariachi.

Harry played *Happy Birthday To You*, while to my immense relief the leader of the mariachis listened gravely, and without the slightest hint of condescension, welcomed the boy into his group of professionals.

Henceforth our son was to play with them at the hotel, carefully following the leader, and striking the same chords almost simultaneously. When a newly-arrived guest tossed him a coin and called for a given melody, his standard response was, "No hablo inglés."

Captain Crosby on *The True Love*

Merle Oberon's Acapulco home

Harry's success turned out to be the finest birthday present my husband ever received. Bing had always remained sensitive to the fact that he had never learned to play any sort of musical instrument.

In his early days with Paul Whiteman's band, this had proved embarrassing, because a convention of the day called for the spotlight to single out various individuals for solos. Those who could sing would then lay aside their instruments to perform vocally.

Whiteman had originally entrusted Bing with one or another of the wind instruments, but had soon substituted a violin with rubber strings because of Bing's insistence on trying to toot any sort of horn. Now our frustrated musician could finally enjoy a vicarious triumph in the person of his namesake.

Last but not least of Bing's birthday presents was a reprieve from the social obligations which he had incurred by importing half of Hollywood. He was a lover of contrast, who delighted in good company to the point of utter exhaustion, after which the old bear just had to crawl back into his cave.

We loaded the three children into the *True Love,* collapsed on the deck, and embarked on a slow cruise to nowhere. It was a week of perfect happiness for all concerned.

Bing wanted to stretch it into at least a month, but I was too busy earning stars in my crown to realize that I was already safe in heaven. In retrospect, it seems hard to believe that I insisted on returning to port so that I could further my projects for Immaculate Heart College.

In spite of my recalcitrance, willy-nilly our second honeymoon continued, as Bing squired me to Mexico City, where he devoted his days to business luncheons and golf matches, while I persuaded Malena Sordo to try to convince her husband Juan to come down off his high horse, and to collaborate with a brace of gringo architects on the design of my dream campus.

For a time, her task seemed hopeless, but she finally extorted a grudging agreement.

I then phoned the sisters, who communicated with their architects, and arranged for a reunion of all hands in Acapulco on May 25th.

Meanwhile, I had been so involved, first in plotting, and then in congratulating myself on the success of my schemes, that I had somehow neglected to keep Bing abreast of events. I hadn't wanted to sound any false alarms, but I now felt perfectly safe in informing him that he was off to Acapulco in the morning.

I was unpleasantly surprised to learn that Bing had long since scheduled a fishing trip out of Las Cruces, with friends who were traveling from Canada to meet him there.

"You'll just have to cancel it," I announced firmly. "I'll never have another such opportunity to get these architects together.

I'm flying one in from Detroit, and the other from Washington D.C. Surely you don't want to waste all the funds that I'm spending on this project."

"I can't cancel the trip now," Bing objected. "Everyone's been counting on this vacation for a year. By the way, whose money is it that you're lavishing so generously?"

On second thought, I decided to ignore crass monetary considerations as beneath me.

Is this a man who would strand a devoted wife in Mexico City?

"Well, simply postpone your voyage then," I insisted. "Phone your friends, and inform them that there has been a delay."

"I can't, damn it. They're already on the way down."

"I'm leaving for Acapulco in the morning, and I need you with me. Would you really rather go fishing with a bunch of men?"

If you ask the wrong question, you can be virtually assured of getting the wrong answer. "Yes," Bing stated flatly, and started for the door.

"Hey, wait a minute. This is important work for your Church. Don't you want the nuns to build their college?"

"Three architects will never agree on anything; there isn't going to be any new college; and you and your nuns are as nutty as fruitcakes."

Bing evidently viewed this as an exit line, for he slammed the door behind him. I was so incensed myself that I decided to await his apologetic return, before permitting him to succumb to my irresistible charms. If I'd had the good sense to glue my ear to the door, I'd have heard sounds of rapid packing.

Without a word of adieu, Bing left within the hour for Las Cruces. In his haste to depart, he had somehow overlooked the fact that he had left me pigheadedly sitting in Mexico City, without the barest necessities of travel.

He'd always taken care of such details as documentation, finances, suitcases, etc. Now I found myself all alone, sans passport, sans pesos, sans luggage, sans hubby, and sans the faintest notion of how to go anywhere or do anything by myself.

To such a pass had this outbreak of male liberation brought me. A stranger in a strange land, I wished desperately that I were back sunning myself on the deck of the *True Love*. If Bing had determined to teach me a lesson, he had certainly succeeded beyond his wildest dreams.

Just what does the resourceful modern woman do in such an emergency? You guessed it, she screams for help.

By sheer coincidence, one of Bing's golf partners was rooming in the same hotel. I wept on his shoulder until he realized clearly that I was wholly his responsibility, arranged for my flight to Acapulco and my accommodations while staying there, pressed a wad of pesos upon me, and heaved a vast sigh of relief as I stumbled onto the plane.

Somehow I actually managed to reach the Las Brisas Hotel, where the meeting of architects was to take place. Wondrous to relate, they had all made it too. Apprehensively I scouted the lay of the land.

This time my Mexican had been so softened up by continual pounding from his better half that he proved almost amenable. My countrymen, on the other hand, still adamantly refused to cooperate with each other, or with anyone else.

"Why," I asked in bewilderment, "did you travel such a long way, just to tell me that you weren't interested?"

"It was your nickel," growled the builder from Detroit, "and besides that, I thought you might have seen the light, and finally decided to give me an exclusive."

The three of them were still circling each other warily when I left the room, found a taxi driver who could take me to Merle Oberon's, threw myself upon her mercy, and begged that she schedule me back into San Francisco, where I should be safe.

99

Winona Love

Francis Brown

Merle had seen far better histrionics in her time, and she refused to be rattled by mine. Coolly she pointed out that I couldn't get back into my country without a passport.

Considering the alternatives, she decided that my best solution would be to return to Las Cruces, where I was so well known that the authorities would be unlikely to ask for identification.

After seeing to it that I had a good night's sleep and a ticket to La Paz, she then had her driver deposit me at the airport.

During the entire flight I worried about traveling from La Paz to Las Cruces in my indigent, undocumented state. The problem was still unresolved when I stepped off the plane and into Bing's arms.

Somehow, on the tip of a peninsula innocent of telephones, he'd managed to receive news of my arrival.

I clung to him desperately and blubbered, "Oh Bing, you've no idea of how terrible it was. I didn't know what to do, and I made such a fool of myself, and the architects still hate each other, and I didn't know where to go, and I'll never travel without you again, and I'm so glad to be home."

"Take it easy, will you, the pilot's watching," Bing grinned, as he carried me to our own plane.

I continued sobbing about how wonderful it was to be back where I belonged, and my husband was obviously trying hard not to look too triumphant. Unfortunately he wasn't succeeding. Why oh why was everything so easy for him, and so hard for me?

On May 30th, we all flew back to San Francisco, where Bing and I supervised the children's last weeks of formal study, and shopped for the safari clothes that we planned to wear in Africa. As soon as school was out, the whole family left for the Mauna Kea Hotel in Hawaii.

We were met at the plane by Bing's golfing friend, Francis Brown, and his lifelong companion, the comely native Hawaiian dancer Winona Love.

Since they were the most compatible couple I'd ever met, I finally plucked up the courage to ask Bing why they had never married.

It seemed that Brown was a descendant of one of the first Scotch families to settle in Hawaii. His forebears had had a horror of miscegenation, and rumor had it that a grandfather had placed a clause in his will, which disinherited Francis if he married a native girl.

If this were true, it had cost the adolescent grandson dearly one night, when he was too inebriated to drive his car home from a party. An island beauty at the wheel had demanded that he marry her.

When he refused, she had driven straight into the nearest tree, killing herself outright, and leaving Brown with injuries from which he never fully recovered.

We all love a story with a moral, but in this case it had somehow been reversed, since Francis renounced not liquor but matrimony. After a round of golf, he invariably toasted his victory or drowned his sorrows, and then invited everyone in the men's bar home to dinner.

He would seat as many as thirty at his immense table, raise a final glass in a toast to the assembled company, and march cheerfully off to bed, leaving Winona to feed and entertain his puzzled guests.

Golfing amid the palms

While Bing and Francis toured the island's golf courses, I pursued my hobby of shelling to its ultimate conclusion. After a half-hour lesson in the hotel pool, I donned a baby scuba tank, plunged into the Pacific, and followed a trail along the bottom until I arrived at a hillock of sand, whence I brought up a large auger.

Encouraged by this triumph, I next uncovered and brought to the beach a gigantic cone shell, which the nearest Hawaiian promptly knocked from my hands, prior to explaining that its denizen packed a lethal barb.

The locals were peculiarly sensitive to this fact, as a consequence of a recent incident. A professor of marine biology had collected several fine specimens in her heavily-gloved hands, and placed them in a convenient sack.

Then, in a sudden lapse of sanity, she had thrown the bag over her bare back, and dropped to the beach dead.

If fate had any such dramatic demise in store for me, it was not yet ready to spring its big surprise. Nonetheless, I did manage to throw a scare into my spouse.

Having promoted another baby scuba tank, I attached it to our first-born, and introduced him to the wonders and perils of the deep.

For the most part, our procedure was straightforward enough. Since the wary crustaceans, who constituted our quarry, fed on the coral reefs at night, and buried themselves in the sand to sleep during the day, we followed each trail until it ended in a mound, and then exhumed its indignant inhabitant.

The only excitement derived from the fact that there were other predators afoot, or rather afin. Sharks too hunted through the coral reefs, in search of the schools of smaller fish which habitually congregated there.

We soon learned that if we left the gray killers strictly alone, they in turn paid no attention to us.

But I warned Harry not to discuss the matter with his father who, though formerly a swimmer and diver of Olympic quality, flatly refused to don a tank and "make like a poor imitation of a silly fish."

"Someone has to preserve enough breath to give you mouth-to-mouth resuscitation when they drag you out," he had remarked dryly.

A boy in his tenth year has a short memory and a strong sense of adventure. One evening at dinner, Harry followed the accepted Crosby custom of raising his hand to demand equal time to join in our endless conversational melee, and cheerfully announced that he had dived down on top of a monstrous tiger shark, and driven it out of the coral reef.

Much as I hated to spoil a good story, I was quick to explain that the leviathan in question had in fact been a harmless, basking, five-foot sand shark, which the advent of a determined man-child in full scuba gear must have frightened out of its few wits, but the hound of heaven was now in full cry.

"Why do you have to go to such extremes in everything?" Bing demanded of me. "If we're staying at the beach, why can't you sunbathe, or swim, or read, or stroll, or find some other way of imitating normal human behavior?"

"But you've always approved of my shelling," I reminded him.

"That was because I hoped against hope that it would keep you out of trouble. It did seem harmless as long as

Under water with Kathryn

and a star fish

you were just picking them up along the beach, but then of course you had to extend the scope of your activities.

You waded after them, swam after them, dived after them, and now you're fighting sharks for them, and risking the life of my namesake in the bargain.

I had promised my sainted mother to protect her grandchildren against evil influences, but somehow we failed to foresee the likes of you."

Of course I swore to be more careful, and privately guaranteed Harry a licking if he didn't learn to guard his tongue. For the next few days, we waited until Bing was safely off the first tee, before returning to the reefs.

Not that we fooled him for a moment. He glumly watched the cowries and miters pile up in the acid baths in his kitchen, prayed for guidance, and anticipated trouble.

To my delight, he also tried to distract me from my submarine jousts with death, by challenging me to a series of tennis matches. It was the one sport in which I could compete full-out with him.

I had devoted much of a misspent youth to hitting a ball against the side of the house for hours, until discouraged by the inevitable broken window, to imitating my brother and sister, who were both of championship quality, and to playing on my high-school varsity for four years.

Bing, on the other hand, had picked up the game later in life, and had no style to speak of. Breaking his wrist in defiance of all the experts, he calmly ran me to death with lobs and cuts that my slashing forehands alternately dumped into the net, or out of the court.

Like many of his other opponents, I wasted my time trying to ferret out the secret of his unconventional success, before finally admitting that he was exasperatingly coordinated.

His athletic ability was put to another test, as he partnered Francis Brown in a series of golf tournaments. Brown had Walter Hagen's gift for partying all night, and still arriving clear-eyed at the first tee the following morning. Bing had an insomniac's need for precious sleep, and no shred of tolerance for alcohol.

At length, an incident showed him the way out. After supporting Francis, as the latter wove his way through a series of bars, our crooner ordered squab for them both at Canlis Restaurant in Honolulu. There Brown recalled through his haze that he had promised George Kaanapau to bring Bing to watch his act at the Royal Hawaiian.

So the squab went into little brown bags, and the golfing buddies traipsed off to occupy front-row seats and calmly munch their picnic lunches, to the horror of the *maître d'hôtel,* and the delight of the singer and all his fans.

When George Coleman joined the picnickers, the trio planned a visit to the Hilton Hotel's Hawaiian Village, where the bar served only the finest Okuliau, their celebrated brandy.

There, by some stroke of good fortune, the doorman failed to appear, and Francis, a famous personage on the island and a lifelong senator, complained bitterly of the lack of service.

"Right," observed Bing. "If they're going to treat us this badly, we might as well go home."

To his amazement, Francis concurred wholeheartedly, with the result that Bing arrived for their 8 AM tee-off as bright-eyed and bushy-tailed as his genial partner. Thereafter he always

With Francis Brown and George Coleman

complained of imagined slights from the staff, when he needed to drag Francis out of a given den of iniquity.

While the men played in their final tournament, I packed for myself and the children, and then killed the last hours of waiting by accepting an invitation to inspect the facilities at a local hospital.

I donned my Nurse Jane Fuzzy Wuzzy costume, and first observed, and then assisted in obstetrics. My initial patient was a tiny Japanese woman, who was wheeled in, rejected all sedation, was delivered of her baby in fifteen minutes, thanked us profusely, and was wheeled out again.

Patient number two was a stout Hawaiian matron of some forty summers, who had already given birth to seven children at home. This time, however, she needed assistance. Her present child was two months overdue. The mother had been in labor for nine hours, and was clearly in dire straits.

The hospital's sole anesthetist was away on a prolonged fishing trip to the outer islands, so our patient had received only oral sedation, before the obstetrician and assisting intern tried to deliver the new baby with high forceps.

When this procedure failed, the obstetrician decided to inject a spinal himself, in order to perform a Caesarean section. The resulting nightmare rivaled the worst scenes that I'd witnessed during my training.

The eleven-pound child was anacephalic, with the mask of a face but no skull or brain. The intern thrust it at me, so I fashioned a towel to hide the missing skull, and showed it to the waiting father, while both physicians turned their attention to the mother, who had lapsed into deep shock.

"What should I do now?" the father asked in bewilderment.

He had come up with a good question. "Perhaps you'd best go away for a while," I decided, and he accepted my suggestion with alacrity.

I returned to the delivery room, and assisted the two physicians in trying to stem the flow of blood from the hemorrhaging mother.

When it became obvious that we had failed, and that the shock would soon be irreversible, the obstetrician resolved on heroic measures, commencing with a Porro hysterectomy.

For the next two hours, I administered blood transfusions, while the physicians tried to stem the outflow, all to no avail. At the woman's request, I became the godmother of her "beautiful child," and baptized it *Theresa*.

It expired shortly after the mother had slipped into a coma. In spite of all our efforts, she too died an hour later.

I was wondering dully what to say to the husband upon his return, and how he would care for his seven motherless children, when Bing and Francis arrived to pick me up.

They burst in like emissaries from the land of the living, eager to relate their triumphs on the links, but their smiles turned to dismay when they focused on the bloody zombie into which I'd been transformed.

"Good God, what happened?" Bing demanded.

"Never mind. Just let me wash and change, and then get me out of here."

"Isn't there anything I can do?" Bing asked, when we reached the airport.

"Yes, you can escort me into the bar, and buy me a strong drink."

Hunters by the fire

Our tent

Trader Vic cooking

Bing was flabbergasted. In the entire course of our acquaintance, the extent of my tippling had been the occasional glass of water over ice, flavored with a thimbleful of Blue Nun. He was minded to question my sanity, but Francis welcomed a new convert.

"Come on, girl," he urged. "Let's ditch this missionary (his one and only term of invective)."

Brown hustled me into a seat at the bar, with Bing trailing us bemusedly. Aside from a brush with a pub in Ireland, this was my first encounter with such an establishment. I found the atmosphere cool, dark, quiet, comforting, and curiously religious.

The banana daiquiri which Francis recommended hit me even harder and faster than my customary thimbleful of wine. Soon I had so far recovered that I was gazing vacantly and amiably about the room.

My eye chanced upon a vaguely familiar native face. "Do you know that man?" I asked Francis, who seemed to be personally acquainted with half the inhabitants of the isle.

"Can't say that I do," my guide replied, "but the peroxide blonde with him is a well-known professional."

Just then the object of our attention caught my eye, returned a stare in which amusement gradually melted into surprised recognition, picked up his blonde, and left hurriedly.

I now recognized him too. Indeed it was Theresa's father. He had probably feared that I would tattle to his wife. He couldn't yet know that all his secrets from her were now safe forever.

I reflected that it was I who had suggested that he leave the hospital, and rushed out of my new-found sanctuary to be very sick indeed.

The flight back to San Francisco passed in a blur of nausea and nightmares. Once safely home, Bing and I devoted ourselves principally to the children.

Mornings I held forth in our attic schoolroom. Afternoons we all swam and played tennis at the Burlingame Country Club.

On July 24th, Bing and I flew to Africa. We spent our first night in a Nairobi hotel which, with its screened-in verandas and exotic caged birds, resembled something out of a British movie of the 1930s, possibly entitled *The Far-Flung Empire*. Just to complete the picture, we discovered William Holden and Jimmy Stewart, gallantly supporting the enormous bar.

The next day, we flew to our campsite, in high meadowlands some fifty miles from Arusha. It was an imposing installation, boasting three English hunters, 26 African guides, bearers, beaters, skinners, and camp attendants.

Bing and I occupied a luxurious tent for two, complete with ground cloth, oriental rug, reading tables separating our cots, and a clothes closet for our tin trunks, and for whatever garments we chose to remove from them to suspend from hangers.

The entire camp was under the supervision of Jeanne Mathews, wife of Terry, our lead hunter and safari organizer. Amazed at the way she directed a dozen simultaneous activities in four languages, I asked if nothing ever fazed her.

"Well," she admitted, "it was a bit dicy during the Mau Mau insurrection. One of us had to be on guard at all times, so neither Terry nor I had a decent night's sleep for three years.

How about trading a shuka
for a land rover?

Ultimately mollified Masai

Searching for honey

After that, I thought that nothing could bother me, but it's taken a bit of time to recover from that last plane prang."

My further inquiries elicited the fact that *prang* means *wreckage*, and that Jeanne's husband had dragged her from the flaming remnants of a small aircraft, which had crashed on takeoff only a month earlier.

I made a mental note that life on the broad savannas might prove a mite too "dicy" for my taste.

To make matters worse, Bing was in his element. He had more phases than the moon, so I'd already had the experience of watching the beloved husband, whom I thought I knew, turn into various types of athletic stranger on fishing and hunting expeditions, and even in golf tournaments and horse races. But his self-sufficiency in this primitive world was becoming positively threatening.

After a splendid evening meal, and some good stories around the campfire, he bade me good night with an offhand remark to the effect that I "just might hear a few noises."

Within minutes, my inveterate insomniac was snoring softly, while I, the legendary sleeper, was recoiling in horror from every wail and scream that shattered the African night.

Suddenly there was an ominous crunching of bones that seemed to emanate from under my cot, and our tent resounded to what sounded like a combat between two ten-foot tomcats on a back fence.

Without making any conscious decision, I found myself sprawled across Bing's cot, screaming and desperately shaking him awake.

"What's the matter?" he finally murmured drowsily.

"Th-th-th-th-that noise out there," I stuttered hysterically.

Apparently it took him a while to hear me above the din, but then he muttered reassuringly, "Oh that's just a lion scrapping with a couple of hyenas over a kill.

Don't worry, they're as tidy as janitors. There'll be absolutely nothing left by morning"

Grimly I waited for a momentary lull in the combat to register my next complaint, but when it came, all I could elicit was another soft snore. Silently cursing the Dark Continent, hunting in general, safaris in particular, and the institution of matrimony as applied to poor betrayed Texans, I crept back into my sleeping bag, resolved to remain wide awake until daybreak, while suffering the terrors of the damned.

Obviously my timetable must have gone awry shortly thereafter, for I awoke, in what seemed like minutes, to a glorious tropic dawn.

While Bing slept serenely on, apparently uncrushed by the weight of the bad karma that I had heaped all over his cot the preceding evening, Jeanne Mathews and I hiked to the water hole for some animal and bird watching.

Hardly had we settled ourselves, when the native fauna were off in a drumming of hoofs and a whirring of wings. Turning, we saw that a group of Masai warriors were waving their spears to drive a herd of cattle before them toward the water.

"What a fantastic picture!" I cried, popping up in front of them with the new camera that Bing had bought me, and delightedly clicking away.

In a field of ipomoea

All too late, I registered Jeanne's shriek of protest, but two curious phenomena did impinge immediately: The Masai, at whom I had aimed the camera, pulled his red garment up over his head to hide his face, thus revealing the rest of his anatomy in graphic detail. Simultaneously his fellows charged with spears, forcing me to drop the camera and flee for my life.

"Ask me before you try anything like that again," Jeanne hissed.

Resignedly she strode forward, jabbered away at the warriors until some semblance of calm had been reestablished, ransomed my camera with a handful of coins, and shepherded my crestfallen self back to camp.

On the way, she informed me that she remembered when the natives had all gone stark-naked in the countryside in Kenya and Tanzania, but that recent laws required them to wear their red shukas in the field, and trousers in the unlikely event that they entered a town.

Unnecessarily she added that they had an aversion to being photographed, at least until having been properly warned, mollified, and bribed.

Privately I resolved to stick close to Bing for the next few days, strive to do as he did, and ask questions before making any sudden moves.

He and I set forth after breakfast, carefully skirting an area in which the Masai were burning the long grass of the meadow.

When I asked why so many starlings were picking through the still-glowing embers, Bing said that they were seeking out drunken grasshoppers.

It seemed that the warriors' fires passed so quickly that they simply stunned the insects, leaving them as a defenseless feast for the birds.

A mile further on, we spotted a group of natives engaged in a different activity. Bing explained that they were digging for Tanzanite, a beautiful blue stone that had been discovered in the area some weeks before.

Short hours ago, I'd have immediately abandoned all the hunting nonsense for a pick and spade, but mindful of my initial experience with the Masai, I stilled my acquisitive instincts, and continued to follow Bing.

After another fifteen minutes, we came upon one of the hunters, who was sitting in a Land Rover, and watching three of his guides engage in some sort of frenetic activity.

At first I took it for a kind of war dance, but Bing explained that they must have discovered a bee-hive in the ground.

Sure enough, a swarm of angry bees poured forth. Bing and I dived into the vehicle and rolled up the windows, but the Africans simply stood motionless.

This wasn't a perfect defense, as some authorities would have us believe, but the natives suffered relatively few stings, waited until the bees had calmed down, built a smoky fire to tranquilize them further, and dug out six honeycombs, which they tossed into the big canvas sack which was normally used as a glorified water bottle.

Just as I was concluding that the incident had come to an end, the real trouble began: The sugar-starved natives were congratulating themselves on their success, and on the point of returning to camp to share the booty, when the swarming bees returned to select the nearest jacket as their next hive site.

Springtime in Tanzania

Within seconds, the garment's original occupant had thousands of bees coating his back. He panicked and raced for the car, where I helpfully screamed contradictory injunctions to save him and to lock the doors.

Our hunter had yet to learn what a nitwit he had on his hands, so he attempted to follow my mandates to the letter. Locking the door firmly behind him, he leaped to the African's assistance, and was stung a score of times on his balding pate before joining the now-general exodus.

After an hour of further maneuvering, Bing managed to herd the guides and their precious canvas bag into the Land Rover, with only a minimal escort of bees, and we split for home.

On the way, we almost ran over a dead giraffe. After stopping to investigate, our hunter and the guides engaged in a long, inconclusive discussion in Swahili, the upshot of which was that, since there were no signs of attack by a predator, they had no idea of the cause of the giant's death.

Nosing around with the sole hope of getting close to something that large when it was in no condition to bite or kick, I astonished myself and the entire party by solving the riddle. The unfortunate long-necked mother had died in parturition, victim of an unsuccessful footling presentation.

The men were so obviously impressed by my knowledge of basic mammalian physiology that I recovered a bit of self-respect, and was even considering setting forth on my own again, until reason reasserted itself, and I returned to playing the helpless female, and clinging tightly to Bing.

Just before we arrived in camp, the hunter stopped our vehicle and pointed to an enormous acacia tree, full of what seemed to be ripe pears. On closer inspection, they proved to be hundreds of green-and-yellow parakeets.

Of course they weren't game birds, but the ensuing discussion wetted the men's appetite for the hunt, and they resolved to go shooting in the late afternoon.

At twilight, we repaired to a large lake, sat on a levee, and blazed away at silly sand grouse, as they rocketed in from all points of the compass. Dipping, dodging, ducking, and twirling, they described such erratic patterns that they were safe from me until they landed, at which time I was warned that there was a rule against blowing their fool heads off.

Ordinarily I would have amused myself by blasting away randomly at various patches of blue sky, before reloading in my own peculiarly slow but ineffective fashion.

On this occasion, however, the unfortunate hunter who had been assigned to me as loader, kept slapping the shotgun back into my hands before I had recovered from my previous catastrophes. The story got around, and I lost all the kudos that I had garnered from that blessed giraffe.

After an early breakfast the next day, I joined Bing on another voyage of exploration. I asked why we had hunted our birds in the evening, and he answered by pointing out that all except the aquatic species visited their sources of water once early in the day, and then again at nightfall.

Accordingly, we would now have at them in the cool of the morning. We watched several of the larger varieties arrive at our water hole. A secretary bird, with his wings sticking out in

Underneath the banyan tree

back, looked like a dignitary in a top hat with his hands folded behind him.

I gasped as a majestic greater bustard sailed in on his eight-foot wing span, and Bing picked up the feather of a guinea fowl to stick in my hat.

We turned our attention to the lush flora. The long, brilliantly-green grass was interlaced with wild hollyhock, heliotrope, ipomoea, and larkspur.

"The heavy rains have transformed everything," Bing explained. "It wasn't at all like this last year."

We observed two of our guides pounding sticks into the soft trunk of a banyan tree, and using them as a ladder to climb it and bring back the seed pods from which they got cream of tartar.

They tossed some down to us, and I chewed experimentally at first, and then with real enjoyment of the citrus flavor.

Indeed I found it so refreshing that I plucked a leaf from a pretty little shrub, and was just reaching absent-mindedly for my mouth when Bing knocked it out of my hands.

"That's cassia," he snapped. "The Masai use an infusion of the leaves for a purgative and a fish poison. They pour it into a stream, and watch their catch for the day float to the surface."

We approached thick underbrush, in which grew objects that looked like mottled green-and-yellow tomatoes.

"Those are Sodom apples," Bing explained. "The eland love them. Let's sit a while, and see if any come by. We're downwind here, so we might be in luck."

Sure enough, after about fifteen minutes rest, we caught our first sight of the huge antelope, and watched breathlessly while two of them paused to munch on the fruit. Several more

were just coming up to join them, when the original pair suddenly raised their heads, sniffed the wind, and vanished in a thunder of hoofs.

"What could have caused that?"

"If you'll be quiet for a moment, we may find out."

Three minutes later, a mother cheetah and her two cubs passed within a few yards. "Watch what happens when she gets downwind of us," Bing whispered.

As he had predicted, the mother sniffed once, wheeled, spotted us, and was off for the bush like a furry projectile. Then she seemingly remembered something, whirled, raced back to her cubs, cuffed them to get their attention, and herded them at their maximum pace into the nearest thicket.

The evening was devoted to more bird watching at the water hole. Bing added a brilliant blue tail feather to the collection in my hat.

When I asked him to identify it, he assured me that it came from a *lilac-breasted roller.*

I wasn't naive enough to accept this perfectly correct identification at its face value. "Aw come on," I protested. "You just made that up to plague me."

"Right you are," Bing admitted agreeably, "and it was fiendishly clever of you to catch me in the act. It's really from a red-headed, double-breasted, mattress thrasher."

"That's much better. Thought you could fool a tenderfoot for a minute there, didn't you?"

Driving back to the camp at twilight, our headlights picked up a pair of jackals running along the road, and then a white-tailed mongoose, whose huge brush floated out behind him as he scampered away.

The Woods bag an oryx.

Oryx for supper

You meet all kinds at a bush stop.

Though he's not of the cat family, his curiosity almost cost him his life, for he soon wheeled and raced straight back toward the truck, determined to find out just what we were. Only the driver's quick foot on the brake preserved our ferretlike friend to inspect some future vehicle.

By the following day, we were out of fresh meat, and Bing promised to shoot an oryx for everyone's dinner. I sat on a flowering hillside, and watched through binoculars the sudden transformation of my gentle husband into a predator.

After catching sight of the nearly parallel horns of a huge, solitary male, Bing spent half an hour maneuvering downwind of the animal, and two more hours in a slow, methodical stalk, employing every bit of available cover as he glided toward his quarry, and simply freezing when its gaze caught him on the open savanna.

Bing had worked his way to within 150 yards of the oryx. I watched him take slow, deliberate aim, and drop it with a single shot to the heart.

I kept to my hillside, as he directed the butchering of the beast, gave the prized intestines to his favorite guide, and returned, bloody but triumphant.

Halfway along the trek back to camp, I called for a bush stop. I had not yet penetrated a discreet distance into the undergrowth when I heard an odd, loud, grunting sound.

I turned to confront an irate old rhinoceros, whose terrain I had inadvertently invaded. The truth is that I have always been on the slow side, but in this instance I moved with a speed that would have delighted a track coach, and found myself behind the trunk of a large tree when the first charge thundered past.

By the time my adversary had whirled and sighted in on me again, I was up into the friendly, low-hanging limbs of an adjacent bush, though to this day I have no recollection of how I arrived there.

My problem now was that a really determined charge would uproot shrub and all, and whatever that antediluvian locomotive might lack, it surely wasn't determination.

Fortunately my screams had alerted Bing, who was himself trying to break the record for the hundred meter dash, as he came sprinting straight at my foe, waving his arms and howling obscene threats. My relief yielded to horror when I realized that he was unarmed.

For a long moment, the rhino simply stared at his diminutive assailant in utter disbelief. Then a couple of neurons must have bumped together in his dim little prehistoric brain, and concluded that anything which charged him so directly and fearlessly must be dangerous.

He snorted twice more, wheeled, and trotted reluctantly off.

"Jump, Juliet," laughed Bing, holding out his arms to me. "Let's get out of here before that big porker changes what we laughingly call his mind."

"Why didn't you bring a weapon?" I asked breathlessly, clambering down from my insecure perch.

"Nothing short of an elephant gun would have got that monster's attention, and I had no time to think of one, let alone load it. Now hustle."

And so I did with a will, but I remained of two minds about the whole experience. I had hunted with Bing before, but always in relatively civilized and protected spots.

119

Trader Vic and Helen

A Kenyan giraffe

Lion cubs

This primitive provider was a complete stranger to me, and I was beginning to realize that he was in his true environment. Ill at ease in the effete world of Hollywood, which had granted him such rewards as society could offer, he was at home in mankind's earliest habitat.

I, on the other hand, wouldn't have survived an hour on my own out here, where nature was so red in tooth and claw. Truth to tell, I had been annoyed from time to time when glamorous starlets flirted with my husband, but I had never known real jealousy until this moment. Bing's abiding love was Africa, and no woman in the world could hold a candle to it.

"God preserve me from an interesting life," runs an old Jewish refrain. I had had quite enough adventure for the time being, so I spent the next few days safe in camp, assisting Jeanne Mathews, dressing in my fluffiest attire, and generally playing the part of a fragile girl.

Trader Vic joined us on the hunt. One night by the campfire, he commented on the attractions of my dressing gown.

Grateful to find myself cast in a role in which I felt a trifle more secure, I pranced over to him, sat on his lap, and set out to generate a murderous, green-eyed rage in my spouse.

"How do you like my technique?" I inquired demurely.

"It's just great," Bing informed me. "As usual, you're right on target. You're sitting on his wooden leg, and cooing into his tin ear." Not for the first time, I marveled at my faculty for bringing out the primitive beast in men.

The next morning, my husband observed me sadly, as I dug out some unmentionables. "I'm starving to death in the midst of plenty," he sighed. "I forgot to bring any shorts."

"I'll share with you," I offered generously, "if you'll promise to stay away from the lacy ones. People might talk."

"Well if I can't have the lacy ones, I just won't wear any at all," Bing lisped. He flounced out of the tent, stamping his foot in a fit of pique.

A moment later, he minced back in to see if he could borrow my perfume. "Just what is that fabulous scent?" he inquired in a querulous falsetto.

"I didn't notice a thing till you came in," I assured him grimly. "Just how long do you intend to sport the same ratty shorts beneath those scruffy old khaki pants?"

"I always change them regularly on safari," he announced grandly.

"Just how regularly would that be?"

"Once a month, whether they need it or not."

I continued to treat the wilds of Africa with profound respect, though I learned from Jeanne Mathews that my problem at the bush stop was far from unique. Liz Coleman Crocker, later the Duchess of Manchester, had also met up with an irate rhino, when exploring the thickets on just such an errand.

She, however, had advanced to a point where she was forced to sprint for her Land Rover, panties at the knees, and laughing her fool head off. Legend had it that it was precisely this episode which won her the duke's heart and hand. He just couldn't resist a good sport.

Leonora Wood, a fellow Texan who had rendezvoused with us, was less fortunate. She had insisted on following a practice common in her home state, by sitting on the fender of her Land Rover,

With Bruno Paglai at the Olympics

whence she could get off immediate shots at astonished game birds.

Alas Leonora discovered that Africa is not Texas. Large burrowing animals leave concealed holes which can easily break an axle.

When the wheel beneath her perch dropped into one, she was thrown fifteen feet onto her face. I did my best to clean her cuts and abrasions, and to staunch the flow of blood, but I had only tetracycline and hydrogen peroxide in my minimal medicine chest.

We radioed for a plane, and dragged a log behind a Land Rover to ready an impromptu landing strip. Off Leonora flew to civilization, followed closely by my envious gaze.

At last our weeks in the bush came to an end, as I've remarked that all things must, and we flew back to London, which had never looked better. Indeed, after my adventures in Africa, I would doubtless have viewed it as a haven of refuge during the blitz.

We spent four days there, followed by three more in Portugal; then returned to Florida for some scuba diving and luxuriating in the comforts of civilization, which our safari had finally taught me to appreciate fully.

I was reminded of certain medieval artists' representations of Paradise, with the blissful denizens gazing down over the rim at their erstwhile friends and relatives, haplessly frying in the nether regions.

We humans are creatures of contrast, apparently needing to alternate pleasure and pain, if the former is to be properly appreciated.

Bing and I returned to Hillsborough on September 1st, solemnly vowing never to leave home again. Some measure of our resolve may be gleaned from the fact that he departed on the 5th for a golf tournament in Phoenix, returning just in time to wave good-bye to Mary Frances and me, as we flew off to Chicago on the 16th, to start rehearsing *Sabrina Fair.*

On the 17th, Bring wrote the following letter from Hillsborough: "You escaped to Chicago in the nick of time. If you were available, I'd chase you all the way to Crystal Springs, with my trusty 28-gauge kicking up dust beneath your high-stepping feet. In point of fact, I'd be tempted to have recourse to the 12-gauge, but I remain a true sportsman, even when thoroughly aroused.

I have just learned that Johnny Longden phoned on Saturday with an urgent message, which you somehow neglected to pass along. As a direct consequence, our horse Society ran, won, and paid 5 to 1 to anyone lucky enough not to have married a lapsed Baptist who doesn't approve of gambling. It was my one great chance to get even, but oh well, lucky in love....

If you really are planning to let Mary Frances give the prologue, I suggest that you move it to the end, converting it into an epilogue for your own protection. I'd as soon follow a dog show as that little scene stealer.

But on second thought, anything might be preferable to letting her play a role. She does have a way of taking over any production that she pokes her nose into."

On the same day, Bing thoughtfully wrote a long letter to Mary Frances, despite the fact that he was devoting most of his time and energy to trying to save the right eye of Terry Mathews.

A cable from the hunter's wife had described the incident as follows: "My husband thought he was in a safe area

With Merle Oberon at the Floating Gardens

on the far right, but a bird flushed, and his client's gun swung toward him. Terry ducked, and threw his hands up, blocking a few of the pellets, but one of them seriously injured his shooting eye, which surgeons are now trying to save in a London clinic."

A letter from Terry himself depicted the disaster as follows: "I caught most of the pellets from a 12-gauge at about 45 yards. I'm still carrying some 20 of them, which the surgeons persist in considering harmless.

The one that entered my closed eyelid passed through the lens, and reached the interior cavity. It has been successfully removed, but no one holds out much hope for any further use of the eye. I still plan to outfit and conduct photo safaris, but I'll have to find a hunter to take care of the more dangerous game."

Bing did everything possible to unearth the best treatment for Terry, while I struggled with the problems of a theater brat's mother. My daughter had decided that, since she introduced my play each evening, I should repay the favor by serving as her maid and cook in the motel where we were lodged.

Furthermore, she saw no reason to continue her school work, now that she was launched on a performing career.

I solved part of the problem by lugging home an armload of high-school literary anthologies, borrowed from apprentices working on the set. I absolutely forbade my child to touch them, thus guaranteeing that they would be read from cover to cover by an indignant nine-year-old.

Of course her prologue was a smash hit, and the entire play received excellent notices. As a consequence, we gave a series of press interviews, which

I found unnerving because of Mary Frances' proclivity for saying almost anything at any time.

One scribe noted that "she looks like Shirley Temple, but acts like Heloise." It seems that she had confided to him that she was doing her best with lines that were too few and too weak, that she had planned a future as an actress or a nun, or possibly both, and that her mother had yet to raise her allowance as promised.

Also that I didn't do much of a job on stage of kissing all those boys who wanted to marry me, but that she was endeavoring to coach me in the role.

"Ye gods, what are we rearing?" was Bing's comment when he read the last item. It was October 16th, and we were flying to the Olympics in Mexico City, while still competing as ferociously as ever in scrabble.

Bing had completed an RCA special with Bob Hope, Jose Feliciano, Stella Stevens, and Diana Ross who had just left the Supremes. Now he was planning a very merry white Christmas at our ranch.

We watched the Fosberry flop win the high jump, and floated on our own barge through the lush gardens at Xochimilco.

Bing asked our hostess, Merle Oberon, if she thought that their mutual friend, Mary Morrow, then in the throes of romantic quandaries, would enjoy a holiday at the ranch.

"If you're there, I'm sure that she would, Rhonda Flemming would, Joan Caulfield would, Mona Freeman would, anyone would, and as a matter of fact, I would. Why haven't I been asked? You certainly entertained me royally in the old days at Elko."

Mary Morrow

I sat at the other end of the barge, stolidly munching on a hamburger. If Merle kept on teasing Bing about former girl friends, I would doubtless eat enough to sink the boat, and thus avenge myself on the lot of them. Fortunately for all concerned, my husband's attention was soon diverted by the food that Merle's chef prepared.

Bing had to return to Los Angeles for a series of recording sessions, after which we spent two weeks in the wonderful winter climate of Las Cruces. Then he was off bird shooting in South Carolina, while I made yet another desperate attempt to get the children in hand.

Mary Morrow, beauty queen, model, faithful friend, and social butterfly, arrived December 8th at the Reno airport, where my brother-in-law picked her up.

On the drive to the ranch, they stopped at a tiny diner in Susanville. Continuing the trip, they had almost reached their goal, when Mary touched Leonard on the arm, and suggested that they return immediately to the restaurant.

Revisiting the booth which they had occupied, they found on the floor Mary's cosmetic case, with its seven million dollars worth of jewelry still intact.

Lacking Mary's classic beauty, I still tried to imitate her light touch and easy social graces, but found the role hard to pull off in the midst of so many children and dogs.

I hoped that a bit of her style would rub off, when we took time out for a fashion show in Las Vegas. There she spied a man's karakul lamb coat with a rich beaver collar, and immediately cooed, "But that's Bing."

We struck a bargain with designer Jean Louis, and acquired the coat long before Joe Namath had his mink. Back at the ranch, Mary always opened the correct bottle of wine to prevent tears as we chopped the onion for our soup, and I was left asking myself, "Why didn't I think of that?"

She told us stories about dates with the great stars of Hollywood whom she had met through Bing, while always requesting his advice and comments, which she found generally unsatisfactory. For example, after an exposure to Clark Gable, she had asked what the inner man was really like.

When pressed for an answer, Bing had thought for a minute, and finally admitted, "Well, all in all he's a pretty good shot."

This launched Bing on a spate of hunting stories involving Clark and Gary Cooper. Trapped by a blizzard in the high mountains above Elko, they had sought refuge in a sheepherder's hut. It's occupant prepared them a great supper, featuring delicious fresh-baked bread.

"What's your secret?" Gary asked.

"Es el agua. I catch it in the rain barrel outside the door."

Clark eased out back to check on the ingredient, and discovered a foot-long rat, sharing the barrel. Unwilling to spoil the party, he waited a year before sharing his discovery with Bing. Gary never did learn the secret of his host's recipe.

Merry Christmas 1968

New Year's Eve found Mary and me sitting before a warm fire, and discussing marriages, hers and mine. She confided that Bing had passed through Palm Springs in the spring of 1957, en route to a tour of the South with Phil Harris.

Our crooner had looked so unhappy that she had finally risked asking him just what his trouble was and how she might help.

"She's only 23," he moaned.

"Is that so important?"

"My friends and relatives seem to think so."

"Well time, which solves all problems, will eventually cure that one."

I stared into the fire through eyes permanently crow's-footed from squinting through the sights of shotguns, folded hands permanently shriveled from dish washing, and through lips permanently pursed from screaming at inattentive children, commented, "The other day, a reporter reminded Bing that he would soon be 60, and that I would turn 30 in the same year." "What will you do then?" the newshound had demanded.

"You know, I really hadn't thought of that, but as you put it, there's obviously no good remedy. I guess I'll just have to trade Kathryn in for a younger woman."

The gang's all here.

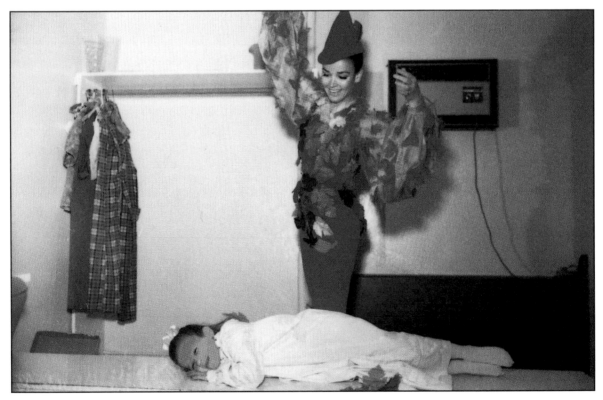

Peter Pan to the rescue

1969

The Crosby family spent a white New Year's day at Wyntoon, the Hearsts' Bavarian fairyland, an hour and a half from our Rising River Ranch.

The snow was so deep that it touched the eves of our barn, permitting the children to slide from the rooftree directly into it, a circumstance which initially led my brother-in-law, Leonard Meyer, to oppose my plans for an expedition.

At my further insistence, he gruffly helped to pack our picnic lunch, five adults, three children, and voluminous snow gear into his station wagon. Sure enough, we bogged down in deep drifts the moment we abandoned the plowed highway, before reaching even the outer gate to Wyntoon.

Bing and Leonard climbed out, dug in manfully with their shoulders just above the rear bumper, and made loud puffing noises. The children piled out to cheer them on. Mary Morrow remarked on how secure she felt with such strong

men about, and I, the immediate cause of the catastrophe, remained safely behind the wheel, helpfully warbling random stanzas from Peter Pan.

At length, Leonard sidled up to the car door, allowed as how he believed in magic, and could use some help from Tinker Bell, slipped, fell into a drift, and finally marched glumly off towards the caretaker's house, a long snowy mile away.

Scarcely an hour later, he returned with the caretaker in a huge four-wheel-drive vehicle, carrying two snow-mobiles, which they unloaded while I was transferring myself and the picnic lunch to the truck.

I was about to call for a driver, when an ear-splitting roar drew my attention to the lead skiddoo.

To my amazement, I saw my hopelessly unmechanical spouse seated proudly at the wheel, with Mary firmly ensconced behind him, looking for all the world like a biker and his bird.

131

Wyntoon

In a deafening crescendo of sound, they whirled off along the trail, with Mary's full-length mink flying out behind them like a comet's tail.

"That looks like fun," I remarked to no one in particular.

"Don't fool yourself," Leonard cautioned. "Bing's never driven one of those things before, and I've seen him take five runs at removing the cap from a Coca-Cola bottle. If you ask me, that lady's in a heap of trouble."

"Nonsense. Anyone can see that they're doing fine. Now it's my turn. Surely I'm at least as inept as Bing is."

I vaulted down from the truck, forged my way through the drifts to the second snowmobile, and issued a blanket invitation to anyone in the group who wished to join me.

Curiously enough, there were no immediate takers. "Don't any of you children want to ride with your mother?" my sister finally asked.

Three small heads shook as one. Just what is it about me that inspires such confidence?

"All right," I decided, "if that's the way you feel, I'll go it alone. Where's the starter on this silly thing?"

The caretaker had just finished showing me, when Leonard realized what was happening and shouted, "No, no, no! Stop her before she kills herself. She's too dumb to be scared."

With a desperate lunge, Frances Ruth threw herself onto the back of the machine, just as I took off in gleeful pursuit of Bing and Mary. Within seconds, I noted with satisfaction that mine was the faster machine, or perhaps that I simply had more gas on. However vague I might be about mechanical details, there was no disputing the fact that I was racing

along at a smart pace, and rapidly reducing the distance between us.

"Throttle back," my sister shrieked. "You're going to run them down."

Privately I wished that she would stop making meaningless noises, and suggest a way to pass Bing on such a narrow, woodland trail, but I wasn't silly enough to waste my breath telling her so.

I was much too busy dodging Mary's billowing mink, and trying to get into sync with Bing's suddenly erratic steering. So far as I could see, his passenger wasn't helping him much by shouting some sort of hysterical warning into his right ear.

"It's Kathryn, I tell you," she was yowling, as I later learned. "Get off the trail before she catches us!"

"How in hell do I do that? It's solid trees on both sides."

"Well you'd better think of something. Here she comes!"

For my part, I was delighted to see that Bing had veered sharply to his right, plunging through some minor undergrowth in the process, but leaving a clear path for a horse that could run.

With a triumphant rebel yell, I surged forward directly into Mary's mink, which had somehow zigged when Bing zagged. In her favor it must be said that she shed it with creditable speed, and I was off at last on a clear track, with the coat wrapped about the front of the skiddoo like a trophy on a knight's helm.

I had covered scarcely another quarter mile, when my better nature asserted itself. In justice to Frances Ruth, I must admit that my stroke of conscience was aided and abetted by her insistence that I had wrecked my husband's conveyance, and abandoned

With Frances and Leonard Meyer

his Southern-born friend to freeze coatless in the deep snow.

"No problem," I pronounced womanfully. "We'll go back and pick them up."

"Noooooo!" was Frances Ruth's less than helpful contribution. "You can't turn around here."

My older sister was generally acknowledged to be taller, stronger, wiser, and prettier than I, but throughout those long, golden, childhood years, I had always considered her to be the weakling of the family. Fortunately I still had courage enough for us both.

I whipped the wheel around, surged through a series of brambles and branches, dodged a mighty pine which sprang threateningly into my path, and in a trice had reversed our progress, to barrel back along the trail on a mission of mercy.

All to no avail as it transpired, for Frances Ruth's dire warnings to the contrary, Bing and Mary were not lying bruised and bloody in the snow. There they came, dawdling pusillanimously along the path, a bit the worse for wear to be sure, but still decidedly mobile.

"Good God, there she is again," Mary screamed. "Stop this crazy machine, and let me off."

"Couldn't you just drag your feet or something? The contraption doesn't seem to have a brake."

"Then turn back into the woods before we crash head-on."

And that was exactly what the silly things did. Just as I swept up to deliver the coat, their skiddoo leaped a bank, crunched through a tangle of tree limbs, and dived full into a profound trailside drift.

The whole maneuver was really quite impressive in its way, and I might have stopped to congratulate Bing on

pulling it off, if only I had known how. As it was, I found myself whizzing back along the path toward the rest of our party, who were still maintaining a sedate pace in the big truck.

I hailed them joyously, and was just dashing up to acquaint them with the details of Bing's latest feat, when they swerved abruptly to port, and disappeared into the depths of the forest.

Oh well, it was a fine day for a ride in the country. I cheerfully retraced the entire route, and circled our stalled station wagon, before returning regretfully to retrieve my errant relations.

I found them happily reunited. Those in the truck had apparently escaped unscathed from their passage through the woods, regained the trail, and followed it until they met Bing and Mary, just emerging from a huge drift, and looking for all the world like the snowmen which the children had fashioned the preceding day.

Since it was obvious that Mary was in dire need of her mink, I proposed to deliver it *en passant*, providing of course that I could find a way by, since the truck and the upturned skiddoo were contriving to block my path.

It was at this very moment that my spoilsport of a sister climbed my back, and jabbed frantically at a gadget which she later identified as that silly throttle that she had been making such a fuss about. Our little machine spluttered ingloriously to a halt, and the entire party descended upon me with dark and accusing stares.

I remained unperturbed, since I can recognize base jealousy when I see it. After all, wasn't I the only one who hadn't had an accident?"

In the sequel, Mary retrieved her coat, and the caretaker glumly stashed

Father of the bride

the snowmobiles back into the truck. We all proceeded with him to Wyntoon, where we ate our picnic lunch under forty-foot ceilings, before a fireplace in which a tall man could stand upright.

We inspected the still-unfinished stone and timber castle which Hearst called *The Gables,* near the bend of the swift McCloud River. And then it was off to Marion Davies' house, and to the three Bavarian chalets covered with Willy Pogany's illustrations from fairy tales, which were dubbed *The Bear, Cinderella,* and *Angel House.*

While the children clambered atop the gothic furniture to stage mock battles, or swung from the staghorn chandeliers, I nursed a hot toddy before the fire, and observed Mary's futile efforts to dry her mink.

"It's the last time I'll run off with your husband," she assured me. "It seems to bring out the fiend in you."

"I wasn't angry," I stated truthfully.

"May I never meet you when you are," Mary sighed, "but this really is an enchanted spot. What did they do here when the snow wasn't quite so deep?"

"Marion Davies made quilts while her guests fished. They could cast right from the back porch. Maybe Bing will bring us here to try it next spring."

Back at Rising River Ranch, Mary snapped the picture of the Crosbys hanging on the gate, which became our Christmas card for 1969.

On January 11th, I hauled Bing off to Southern California, to attend the wedding of Bob Hope's daughter Linda, in a ceremony presided over by a priest and a rabbi.

While both clerics made their initial speeches, I tried unsuccessfully to explain matters to my spouse, who had learned too well from the nuns in childhood that his Church permitted mixed marriages with fellow Christians "only to prevent a greater evil," and forbade any species of association with those outside the pale.

I, of course, had converted for his sake, reasoning that Paris was well worth a mass, and Bing had thought himself justified in demanding similar sacrifices from his friends.

However, since Dolores Hope was unquestionably a paragon of Catholicism, my husband grudgingly accepted the fact that his side had somehow blessed this union, or would do so as soon as Dolores had explained the new dogma to the Pope.

In spite of my efforts, Bing continued to look as uncomfortable as the rabbi throughout much of the afternoon. But the ceremony, whatever it was, impressed everyone.

The church was crammed with Hollywood notables, each in his own version of what constituted correct attire for a Jewish-Catholic wedding. The odor of incense mixed with the scent of thousands of flowers, the voices of the choir mounted heavenward, and a good time was had by all.

At the subsequent reception at the Hope home, rivers of champagne flowed through the huge tent which covered most of the back yard. The bride was radiant, as were Bob, Dolores, and even the confused parents of the groom.

When questioned about the authenticity of the ceremony, and about his general tendency to assist in fundraising for all religions known to man, Bob queried, "Wouldn't it be a shame to be excluded from Paradise on a mere technicality?"

Warbling native boy with trophies   It couldn't have been that hard.

All in all, the ministrations of priest and rabbi, and the congratulations of friends and relatives, must have taken reasonably well, because the happy couple had a record-breaking run in their own version of *Abie's Irish Rose* before the inevitable separation.

On our way out, Bob mentioned slyly to Bing that it would be Mary Frances' turn soon enough, and guffawed as he watched his longtime co-star turn green about the gills.

A number of other old partnerships were severely tested by the 28th Crosby National Pro-Am, which was played under the worst conditions in the history of the tournament. The first day was actually washed out by high winds which brought rain and hail, and the rest of the mess was conducted in what Phil Harris loudly termed "double-bourbon weather."

This was the year when Bing first invited Pat Ward-Thomas, the famed golf correspondent for the *Manchester Guardian,* who polysyllabically described the play of Dean Martin, Jack Lemmon, Sean Connery, James Garner, Andy Williams, and a host of others, while somehow the porous strata of soil and sand absorbed one of the rainfalls of the century.

Six-foot-seven-inch George Archer, who had first visited The Crosby as a caddy twelve years before, won by a stroke, and pocketed $25,000, a huge prize for those days.

For my part, all I derived from the affair was a nasty case of the flu which, with my susceptibility to respiratory ailments, bordered on pneumonia, leading Bing to convey me to Las Cruces on February 1st, for some hunting and fishing in the hot, desert sunlight.

My husband soon tired of playing nurse, and flew off with George Coleman to bedeck their hats with branches, and try to repeat Charlie Jones' 1966 success with the elusive brant.

Meanwhile I recovered rapidly, and devoted myself to vigorous but unproductive fishing from the back of the Dorado, and to journeying to Todos Santos, for an uncharacteristically successful pursuit of the swift white-winged doves, which for once seemed determined to dive straight down the barrel of my gun.

Simba, my warbling native boy, joined me just in time to start training for our forthcoming African safari, by acting as the bearer who lugged the trophies home. The pictures of my triumph were designed to make our son Harry, who had the requisite talent and gender to supplant me in the hunt, eat his heart out one last time.

On February 10th, we flew back to Los Angeles, where Bing taped a Hollywood Palace show. Between scenes, he was on the phone continually, leading his resident paranoiac to conclude that it must concern some (sob) old or (horrors) new flame. At length I demanded an explanation, and succeeded in forcing the word *poison* from his lips.

My onboard computer processed the fact that all three children were with us and presumably safe, so the calls had to concern one of our other relatives. I wormed the truth out of Bing, and my worst fears were realized.

Cindy, my adored Labrador, who shared my life and guarded it with her own, had somehow got into oatmeal that had been treated with rat poison. She was in agony, and the consulting veterinarians had decided that she must be put to sleep.

Lynn Revson, my first contributor

Bing had vetoed that suggestion, and had insisted on massive blood transfusions, which had indeed saved the little dog's life. All this without subjecting me to needless worry and indecision. So much for lovers, old or new. I relapsed into my normal state of acute paranoia.

On Monday the 17th, we were off to New York, where Bing received the initial Golden Tee award, in recognition of his contribution to the world of golf.

Bing had contemplated a week of relaxed theater-going, during which he wouldn't have to share his wife's attention with children and charities. His first unwelcome surprise was the discovery that the Mother Superior of the Immaculate Heart Sisters was quartered at our hotel.

"What's that nun doing here?" he inquired in tones of dark suspicion.

"Well, I thought that as long as we were going to be in New York, I might as well do a little promotional work for your Church."

"So it's my Church now, is it? Certainly it's grown more affluent than anything I remember. Was it a Jean-Louis original that the good sister was sporting in the lobby?"

"She has to look presentable if she's to meet with important people," I insisted, prudently refusing to discuss the financing of the gown in question, or of the other racy numbers in the Reverend Mother's spiffy new wardrobe, or, for that matter, of her luxurious rooms in the hotel.

"As I've often warned you, I won't have you running around New York, begging money from my friends."

"How about friends of friends?" I asked with due subservience, mentally reviewing my list.

My experienced quarry sensed a trap: "I'll have none of that either," he stated decisively.

By the end of the week, the whole discussion had proved academic. Sister Anita and I had visited seven foundations and the home offices of a dozen major corporations, but neither friends nor friends of friends had coughed up a single dime.

As a last resort, I invited the remnant of my potential victims to dinner at the Grenouille Restaurant, where Reverend Mother uttered her last piteous plea. Charles and Lynn Revson looked inquiringly at Bing, who was caught between sinking beneath the table in embarrassment and glaring daggers at me.

"I do remember," Lynn told her husband, "that in Immaculate Heart College the plaster on the ceiling of the President's office was doing its best to decorate her desk. For purely cosmetic reasons, if none other, I think we should make a contribution."

"Would ten thousand dollars help?"

"That would be wonderful," I shouted, overjoyed at having obtained my first contribution ever. At long last, the Church and I seemed destined to be business partners.

My elation was somewhat dampened by a sharp kick in the shins, and a hissed, "Kathryn, stop it! This is outright blackmail."

But Sister Anita was seated at the other end of the table, out of range of flying feet or whispered threats. She expressed her gratitude in a heart-rending narration of the years that she and I had spent as inept mendicants, without a sous to show for our travail.

At this point, even I feared that her tale of woe might be a trifle *de trop*

On the steps of Merle Oberon's Acapulco home

At lunch with the lady herself

under the circumstances, but it struck a responsive chord in a most unlikely breast.

Malcolm McLean, stout agnostic, billionaire industrialist, and originator of containerized transport, had started life as a simple lumberjack.

Not only did he identify with poverty, but he knew what it was to have a petitioner in the family. His school-teacher spouse, Margaret, had marched for most of the worthier national causes, too often with results that rivaled mine. Now he launched into an uncharacteristic harangue:

"My wife went to see one man after another that I'd handed millions worth of business to, only to be told that they'd already given to charity. How many more orders do you suppose those deadbeats got from me?

I know just how all that begging must have made you feel, so I want to pledge $100,000, for whatever purpose Kathryn considers most appropriate."

Said Kathryn was too busy guarding her shins and gazing steadfastly down at her plate, to acknowledge such overwhelming generosity. When she finally did sneak a sidelong glance at her inarticulate mate, she watched his color change from beet red to ghastly greenish white.

His long friendship with McLean had been firmly grounded in his delight in the latter's booming banana ball, which had led Malcolm to construct a private course in which all doglegs curved to the right. Bing, who hated debts of any description, had now been placed under an obligation which only huge contributions to Margaret's causes could ever repay.

The sequel had to be a bidding war against an opponent of far greater resources, tantamount to trying to break the bank at Monte Carlo.

Heretofore, I had occasioned my husband only grievous embarrassment; now he was staring bankruptcy full in the face.

Malcolm drove a strangely silent Bing and his exuberant wife to the airport for the flight to San Francisco. On the plane, I made the tactical error of complimenting my spouse on his success in obtaining contributions:

"We'd never received a cent before, and in one dinner with you, we took in $110,000," I rhapsodized. It almost cost me my marriage.

We spent the first days of March in Acapulco, as house guests of Merle Oberon. Chameleon-like, Bing transformed himself from the mate of a mendicant to the center of a brilliant international circle.

I still don't understand how such a lackadaisical specimen managed so consistently to dominate his social environment. He certainly made no effort to perform. So it must have had something to do with his assumption that he was the natural focus of all attention. Since he never doubted it, neither did anyone else.

I, on the other hand, always found myself abandoned just outside the pale. In that glorious tropical setting, surrounded by the political, financial, and social leaders of the world, I found nothing better to do than sneak out the back door with my tape player, to practice ballet on the patio.

Why is it only in retrospect that I can appreciate how silly I must have seemed?

On Monday, March 3rd, we picnicked aboard our hostess's cabin cruiser, while touring Acapulco Bay.

Finally appearing on the runway

Bing sat in the stern with Bruno Paglai, Merle's husband of the moment, and reminisced about the grand old days when Hollywood stars crossed the border on weekends to wager their paychecks at the Caliente race track.

Since the crew's eyes never left Merle's bikini, in the interests of our peace and safety, we had thought it best to station her in the prow. Toward the end of the day, I joined her there, as the boat moved silently across a calm sea into the glowing colors of the tropical sunset.

Since neither of us was knowledgeable about horses, our conversation was more or less limited to men. Caught in an uncharacteristically communicative mood, Merle recounted dozens of tales of her husbands and lovers, involving many of the great and the near great of the mid-twentieth century. Fascinated, I asked her how she had managed to captivate so many male celebrities.

"Are you planning to launch a new career as a temptress?" Merle inquired, with a smile that I found just a trifle too patronizing.

"No, I simply want to tantalize one golfer. Let's concentrate on fascinating a husband."

"That's easy enough. Just keep him off balance For example, when I was married to Lucien Ballard, we attended a ball in Monaco, where I found myself dancing with Count Georgio Cini.

At the end of the number, we walked out onto the terrace, down through the garden, along the dock, onto his yacht, and didn't return for three months. How do you think Bing would react to something like that?"

I knew the answer to that one all right. "He'd hunt me down and kill me,"
I replied solemnly. It seemed that even if I could develop any talent for the role of siren, I still lacked the requisite courage and breed of husband.

Oh well, given my circumstances, at least I was still a *live* coward.

On Tuesday, March 4th, we bade farewell to Merle and Acapulco, and I cheated furiously at scrabble all the way back to the San Francisco airport.

Scarcely had we unpacked, when Bing metamorphosed from social lion into forest bobcat, and disappeared in the general direction of Dr. Sullivan's Guadalupe Ranch. I hardly noticed his absence, so preoccupied was I with preparations for a style show in Oakland, for the benefit of the Children's Hospital Medical Center.

Jean Louis had recently designed new stewardess outfits for United Airlines, which had somehow achieved more worldly success than the nuns' habits which I had sponsored. United was expressing its gratitude by financing a lavish charitable spectacle, featuring ten leading models, and starring the erstwhile Grandstaff sisters.

The theme was a round-the-world flight, with an original musical number for each of the countries visited. Frances Ruth and I rehearsed diligently, and luxuriated in the gorgeous costumes for a week before the fateful day arrived.

On Wednesday, March 12th, our models' chorus, fortunately backed by a choir of professional vocalists prudently furnished by United Airlines, sang its way into the hearts and hopefully the pocketbooks of the Oakland elite.

All went swimmingly, except for a minor problem experienced by the shorter of the Grandstaff girls.

145

One of the costumes from *The Guardsman*

During the rehearsals, I'd had the foresight, or sheer dumb luck, to include in my plans my maid of all work and occasional theatrical dresser, Bridget Brennan.

In the flurry of last-minute preparations, I had somehow overlooked the fact that, by reason of a Nathaniel nosebleed, my faithful retainer had been confined to quarters, so I now found myself in the improvised dressing room, struggling hysterically with the scores of buttons on the splendid costumes from *The Guardsman,* which I had insisted on showing off.

Each number began with the models, in their roles of globe-circling tourists, trouping off the plane two-by-two, like animals descending from the Ark. By about the third attempt, my poor sister had the drill down pat.

While the five couples ahead of her resolutely joined hands, and prepared to trip joyously down the runway, caroling an appropriate local ditty, she hoarsely whispered, "Kathryn, for God's sake pin it up or do something. We're on."

Then, in utter desperation, with no one's hands to hold but her own, she resolutely clasped them behind her back, and danced off alone into the glare of the footlights.

Indeed she carried it off so well that the audience learned to reserve their special applause for the regal being who, after a brief pause for effect, invariably followed her handmaidens onto the stage.

As soon as I got myself more or less buttoned up, it was time to start the reverse process, which in turn took so long that I was laboring under a severe handicap, even if I hadn't had other far more complicated costumes waiting to ensnare me.

Eventually I arrived at a solution of sorts. I would skip every second number, permitting myself to wear whatever costume I had finally worked my way into, appropriate or no.

If fate decreed bikinis in Boston, and furs in Florida, I disclaimed all further responsibility.

My well-deserved triumph came when I joined the grand finale in midstream, after all those tall models had swept only thrice across the stage. Resolutely, I glommed onto my sister, as she passed my place in the wings.

I then bowed as deeply as the next to acknowledge all ten curtain calls, determinedly deaf to occasional cries of "Who's the little one?" or "Where did she come from?"

On good Friday, April 4th, Bing and I flew to Las Cruces with Dierdre, the three children, and of course Cindy. We had left ourselves only two days to perform the annual ritual of cleaning the church, and preparing it for services on Easter Sunday.

As usual, Bing refused to play scullery maid, but he did fly to La Paz with a lengthy shopping list, which included the biggest *piñata* he could find, and hundreds of small presents to fill it.

Since these had to be tough enough to resist determined blows from a baseball bat, they consisted largely of small plastic toys, hard candies, and cookies, to which he would add the hundreds of pennies which we had saved during the preceding year.

There was also the problem of transporting some twenty gallons of ice cream back to Las Cruces, while preventing them from melting. Over the years, Bing had devised any number of ingenious solutions, involving insulated picnic hampers, layers of

Daughter Mary with blossoms in her hair

The littlest angel prepares for Easter

Scrambling for the treasure from the piñata

straw, and chests full of dry ice, none of which had ever succeeded.

Meanwhile Dierdre and I offered the children all sorts of rewards to participate in the drudgery of church cleaning. All to no avail, for our little ones resolutely refused to get down on their knees and scrub for their parents, for Las Cruces, for Mexico, for the greater glory of God, or for a peon's minimum wage of two bits an hour.

At last Dierdre and I concluded that it was simpler to work like mules ourselves than to deal with such recalcitrants, which of course had been the small plotters' plan all along.

Saturday night, we dragged our weary bones back from the now pristine church to stumble about the kitchen, trying to make cakes for the morrow's fiesta.

As I later learned, our consistent failures derived from the fact that we were using a mix prepared for the altitude of Mexico City. At sea level, it sat stolidly in our ovens, burping lackadaisically, but never rising at all.

Bing referred to my cakes as *Hillsborough hardtack,* my sole contribution to the history of Mexican civilization. He assured me that archeologists of the 35th century would make much of such curiously impenetrable objects, since they were certain to be the sole artifacts which survived from our era.

Before staggering off to bed, we dyed the eggs. Early Sunday morning we rose to conceal three baskets of them within a hundred-yard radius of the church.

All during the high mass, we heard flocks of cardinals raucously celebrating the holiday, and leaving nothing but shells for the children's annual hunt.

The *piñata* proved more satisfactory. After several tots had narrowly escaped concussions from their wild-swinging, blindfolded contemporaries, Harry hefted the bat disdainfully, and leveled it with a single blow.

Relatively few of the smaller children were trampled in the ensuing scramble, only a minority threw away the toothbrushes that I had included to counteract the effects of the candy, and we all drank our fill of Bing's ice cream, which this group persisted in finding delicious, having yet to taste it in anything but its liquid form.

Monday, April 7th, saw the opening of the Kathryn Crosby School Abroad. Now that the laborers' children had been shipped back to La Paz, I had only our Mexican housekeeper and gardener, to join my three unruly Crosbys in pursuing Dr. Sullivan's programmed courses in reading, math, English, and science.

For his Spanish program, however, we were accompanied by Bing, Dierdre, and various bored fishermen's wives from the hotel.

Deprived of the first opportunity in a year to explore their beloved seashore, my three urchins proved uncontrollable, so I resorted to barefaced bribery: Only the best-behaved would travel with me to Mexico City at the end of the week.

For the first three days, the odds seemed to favor Nathaniel. Not that he was any less contrary than his siblings, but he lacked their inventive imaginations when it came to deviltry.

By Thursday, Mary Frances had awarded herself the prize. When Harry protested, she slapped his face, and the answering salvo left her with a lovely black eye.

"I was basely struck by an elder sibling."

The winner atop the pyramids

Unfortunately we were invited to a cocktail party that evening, so Dierdre warned our heroine not to tell anyone that Harry had hit her. Not three minutes had passed before a curious hotel guest inquired into the origin of the shiner.

Without a moment's hesitation, Mary Frances revealed cryptically, "I was basely struck by a relative."

Inquisitive eyes turned toward Bing, who promptly disclaimed all responsibility, stating for the record that he struck females "only in self defense."

"Oh it wasn't daddy," his daughter sniffed in disgust. "He wouldn't dare hit me, but I'll give you a hint. It was an elder sibling."

Bing was too astonished to be annoyed. "I was thirty and a father when I learned that word," he admitted. "Where in the world did you come upon it, princess?"

"Reading, after the children are asleep," his darling dimpled smugly.

It was Friday, and Nathaniel's victory seemed secure. After lights out, I stopped by his bunk to congratulate him. It was empty, and coincidentally so were those of Harry and Mary Frances. Hastily checking my inventory, I found that the black light used to hunt scorpions had also disappeared.

Sure enough, there amid the cacti were my youngest and his sister, vying to see who could catch the biggest arachnid by the tail. When I hauled them back to bed, I was delighted to find Harry snoozing angelically, surely a deserving victor.

On Sunday, April 13, Bing and I left with Harry for Mexico City. Not until the children were grown was I to learn that it was he who had organized the scorpion hunt.

He had been safely hidden behind a cactus when I caught his siblings in the act, and had prudently departed while my attention was engaged elsewhere. Newly cemented bonds of mafiosi-style loyalty had prevented the others from finking on him.

All the way to Mexico City and back, we praised Harry's deportment, and the model child accepted our accolades with becoming modesty. Playing tourist, we took him to see the pyramids, and snapped dozens of pictures of our complacent hero, serenely ensconced upon Aztec monuments.

On Tuesday evening, we flew back to Las Cruces, where I spent the rest of the week playing teacher. On Monday morning, April 21st, I was to fly to Los Angeles for a meeting of the Board of Regents of Immaculate Heart College. While preparing to catch the early plane, I suddenly experienced serious passport difficulties.

Incredibly, in this isolated spot, where documents were rarely checked, and I had often come and gone with no papers at all, a newly-appointed immigration officer had decided that, since the three children were on my passport, and I had presumably arrived with them, Mexican law suddenly forbade me to leave without them.

Hesitantly I inquired just what the penalty might be if I disobeyed this novel regulation.

Insofar as I could understand his vile Spanish, the bureaucrat seemed to be saying that the children would then be stranded forever, without passports, in the depths of Mexico.

Hardly able to credit my good fortune, I snatched up my documents to sprint toward the Aeronaves jet and freedom, visions of multi-splendored

Vera Ellen and Rosie sing *Sisters*.

So do Bing and Danny Kaye.

new careers dancing before my eyes. But would you believe it, deprived of the anticipated gratuity, my latter-day Aztec ratted on me. He alerted the flight crew, who in turn informed the passengers that an unnatural mother was abandoning her little ones to an unknown fate, and jetting off to peace and happiness.

Unable to endure the stern glances of my fellow passengers, I sadly deplaned, hitched a ride back to the hotel in Las Cruces, caught Bing just as the Dorado was casting off for a day's fishing, and explained how nobly I had reacted in refusing to abandon my brood under any circumstances.

Chafing at the delay, my disgruntled spouse put in a quick call to Dierdre's sometime swain Carlos, the merchant prince of La Paz, and okayed a hundred-dollar bribe to be added to our grocery bill.

Bing went fishing. I waited an hour for a private plane to La Paz where, by some miraculous repeal of the relevant law, my departure was immediately approved *sans enfants* for the evening flight, with full permission to return and pick them up at my leisure.

And that wasn't all that was revoked. Long before my plane departed, the official in question, ostracized by his fellow workers, threatened with exposure in the newspapers, and the recipient of a terse message from the governor, had hired a taxi for a mad dash to Las Cruces to return Bing's bribe, before his entire world collapsed about his ears.

I arrived late for my Los Angeles meeting, but covered my confusion by reaffirming Bing's million-dollar gift for a new science building. Exhausted and starving, I succumbed to visions, and

voiced my inspiration that the sisters might reach an immediate accomodation with their archenemy by naming the structure after Cardinal McIntyre.

Accustomed to compromise in their professional lives, the businessmen on the Board of Regents deemed this a splendid suggestion, showing how little insight mere males have into the venom that lurks neath clerical robes.

On the following day, the nuns overwhelmingly rejected my proposal, so I made an appointment to meet with the Cardinal.

On Wednesday, I cajoled a reluctant Reverend Mother Humiliata, newly yclept President Anita Caspary to conform with Pope John XXIII's new order, into accompanying me on a visit to his Eminence.

"He's just going to turn your silly little head," she declared uncharitably. "He was a stock broker and investment banker in New York, before he realized how much money there was in the Church, and experienced a sudden illumination.

Here in California, he has reorganized the entire Catholic school system so that all donations pour into his hands. He dispatches twenty innocents like you before breakfast."

Which remarks demonstrated just how ill-informed even a doctor of philosophy may be, for I found Cardinal McIntyre positively charming. Garbed in a simple black suit with reversed collar, he looked more like a dieting Santa Claus turned Episcopalian than a dignitary of Rome.

His twinkling blue eyes, modest demeanor, and overwhelming sincerity instantly converted me to his noble cause, whatever it might be. Gazing appreciatively at my niveous winter

Sister Helen Kelly accepts my million dollar pledge.

coat, he first remarked that I made a beautiful Snow White. He next rejected all thought of naming a building after him, on the grounds that it might give rise to what the Communists decried as "a cult of personality."

For himself, his sole wish was to remain "a simple, anonymous servitor of Mother Church."

The donation, however, was greatly appreciated, and could surely be put to better use than the contemplated monument in stone. He thanked me for bringing the matter to his attention, would give it his most serious consideration, and would present me with a plan for its best and highest use if I would return in a couple of months.

With further expressions of gratitude for the way in which I was helping him to advance God's work on earth, his Eminence escorted a tight-lipped Sister Anita and myself to the door. The moment that it closed behind us, I took her to task for the many times that she had criticized the Cardinal and all his works.

"That man," I insisted in reverent tones, "is the nearest thing to a saint that I have met thus far in life."

Sister Anita simply shook her head. "I told you so," she muttered gloomily, "but you're too stubborn to listen. You just had to march into the lion's den."

"I saw no lion—only a wonderful human being."

"God give me strength," Sister Anita sighed. "Don't you have any idea of what he did? He simply transferred your gift from our campus into his pocket. Now he'll spend the next few months deciding what new toys he can buy himself with a million dollars.

In your next meeting, he'll point out what a great benefactor you've been, and make you feel that it's all your idea. I strongly recommend that we call a press conference immediately, and make a public announcement of your gift to Immaculate Heart College. It won't necessarily stop that lineal descendant of Richelieu, but it may slow him up a bit."

Though considering such pecuniary wrangling unworthy of the good sister, I did consent to a press conference the following day, on the putative future campus of the college in Claremont, where the nuns resolutely linked the Crosby gift to the construction of their new science building.

Fortunately the involuntary donor was far away in Las Cruces, where communications were marginal at best, but his business manager phoned that evening to favor me with a lengthy lecture on the subject of preservation of capital, which affected me not at all, since I hadn't the faintest notion of what he was talking about.

It was back to playing schoolmarm in Las Cruces for the rest of April and all of May, returning to civilization only once, for the ground-breaking ceremony of the Crosby Science Building at the lovely new foredoomed Immaculate Heart Campus in Claremont.

Once again, the college's science faculty was planning to use our Las Cruces home for a summer school, and Bing's boat, *The True Love*, for experiments in marine biology. Mindful of what their winches and dredges had done to his craft the preceding year, he determined to ferret out a suitable sacrifice in La Paz.

Bing's eyes lit up when he chanced upon the *Alejandro Abaroa Gil*, the pride of the shrimp fleet, and the only new boat in town.

The *Alejandro Abaroa Gil,* pride of the shrimp fleet

"At most it will cost us three hundred dollars for the summer," he assured me, "and it will save thousands in wear and tear on *The True Love.* I'll invite the owner to lunch, and settle this thing right now."

During our meal at Los Cocos Hotel, Bing made polite conversation by asking how, when, where, and why the craft in question had been built.

It transpired that the proprietor, Don José Abaroa, was the patriarch of the La Paz Marina, owning all the land adjacent to the wharves, and permitting the fishermen and their families to live on it rent-free.

Recently a new city government had decided that the time had come to tax landowners for each and every "tenant," and had thus wiped out Don José's lifetime savings.

In self defense, he and his four sons had constructed a nautical masterpiece with their own hands, and were applying the proceeds from it to pay the taxes which supported half the town.

He would be proud to rent the boat to Bing, but he insisted that it be inspected first. Back we drove towards the *muelle,* threading our way past the huts of the fishermen, while Bing gazed thoughtfully at roofs of thatched palm fronds, walls of plywood or corrugated tin, windows covered with burlap sacking, and scores of naked children, playing on dirt floors.

The boat had obviously been prepared for our visit. It shone with new varnish from stem to stern. "Could you perhaps afford a hundred dollars?" its proprietor asked.

Absorbed in his inspection of the shrimp nets, Bing seemed not to have heard him. "I used to pay a thousand a

week to rent a good boat in Miami," he mused thoughtfully.

Don José's eyes started from his head, but after a brief struggle, honesty overcame avarice. "In this poor town, you could lease the entire fleet for less," he admitted sadly.

"But of course the boats in Miami were only half the size of this beautiful ship, so they must have been worth about half as much."

"Do you really believe that you might consider two hundred dollars for the entire summer?" Don José ventured. "I could include a crew to handle it for you."

"And in Miami we had to furnish all our own fishing gear, whereas this craft has every bit of equipment that a marine biologist could desire," Bing concluded. "I'll tell you what I'll do. I'll pay you three thousand a week, and not a penny more. No, no. No more haggling. My mind's made up."

After Bing had concluded his bargain with the prepayment of a week's rent, I took him to task for his sharp business practices. "I know it's a jungle out there," I admitted, "and as an entrepreneur, you're a tiger, but aren't you ashamed of taking such advantage of a simple-minded native?"

"A deal's a deal," Bing affirmed, "and west of Cerralvo, I am the law."

On Friday, June 6th, the whole family flew back to Hillsborough to recover from our vacation, and to prepare Mary Frances for her starring role in *Goldilocks,* a matter of some slight concern, since the overconfident director had accepted our tyke on the basis of exaggerated reports of her acting ability, and no first-hand evidence.

Bald as an egg for the first year of her life, she had eventually developed a

Goldilocks

mousy mop which, however bleached by the desert sun of Las Cruces, could by no stretch of the imagination be characterized as golden.

With her over-sized head, hereditary projecting ears, thick, scarred legs, and generalized hostility, our darling was hardly your run-of-the-mill, fairy-tale heroine. Deciding that anything short of cosmetic surgery was in order, I began doctoring the worst cuts and bruises, and experimenting with dyes and rinses.

On Tuesday, June 10th, the family flew to Los Angeles. The next day, Bing recorded the songs *Take a Longer Look, The Human Race,* and *Don't Settle for Less,* while Mary Frances attended her first rehearsal, whence she was immediately bounced back to me, with pleas to do something about her hair and attitude, at a bare minimum.

Reaching back into my own experience, I recalled numerous girl friends whose change in the former had greatly improved the latter. At 2 PM on Tuesday, the famed Beverly Hills hair stylist Carrie White transformed our nondescript tomboy into a platinum blonde, and with this single stroke, our ugly duckling became a swan.

Somehow the radiant halo about her head masked her physical defects, while her first glimpse in a mirror stunned her into a state of temporary malleability, in which she began dutifully rehearsing the role of girl.

She did decide that she was a big star now, and entitled to choose her own billing, so her stage name henceforth would be *Mary Crosby.* She'd had quite enough of the *Mary Frances* bit.

I agreed to go along, thus permitting the rest of us to film the picnic scene, after which she was to fall asleep, and then join the animated cartoon characters in her lengthy dream.

While I was being readied for my own brief part, the makeup man discovered three gray hairs. This was too much. Here I was, playing an introductory role in my daughter's starring vehicle, after which I would represent only the voice of a fat bear.

And henceforth I, who was still waiting to be discovered for ingenue roles, was slated in real life for that of withered crone.

Furthermore, there was the little matter of my forthcoming theater role as Jean Brodie, which I hadn't quite got round to mentioning to Bing. Was fate trying to tell me something? Could I be destined to play the auburn-haired Scot without benefit of wig or subterfuge?

Resolutely I usurped my daughter's first touchup appointment with Carrie White, and emerged as what I fondly deemed to be a ravishing redhead.

Bing, on the other hand, was horrified. He compared my tresses unfavorably with those of Patrick J. O'Toole, my late unlamented Irish setter, and demanded that I change them back immediately.

I refused adamantly, citing the example of his own Mary Frances, er, Mary that is.

"I liked her better as just a little girl," Bing insisted. "All that business about blondes having more fun is just Clairol propaganda."

"Then why isn't our present undertaking yclept *Coaldilocks* or *Brunettilocks?* Why do I have to be the only drab original left in Hollywood?"

We finished *Goldilocks* on Friday, June 20th, and flew home that evening. Saturday morning, Bing caught me packing. "Well?" he asked. "Well?"

Auburn-haired *Jean Brodie*

"I've agreed to do *The Prime of Miss Jean Brodie* this summer," I admitted stolidly, and awaited the inevitable answering volley.

"So that was the grim secret behind the flaming tresses," Bing sighed. "Evidently I'm to be abandoned once more to my own devices, and I suppose you think I'm going to devote my entire summer to your children.

You've left me with no alternative. As I see it, it's time for Iceland."

"Iceland?" I inquired numbly. "What sort of women do they have there?"

"Blondes, a whole nation of volcanic blondes, busily having more fun disporting amid the ice floes!"

On Sunday, June 22nd, I relieved Bing of one-third of his burden by spiriting his daughter off to Corning, New York, where she began learning the role of Jenny.

Prior to the first rehearsal, however, she ran afoul of the director, Dorothy Chernuk, who informed us that the part was taken.

Since Mary had been promised the job to induce me to sign my contract, I lodged a strong protest, but was told that the original New York cast of diminutive adults would portray the leading children's roles.

Jenny, for example, would be played by Elizabeth Howard, a voice teacher with a master's degree from Julliard. Miss Chernuk would be pleased to consider Mary for the nonspeaking role of second schoolgirl.

Foolishly, I offered my daughter the choice of accepting her demotion or returning to spend the summer at our ranch.

When she furiously opted for the ranch, I phoned Bing, who stalwartly declined to take her back.

It was indeed fortunate that she had a nonspeaking role, for she resolutely refused to communicate with anyone on or off stage for the next two weeks.

Meanwhile I learned my part with relative ease, but at our first dress rehearsal on Sunday, I ran into a problem of my own.

While sitting off-stage, scanning the script and waiting for my cue, I noticed that Peter Duncan, who was playing the role of the artist Teddy Lloyd, was stuttering badly, and generally making a hash of his performance. As my gaze swept the stage, the twin causes of his confusion were all too apparent.

Like Peter, I found myself staring at Linda Sherwood, who had been instructed to play the scene, in which she posed for her portrait, nude from the waist up.

I rushed out into the auditorium to notify the director that someone was making a terrible mistake, only to be informed that the scene had been played the same way on Broadway, and that was that.

I resigned on the spot, summoned my bored daughter, and repaired to my room to let Bing know that we were returning home.

Miss Chernuk arrived just as I was launching into my explanation, and I had a sudden inspiration:

"Here," I smiled sweetly, offering her the phone. "Would you kindly explain to my husband just why your artistic integrity requires a nude scene?"

I spent the next ten minutes trying to squelch Mary, who was fascinated by the way our director managed to make her double chins tremble and her thyroidal eyes pop, and was busily

Pursuing the wily trout at Rising River

adding the same novel expressions to her own repertoire.

I never did learn what Bing said, but it was obviously no contest all the way. So incensed was he at the thought of employing cheap pornography to entice theatergoers that he quite overlooked a splendid opportunity to have me dispatched back home. Miss Chernuk apologized profusely, I withdrew my resignation, and Sandy thenceforth modeled in a camisole.

Troubles never come singly. The role of Miss McKay, the headmistress, was played by Guy Kibbee's niece Lois, last of a celebrated theatrical family.

At the final dress rehearsal on Monday, June 30th, all went swimmingly until Act II, Scene 7, when Miss McKay, trying to thread her way through the darkness offstage without the assistance of the promised guide lights and guard rail, plunged eight feet into the midst of the startled cast, and suffered a severe concussion.

As the ambulance raced Miss Kibbee toward the nearest emergency ward, the director's last words were, "You'll have to have her back here for the opening tomorrow night."

Indeed someone must have obeyed that severe injunction, for the cast at our Tuesday night debut included a headmistress with a vacant stare, and a tendency toward new and lengthy pauses in the middle of key speeches.

We all cooperated in steering her in the right direction at critical moments. Later, when sufficiently recovered, she threatened to upstage the rest of us by repeating her original entry every night, even if she had to add a parachute to her Scottish weeds.

We opened with good reviews, and all went smoothly for the next few days, with my daughter's glowering silence generally accepted as cooperation. Bing, however, had once remarked that summer theater casts were composed of has-beens, might-have-beens, and never-could-have-beens.

I'm sure that he included me in the last category, though he was discreet enough not to say so, but the veteran character actor, who played teacher Gordon Lowther, was definitely a might-have-been, and his problems, like those of most of the breed, came straight out of a bottle.

After he had stumbled about the stage for three consecutive performances, I summoned him to an interview, and staying right in character as Jean Brodie, administered a tongue lashing that poor little Kathryn Crosby would never have dreamed of attempting. To the amazement of all concerned, my version of shock therapy kept him reasonably sober for the remainder of the summer.

Not one to waste our location in Corning, I bought Bing a twelve-piece setting of every available variety of Steuben glass. Then it was off to a week's run in Denver, where my parents joined me, and I invited them to a matinee showing of *Die Fledermaus* in Central City.

Whereupon it was my turn for a reprimand. Lois Kibbee upbraided me furiously, reminding me that I was the star, and must therefore devote all my time and energy to the role. Indeed I was so exhausted in the evening that I gave my worst performance ever, and dragged the rest of the cast down with me. Repentant, I promised not to play hooky again.

Meanwhile Bing, apparently unmindful of his threat to abandon me for

Nathaniel on Mineral Oil, Harry on Castle Bill

Uncle Leonard's newest working cowboy

some Norse goddess in Iceland, was spending his days with Harry and Nathaniel. His letters contained the following information:

"July 4th, 1969. Back at the ranch, all is serene. Shasta is sparkling to the north, and Lassen to the south; gaggles of tiny geese are earning their wings by taking swimming lessons from their mothers; mallards are nesting at the water's edge; and the occasional teal is whistling upriver.

Nathaniel, in complete uniform, is organizing baseball games in the front yard. A purist, he has discarded his Pittsburgh cap today because the Pirates have been rained out.

His brother has learned how to operate all the heavy machinery, but if I didn't insist, neither child would brush his teeth until Alan Fisher caught him next fall. I'll pause now, since Harry is desirous of appending a brief missive of his own."

"Dear Mom: Today I ran the motor boat. Dad was going fishing, so I dropped him off in a swamp, and cruised down the river alone, looking for more arrowheads.

When I thought of him again, it was getting dark, and Dad was trying to keep from sinking into the swamp. He says I am very forgetful, and other, stronger things. I hope your play goes well. Love, Harry. PS I'm sorry that I took all the rest of Dad's writing space."

On Friday, July 11th, Bing arrived unexpectedly in Denver, watched our performance, and sang duets with his daughter at an impromptu party, thrown for him by the cast.

After admonishing me for allowing Mary to stay up so late with "strolling players and tipsy crooners," he departed at the crack of dawn for Iceland.

So he hadn't been kidding after all. I made it a point to pass by the local library for some informal research on creeping glaciers and Nordic blondes.

We spent the third week of our tour in Laconia, New Hampshire, which was suffering through its worst heat wave in recent history. Bing's first letters from Iceland made me envy him his cool retreat:

"July 14, 1969. Here I am with the production crew of *The American Sportsman,* an ABC television feature, to shoot a segment on fishing for Atlantic salmon.

As we circled over Reykjavik, I was amazed at its spotless appearance. We saw no slums, no cheaply constructed tract houses, no visible rubbish—just substantial, shining, white buildings.

Later, touring by car, I encountered only immaculate streets, with no billboards to deface the landscape.

We next flew on a DC-3 to Husavik, on the northernmost tip of the country, threading our way through green valleys and skirting vast glaciers, with only the occasional isolated dairy farm as evidence of man's existence. It would be an easy country to fall in love with.

We arrived at our fishing lodge well before lunch, and took a stroll by the river, reaching its bank just in time to watch one of the guests try to land a twenty-pound salmon without a gaff or net. He rejected all offers of assistance, averring that he catches all his fish that way, and then proceeded to lose his prize.

A renowned expert, he next informed us that he had taken his 600th salmon earlier in the week. So at dinner that night, when the roast lamb appeared, and a question arose as to who was to carve the meat, I volunteered

In Iceland with guide and Bud Boyd

for the task, modestly letting slip the fact that it was the 600th leg of lamb that I had carved in the course of a long and bloody career.

The Laxa is a lovely river which is very easy to fish, since not a tree lines its bank, and it is also innocent of brush or high grass. In fact, I am told that the only trees in Iceland are in a nursery. The story is that the Vikings stripped the available forests for ships and firewood.

The water is crystal clear because it has a lake for its source. By contrast, streams which emanate from glaciers are inevitably cloudy.

Since the salmon have arrived to spawn rather than feed, they are reluctant to hit the fly. It's only the odd one that reverts for the moment to his salad days, and graciously accepts my offering.

In my three days of fishing, I have taken five salmon a day, the largest weighing in at about 24 pounds. But it's not boring. There is continuous action, because I see fish constantly, and always have something to aim at.

The techniques employed are universal. I cast above the fish, and let the fly float downstream. When it reaches the end of its course, I retrieve it in short, abrupt motions, and it's then that a fish is most likely to strike.

Hookups follow the same pattern each time. After dozens of fruitless casts, I find myself dreamily and automatically repeating the procedure, when I am suddenly surprised by a mighty wallop. The salmon then takes off with a rush downstream, leaping and twisting as the line peels off for a good 200 yards.

I race along the bank, hurdling one fence and ducking under another, to thrash through rocks and weeds to a point where I can stop the fish. All of them are very active Each costs me half an hour of chasing up and down the bank, until I finally catch him by the tail, and haul him onto *terra firma.*

I need the occasional strike just to keep warm. Iceland's skies are a mystic blue, and the hills and valleys remain a rich green, but it's frigid here, even in July. A piercing wind sweeps down off the glaciers and whistles through the gorges.

Fortunately it's no colder at night because there isn't any. Just envision your friendly neighborhood insomniac wooing Morpheus at midnight, with bright sunshine streaming through gauzy curtains.

If I were a resort operator, I'd install blackout shades, and I'd recommend that any visiting angler add a sleep mask to his equipment. As usual, I was unprepared.

I do, however, have another observation. Iceland may have the least exploited trout fishing in the world. On my only afternoon off, I laid hold of a jeep, and followed the river forty miles to its head waters.

There wasn't another angler to be seen, but I immediately started picking up brown trout, ranging from one to three pounds, and observed many larger fish.

Returning to Reykjavik, I had just one free day before leaving for England, so of course I went salmon fishing in the river that runs right through town to empty into the sea.

For a couple of hours, during which I had no luck at all, I worked my way toward a large bridge.

I remained there, trying different flies and casting to some rises, until I

The successful angler

Lunch on the Laxa

happened to look downstream and see Bud Boyd, the fishing editor of the San Francisco Chronicle, pointing his camera at me.

When it tilted up, I raised my own head, and saw a thousand silent people standing on the bridge, with traffic backed up as far as the eye could see.

At precisely that moment, I got my first strike. The river bottom was covered with slippery rocks, so I slid and stumbled up and down stream, somehow managing to keep a tight line, while envisioning my chagrin at losing a fish within sight of such a large and knowledgeable audience.

As you well know, I am hardly a bundle of nerves when performing in a film, but I must confess that on this occasion my knees were knocking and my brow was damp. At length I beached a ten-pounder, and held him up to the watching crowd.

This produced some light applause, a few bravos in Icelandic, and finally an orderly evacuation. If I live as long as Winston Churchill, this will have been my finest hour. On to Africa!"

Well, I might have known that my real competition in Iceland would be salmon, not sex. Africa, however, might take a bit of explaining. I had warned my agent that I would be available only through the third week of July, and he in turn had so instructed the organizers of the tour.

But somehow the buck had stopped there. No one had thought to provide a substitute for me in Paramus, New Jersey, the next stop on our itinerary.

As a consequence, I was now facing a furious director and producer, who had to move their entire schedule back a week while Kim Hunter was rushed in to learn my part.

Years later, I discovered that I had consequently been blackballed by the network of summer theater impresarios. I had remained blissfully unaware of the fact, since my husband had finally put his foot down, and restricted me to quarters.

Miss Brodie and I would have a six-week stint in St. Louis in the fall of 1969, and a week at the University of Texas in October of 1970, but not until 1976 was I to tour again.

On Wednesday, July 23rd, my daughter and I boarded a plane for Shannon, where I left her with Dierdre, who had returned home to be married.

On the 25th, I flew to London, where Bing met me at the airport. On Saturday, we attended the theater to watch Sir John Gielgud star in *Forty Years On*, and visited him afterward in his dressing room. As we took our leave, Sir John bowed and kissed my hand.

"When are you going to assimilate some of that continental charm?" I inquired of Bing.

Nothing daunted, he biffed me on the shoulder and said, "We good old boys don't aim to spoil 'em. Try to make that last."

On Sunday, Bing agreed to dine with Billy Wilder and his wife Audrey, a move which I'd have vetoed if I'd been consulted.

I had nothing against the beautiful dancer, but the last time that I saw Billy, I'd been playing a bit part in *Sabrina Fair,* and he'd complained in his strong German accent that I "valked like a wirgin."

The remark had elicited raucous laughter from the film crew, and had left me in a quandary, since I had nothing to do in the scene but amble across a tennis court, and even that

With Terry Mathews in Nairobi Airport

Our group of hunters

minimal contribution was evidently unsatisfactory.

Humphrey Bogart had earned my eternal gratitude by grabbing his friend Wilder by the shoulder, spinning him around, shaking a fist under his nose, and demanding that he "Leave the pretty little lady alone."

To my surprise, I enjoyed the evening. Lovely Audrey and I sat wide-eyed while two of the finest living raconteurs outdid themselves in topping each other's stories, and Billy exhibited a talent for improvisation which rivaled that of Phil Harris.

Our mutual friend, Blake Edwards, had just complained that he was $17,000,000 into the shooting of *Darling Lili* for Paramount, when he had suddenly realized that he had no good way to bring Rock Hudson and Julie Andrews together at the end. Bing wondered whether Wilder's creative imagination might proffer a solution.

"Why not?" replied Billy without a moment's hesitation. "I see it all now. We just change it from a dopey comedy to a tragedy that makes Hamlet look like a Sunday-school picnic.

We start with a Greek chorus of all the bankers who backed the picture. While they moan about fate and curse the gods in the background, the camera pans across their $17,000,000, which Rock and Julie are dumping into a heroic-sized commode.

After a moment's pause to appreciate the true horror of the situation, the star-crossed lovers join hands, leap in, and pull the chain. We then listen to the bankers final lament, as their high-priced stars and all them bucks go belly-up down the drain.

Talk about tragic catharsis! That ending would make a rhinoceros, or

maybe even a producer, cry like a new-born baby."

On Monday, July 28th, Bing and I flew to Athens, where we visited the Acropolis. After the long climb upward under a blazing sun, we paused before the Parthenon to contemplate a fallen slab weighing some fourteen tons, which had once served as a crosspiece to brace the front columns.

A guide informed us that the stone had been lying there for eleven years because the best modern engineers and architects could come up with no way to replace it.

Regarding the huge fragment, Bing waxed philosophic: "We've learned a few tricks from our forebears," he admitted, "but we've certainly forgotten others. And each man's life recapitulates history.

We comfort ourselves with the belief that we accumulate wisdom, and an old man's decisions do seem easier than a youth's, but it may be simply that he's forgotten the wondrous secrets that the boy knew."

"We little girls aren't any slouches either," I reminded him. "Will you accompany me back to the hotel, oh sage, where I may help you to recall the lore of your salad days?"

"Faced with such an object lesson," Bing sighed, "I take it all back."

That evening, we were sitting in the airline terminal, waiting for our plane to Nairobi, when a willowy English blonde of some twenty summers staggered in under armloads of suitcases, favored Bing with a dazzling, helpless smile, and dropped them at his feet.

To my amazement, a man whose bursitis had lately limited even his golf game, readily packed them off to the baggage counter, and returned for the

The hunters at lunch

even larger ones which she had prudently parked outside the door.

Each time they passed, I caught snatches of her conversation, and gathered that she was a computer operator on her way to Zambia, to enjoy herself and fulfill an eighteen-month contract.

When all the heavy suitcases had been safely stowed away, Bing was burdened only with the blonde's carry-on luggage. Simple politeness ordained that she invite him into the bar for a drink. With a wicked grin and a wink at me, he followed her through the door.

Twenty minutes later, when East African Airlines Flight 713 was finally announced, "Miss Zambia," as I had now privately dubbed her, was still holding forth to my husband about her future prospects.

"And what do you do, Mr. Croveny?" she at length got around to asking her silent companion.

"Well I used to sell almanacs to aardvarks, but I now design firemen's and postmen's hats."

"How fascinating! Now I want you to sit next to me on the plane and tell me all about it."

But Bing had tired of his little joke. "That certainly is an appealing invitation," he averred, "but first I'd like you to meet the mother of the last eight of my children."

Whereupon he tried to steer his computer operator toward a gigantic Greek mama, surrounded by her brood of squalling brats. Somehow the blonde became lost in the shuffle, and Bing returned to escort me onto the plane, still oblivious of one vital detail.

No sooner were we seated, than Miss Zambia appeared, glaring daggers at us both, and reclaimed the carry-on bag that my husband had slung across his shoulder. Not for the first time, I confronted the fact that, even if he hadn't been Bing Crosby, I would still have had to face frequent competition from nubile maidens.

Bing was one of the greatest white-knuckle, backseat pilots of all times. Our standard operating procedure in planes was for him to crouch, desperately holding the wings on, while I snored peacefully.

In this case, a heavy Greek dinner, topped off with a sip of ouzo, added to the soporific effect. I was out before we had left the ground.

The next thing I knew, Bing was shaking me. "Wake up, damn it. The plane's on fire."

Gazing languidly out my window, I saw that the nearest engine was indeed in flames. Even as I watched, however, the pilot or flight engineer must have thrown a switch, for the propeller stopped rotating, and the fire died.

"There," I mumbled indistinctly. "S'all taken care of."

For some reason, Bing found the incident irritating in the extreme. As I sank back into oblivion, I heard him muttering, "If we run into cannibals on this trip, and they drop you into a cooking pot, they won't get much satisfaction out of it. You'll sleep through the whole procedure like a lobster, too torpid even to notice what's happening to the temperature of the water."

Bing was left to continue holding the plane up, which he managed so successfully that it brought us safely into Nairobi on three engines.

There we were met by our hunter, Terry Mathews, with a new black patch over the eye that he had forfeited to his trade.

The game birds flocked to the few remaining water holes.

Dik-dik on the game trail

He drove us to the Norfalk Hotel, where he and his wife Jeanne transferred our gear into tin trunks, while I ate and Bing finally slept.

Then it was back to the airport, and on to Camp 17, in a minuscule, single-engined Cessna, which once again Bing helped to fly while I snored.

My first view of our campsite was disappointing. There had been no rain, and the lush green carpet of the preceding summer had been replaced by arid desert. The bed of the river, which had run behind our tents, was now not only bone dry but rock hard.

Moreover the heat was intense. "Much better for hunting birds," Terry observed. "They'll flock to the few remaining water holes."

That first night, Bing slept as he could only in Africa, and even I was now sufficiently experienced to recover quickly from the frequent loud noises, whose source became apparent when I awoke in the morning to watch a pair of dik-dik bounce past, and realized that our tent faced on a game trail. Immediately thereafter, a francolin dropped in to perch on my shoulder and share my makeup mirror.

While Bing sallied forth to scout the terrain, I settled down with a copy of Hemingway's *The Green Hills of Africa*. Always an admirer of Ernest's Attic prose, I nonetheless had to fault his powers of observation.

The hills of Africa are purple, tinged with gold when the tiny yellow flowers bloom, fading into pink at dawn, and something between rusty brown and charcoal after the Masai have burnt off the vegetation, but except for some possible moment in spring which had wholly escaped me, they are never, never green.

My scout returned at lunchtime with the news that three of the four Masai watering holes were dry. We decided to sleep through the rest of the scorching day, and to rise in the cool of the evening, when the doves visited the remaining oasis.

There Terry stationed me in the shade of a bush with two of the bearers to load for me. Fired with energy after my nap, and aware that I could properly lead only birds flying from right to left, I determined to concentrate on those favored few.

They came by the hundreds, swooping in from all directions, and I confidently emptied two boxes of shells at them with no visible results. Since my weapon's kick drove me back upon my loaders, who made me nervous anyway, I resourcefully blamed them for the debacle, and dispatched them to the protection of a distant tree.

I had been waving my gun about somewhat erratically toward the end, so they displayed little reluctance.

Finally the doves dived upon us in such dense clouds that even I began to take my toll, and actually seemed to be outdoing Bing. I started to rub it in, until I realized that he was sportingly refusing to participate in a slaughter.

While the other hunters boasted of their huge bags, he declared that he had stopped firing after the first shots because his shoulder was giving him fits. Recalling his Herculean efforts for Miss Zambia, I reflected that there might even be an element of truth in the excuse.

The next morning, the sky above the solitary water hole was again dark with doves, and Bing quit in disgust after scoring two doubles and a rare triple with his first eight shots.

Guinea fowl still life

Kisio, Chambi, and Kudu

"Sport is one thing, and mass execution is another," he grunted disgustedly. "I could close my eyes, fire straight up, and fill my bag in half an hour. Let's see if the francolin lead us a better chase."

That they did. African partridges, midway in size between quail and pheasant, they exploded from cover like feathered meteors, causing me to drop my puny 28-gauge in alarm and hide my face, and requiring all of Bing's savvy to bag our lunch.

When he tired of the francolins' antics, Bing took off after guinea fowl, which made him chase them for hundreds of yards, as they raced through the dry grass like miniature ostriches, before finally becoming fair game when they lifted into the air.

Following a long afternoon of "The Guinea Fowl Olympics," as Bing had dubbed their chase, even he nodded to sleep by the fire.

The following day there was joy throughout the camp when Bing was talked into stalking an eland.

Bearers, skinners, trackers, and camp hands were all involuntary vegetarians, who ate meat solely on safari, and then only when serving a competent hunter. Their delight when Bing sallied forth was a tribute to the reputation that he had established over the years.

But this time they were doomed to disappointment. After trailing a big buck all day through treacherous country, consisting largely of pot holes and impenetrable brush, Bing finally came up with him, fired, and watched him spin and go down.

Arriving on the spot, however, he found that the eland had disappeared. He tracked the beast until dusk, when he had to return to camp, frustrated and depressed at the thought of leaving a wounded animal.

Unencumbered by Bing's scruples, but sharing his disappointment, his followers sadly rubbed their empty stomachs, and implored him to renew his efforts the following day. Which he did, hauling me along in the Land Rover on the trail of an elusive lesser kudu. As we banged along over terrain, which did fearful things to my innards, Bing suddenly halted, leaped from the vehicle followed by his tracker, and vanished into dense brush.

Dispelling the tension after my own fashion, I once more opened *The Green Hills of Africa,* and immediately struck upon a surprisingly appropriate passage, wherein the author assured me with his customary delicacy: "One shot—much meat. Two shots—maybe. Three shots—heap shit."

Just as I was marveling at Hemingway's erudition, Bing's rifle cracked once...twice...and thrice. Proud of my newly-acquired lore, but sad at the thought of Bing's failure, I piloted the Land Rover toward the source of the noise.

There stood my hero beside a splendid buck! Couldn't Ernest get anything straight?

Well, in a way he could. When Bing and his tracker came upon the kudu, all they could see was a couple of gray stripes, deep in the bush.

The African insisted that the animal was facing left, but Bing, whose color blindness permitted him to see through most camouflage, decided that its head was to the right. He fired, and hit the startled beast in the rump.

The kudu took off for taller timber, and Bing's second try was a clean miss. The third was a brilliant head shot

Prospecting for treasure

A river bed full of crystal

while the animal was in full flight, a feat so unlikely that it fully justified Papa's pessimism.

The feast that evening left nothing but the kudu's horns. As the man of the hour, Bing was again encouraged to sally forth to bag an eland.

Off we went the following morning, with me driving in self-defense. Not that I hit fewer potholes, but I struck them appreciably slower.

We had covered about six miles when I screeched to a halt, shouting "Look there!"

Bing leaped out, whipped his gun to his shoulder, and then dropped it sheepishly. "What did you think you were pointing at?" he inquired with some asperity.

Ignoring him, I darted forward twenty yards, and returned with a large, glittering quartz crystal.

"What's that?" asked my perplexed comrade in arms.

"I don't know yet," I yelped, "but I soon will. Follow me!"

Which he did, but reluctantly and at a safe distance, as I scrambled down into the arid river bed, where I spent ten minutes digging about frantically.

"Sure enough, it's full of rocks and dry dirt," Bing mused philosophically. "Now that you've determined that much, may we resume the pursuit of my eland?"

"Not just yet," I exulted, diving upon a rock with a broad glittering vein of brownish quartz.

"Is it that shiny stuff you're looking for? Why didn't you say so? Half a mile upstream, the river bed's full of it"

"Good Lord, why didn't you tell me?"

"How was I to know you'd gone crazy over rocks. It was shells the last time I looked."

Bing led me to an extensive deposit of quartz, disturbed only by random. jabs from Masai spears.

Obviously the source of the stone that I had discovered downstream, it offered crystals in seemingly infinite variety, many of them creased or actually milky, but others beautifully clear, and in colors that I was sure must be characteristic of emeralds and rubies, or at the very least opals and aquamarines.

I dispatched my husband for reinforcements. By late afternoon I was directing a full-scale, open-pit, mining operation, but eventually the bored hunters wandered off.

Just as I tore the last finger out of my gloves, I heard shots from the vicinity of the water hole. Disgustingly easy as they might be to bag for dinner, the doves were obviously preferable to the alternative that I represented.

The shades of night were falling fast when I headed for home, my Land Rover piled high with chunks of quartz. When I arrived, I remarked on our good fortune in sighting no eland, and Bing muttered something that I failed to catch about the ease of securing an African divorce.

On Wednesday, August 6th, dawn found me washing rocks in front of our tent, and speculating on the extent of my new-found wealth. Behind me, a Land Rover started up, and I turned to find Bing abandoning me for the chase.

Hating to be left out of anything, however painful, I leaped into the path of the vehicle, and insisted on joining the party. Bing rolled his eyes in exasperation, but Terry suggested that I drive while the men looked for spoor.

On we rolled through the cool of the early morning, until Terry called for a

Mother was not amused.

I finally did pull out my camera.

bush stop, and I safeguarded the men's privacy by parking some hundred yards further on.

Hardly had I pulled to a halt, when a tiny elephant emerged from a thicket of wait-a-bit thorn almost at my elbow. It was the work of a moment to snatch up my camera, leap from the Land Rover, and capture his image in my view finder.

Showing no sign of fear but considerable curiosity, he advanced toward me, while I snapped away furiously, so preoccupied with keeping him in the center of my view finder that I paid scant attention to the rumbling noises emanating from dead astern.

When they finally forced themselves on my attention, my first thought was that one of the men had been guilty of an enormous indiscretion, but this notion was dispelled by the sight of Bing and Terry approaching at full gallop, their speed somewhat abetted by covert glances at a behemoth bringing up the rear.

In order of appearance, Bing fixated upon baby elephant, wife, and camera. "Kathryn," he gasped, "dive into the car right now."

"I just wanted to snap a few pictures of this adorable little animal," I demurred. "I didn't think that anyone would mind."

"It seems that someone does," Bing insisted.

Without further ado, he picked me up, and pitched me headfirst into the Land Rover, waited for Terry to spring in on the passenger's side, and drove away at top speed. By the time I righted myself, we had already covered several hundred yards.

"Is that any way to treat a lady?" I inquired huffily.

"Sorry," Bing sighed. "It didn't seem to be the appropriate moment for an in-depth discussion of photography."

"What was your hurry? Weren't we safe in the Land Rover?"

"Safe?" he snorted. "That big cow would have treated this jalopy like a paper bag. The next time you get a notion to photograph a baby elephant, make sure that he's safely behind bars in a zoo. Out here, older relatives are never far away."

Pride goeth before a fall. I was still smarting from Bing's reprimand, and fiercely resenting his superior air, when Terry pointed to a lioness with three small cubs.

"Lucky we're mobile," our hunter remarked. "That lady could be as nasty as a cow elephant with a calf."

"I'll just swing by and take a closer look," Bing decided, pulling up within a few yards of the animals.

The mother lion went into a tail-switching crouch, and Terry suggested diffidently that it might be well to move on. Whereupon Bing trod heavily on the gas, and stalled the vehicle.

His passengers' admonitions to "get the hell out of here" led to a futile churning of the starter motor, and further pumping of the gas pedal.

"You'd better stop now," Terry advised. "I think you've flooded it." A diagnosis which was shortly confirmed by a strong odor of gasoline.

Slowly and unobtrusively Bing and Terry reached for their rifles, while I huddled in the rear seat, and pretended not to know them. If the final score was to be Lions 2, Christians 0, I wanted to make it perfectly clear that I was merely a neutral observer.

After several more excruciating minutes, during which all participants

Jeanne and I went hunting.

Sultan Hamud mountain range

in our tableau, except the gamboling cubs, remained absolutely motionless, and I longed for the courage to pull out my camera, mama lion deduced correctly that her glare had paralyzed the foe, cuffed her cubs into a semblance of order, and stalked contemptuously off.

It took a sheepish Bing ten minutes to restart the Land Rover, after which he patrolled the veldt for the remainder of the day, grimly determined to redeem himself, but encountering nary a trace of the vast herds of eland promised by the game warden.

That night around the campfire, we discussed my quartz find which, however beautiful to me, had been pronounced worthless by our resident expert. My early reading of H. Rider Haggard's magnificent romantic prose still colored my view of Africa, so in my disappointment, I brought up the subject of King Solomon's Mines.

To my delight, Jeanne Mathews informed me that a hunter had sighted an abandoned shaft, not five miles away, with garnets as thick as raisins in a rice pudding. Since I had been feeling superfluous for some days, I decided to let Bing chase his own eland on the morrow, while I prospected for gems.

In the event, the five miles were somehow transformed into twenty, as Jeanne and I bumped through countless chuck holes to the base of what seemed to the highest mountain in the Sultan Hamud range. She had diffidently mentioned "nipping up a little hill," and I, weaned on Texas hyperbole, saw that I had succumbed once more to lethal British understatement.

I tried to conceal my terror of heights, and followed doggedly after a woman who leapt from rock to rock like a klipspringer. As my collapses became more frequent, she shrewdly deceived my oxygen-starved brain with mendacious assurances that the mountaintop was within easy reach.

I had long since ceased to believe in it, when she finally announced that we had arrived, and I pitched gratefully forward onto my face, hugging the dirt of the summit.

When I risked a downward glance, the African plain was spread out before me like a rich banquet. I could easily descry numerous giraffe, impala, gerenuk, and yes, even a small herd of the elusive eland.

After ten minutes of heavy breathing, I managed to rise and accompany Jeanne in the pursuit of my garnet mine, but our task was complicated by the heavy undergrowth, which covered most of the higher elevations.

I focused on the nearest thicket, and was about to enter it when I heard a crashing sound, and was restrained by Jeanne, who remarked diffidently that the copse reeked of cape buffalo.

My surprise momentarily conquering my terror, I asked how so large a beast had managed to ascend the sheer cliffs that we had traversed with such difficulty.

"There are plenty of animal trails up the other side of the mountain," Jeanne assured me.

"Fine, I'll go down that way."

"Don't you want to continue hunting for the mine?"

"No, I've suddenly realized that I don't even like garnets."

"Isn't that a bit of sour grapes?"

"Yes. Now let's get out of here."

"It will be longer and more dangerous to follow the animal trails down, and we'll have a stiff hike back to the Land Rover."

183

The vehicle that brought

our English nurses

"All the more reason to get going." And that was just what we did.

Back at camp, I discovered that Bing had also had a fruitless day. When I mentioned my failure, he informed me that five years previously a Masai burnoff had got out of hand, and incinerated not only the fields but also the nearby mountains, revealing a mine shaft, which had gradually again become overgrown with brush.

"Couldn't you have told me about that last night?"

"I'd have been happy to if you'd asked, but you place a premium on making your own decisions."

Touché, and I generally got away with it, more or less, as long as I practiced in relatively civilized environments, but I vowed to be more cautious on the Dark Continent. On safari with Bing, things might get a bit rough, but they went infinitely worse without him.

On Friday, August 8th, I volunteered my invaluable assistance in the still unsuccessful eland hunt. But some unfortunate waving of firearms led Bing to suggest, "Suppose you just forge on ahead to draw hostile fire and trip land mines."

Aggrieved, I withdrew, and accepted an invitation from the Flying Doctor Services of the African Medical Research Foundation, where I teamed up with three English nurses and a Masai physician named Ismael Nganiki.

With them, I visited my first menyata, a temporary Masai settlement, consisting of huts and cattle pens made of brush, dung, and red dust, and surrounded by a thick wall of the same handy materials.

In the shade of a huge acacia tree, waited my first patients, dressed in their best beads.

While the regular team cared for accident victims on the left side of the ambulance, I stood to the far right, vaccinating the children for smallpox, and inoculating them against the worst of the childhood diseases, such as diphtheria, whooping cough, and tetanus.

The needles that I employed resembled the points of blunt pencils, so I requested new ones, only to be told that mine were indeed two years old, but there were no replacements. The ones I used were to be sterilized by dropping them into the pot in which the team's coffee was boiled.

The headman of the village had the women superbly organized. One by one the mothers stepped forward and presented their children to be vaccinated, while I achieved a nodding acquaintance with essential terminology. Something like *sindanos* seemed to be the Masai word for *injection. Edipi* meant *it is finished,* and *olisere* was *good-bye.*

To administer the polio vaccine, I had to say *tangaaunkotok,* which approximated *open your mouth,* and was the signal for a mother to pry apart clenched jaws, revealing brilliant white teeth and a tongue forced outward to catch the drop of serum.

Next came the expression *sidai,* which hopefully combined the meanings *it is good, swallow it, or we'll have to do it again,* and *that wasn't so bad, now was it?*

When I had completed the immunizations, I assisted in therapy, treating many of the same mothers whose children had already passed through my hands.

As a consequence of nursing their babies up to the age of four, they

Volunteering with the flying doctors,

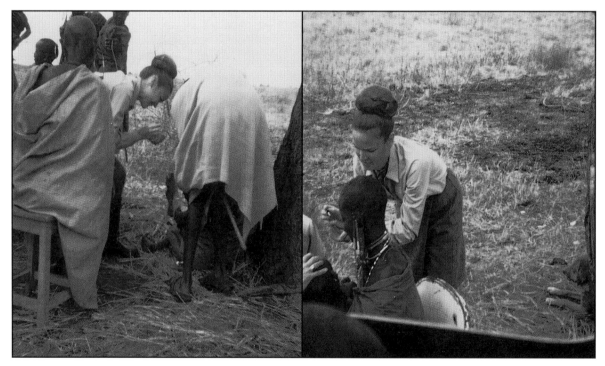

I specialized in inoculation.

suffered from mastitis, so I applied kaolin plasters to the pendulous, inflamed breasts "to draw out the poison," a practice which had been discontinued in the developed countries since the advent of antibiotics.

When I questioned it, a nurse admitted cheerfully, "We lack the necessary medicines, so we do what we can. For example, last year an American donor flew in a ton of Ex-Lax, and we had to pay duty on it.

You can imagine how useful a laxative is for people whose diet consists of milk and cow's blood, but we administer it in small doses as a placebo, when we have nothing else."

Some of the problems that I treated were strikingly similar to those encountered in any clinic back home. During the unusually cool spell which had accompanied the last rainy season, many of the shoeless children had contracted bronchitis, and their parents were suffering from various other respiratory diseases acquired during the same period. There were also numerous cases of the middle ear infection known as *otitis media.*

By the time we had finished with our last patient, it was nearly noon, the heat was intense, and I, who had been on my feet since dawn, was ready to drop. Gratefully I piled into the back of the truck, washed a cheese sandwich down with coffee, and fell fast asleep, expecting to awaken back at camp.

When I was shaken into some semblance of consciousness, I found that we had abandoned the arid community of Mokutani for the water hole of Ngamba, where we stretched awnings on either side of the truck, to offer some protection from the blistering sun. I also donned orange sunglasses, which

made an enormous hit with the ladies present, and led to an exchange of hints on makeup.

The Masai girls wore black dye in a semicircle under their eyes, beads and buttons at the tops of their ears, and heavier ornaments such as corks or film cans, which stretched the lower lobes. I had comparatively little to offer, but made a show of applying lipstick and eye liner, wishing that I had worn a fall and false eyelashes, which I surely could have removed to a standing ovation.

Throughout the afternoon, the doctor and nurses continued to treat the injured men and boys, while I dealt with the women and their remarkably well-behaved children, vaccinating all and sundry, and then trying to unearth the specifics of intestinal disturbances, and of the lower back injuries resulting from filling heavy water jugs at the bore hole. I was saddened to discover that I could offer only antacids for the former, and liniments for the latter, both of which, however, turned out to be universally prized.

Toward the end of the afternoon, I was viewing reality through a haze of heat exhaustion. I was only dimly aware of being bundled into the truck and delivered back to camp, where I woke long enough to decline an invitation to repeat my ministrations on the following day.

I had nothing but admiration for the remarkable people who devoted their lives to such tasks, but with the best will in the world, I lacked the stamina to imitate them.

I was delighted to learn that Bing had had an equally exhausting but less soul-satisfying day, spent once more in vain search for the elusive eland. The

Terry smiles in satisfaction

as Bing bags his mighty eland.

next morning, however, he chanced upon the track of a wily old bull, which he followed for three hours, unable to approach near enough to try a shot.

Then he adopted an old stratagem. In addition to his safari attire, he donned a borrowed shuka, and rubbed red dust over his face and hands, thus convincing himself that he had been transformed into the spitting image of a Masai herdsman.

Obviously his bearers thought that he fell somewhat short of the desired effect, because they became much too busy rolling in the dust and shaking with laughter to be of any further use.

Nothing daunted, Bing put his thespian talents to the ultimate test, strolling about in full sight of the eland, in the role of a diminutive Masai with no interest whatsoever in native fauna.

Imperceptibly, he drew closer and closer to the perplexed animal, which presented a very difficult shot since it continued to face him.

When he finally arrived within two-hundred yards, Bing whipped his rifle out from under the folds of the shuka, and dispatched the eland with a perfect shot through the neck into the heart.

The hunting party rushed to the scene, and a bearer made a remark which led to more laughing and rolling about. When Bing demanded a rough translation, a guide finally gasped out the following: "Bwana may not look like much of a Masai, but he sure does hunt like one."

That evening, there was roast eland for the entire camp. Unfortunately, all the hyenas within a radius of twenty miles must have felt that the invitation included them.

Their convention, complete with hors d'oeuvres, was held in and about our tents. Evidently they saw no reason to limit themselves to inanimate flesh. At one point I was convinced that some luckless animal had expired beneath my bunk.

Fond as my companions were of hyenas, and grateful to them for consuming leftover bones that might otherwise puncture the tires of our Land Rovers, on the whole I rather preferred sleep.

With the dawn came news that a leopard had been feeding on the bait hung from a tree along a nearby game trail. All day, Bing and Terry sat in a blind, which was prudently located well back from the path, lest the big cat drop in unexpectedly.

In the event, the leopard visited neither the bait nor the blind, but every time Bing turned around, something else was staring at him. After being joined by a pregnant cheetah, three wart hogs, two monkeys, and a jackal, Bing conceded that his patience was wearing thin. Then five francolin strutted straight into his hiding place.

The *coup de grace* was administered by a solitary vulture, who perched on a branch above the blind, and divided his somber stares between bait and hunters, before liberally dousing the latter.

"It's a lucky thing," Bing commented grimly, "that elephants don't fly. I'm tired of trying to shoo spectators away. Let's leave the blind to the groundlings, and the bait to the bird."

That night, there was another eland dinner, followed by an even livelier hyena party. The news was evidently getting around.

I never managed to close an eye, but it was only at sunrise that my roommate awakened, wrapped himself in the nearest shuka, and sallied forth

Dancers at the Mount Kenya Safari Club

A crested crane on the lawn

indignantly to disperse the last of the revelers.

Bing's intentions were noble enough, but he made more noise than the hyenas. Terry stuck his nose out of his tent just in time to see a bewildered animal flash by, pursued by what he took to be a native girl in a sarong.

When he twitted the returning Bing about his costume, my husband replied sourly, "Thees ees ze customary night garb of honorable Kenya citizen."

And then with a little skip and a darling entrechat, "Also occasional day garb of slightly less honorable citizen."

As the only one who had slept for two long nights, Bing was surprised to learn that the majority opinion was that the hyenas had won.

He nonetheless yielded to it, and agreed to leave. We dismantled our tents, and flew to the Mount Kenya Safari Club.

As I have had occasion to remark previously, we are creatures of contrast, appreciating the goods of this earth in terms of comparisons with their immediately-experienced opposites. The club replaced the tangled beauty of a tent beneath a spreading acacia with the classical geometric precision of manicured lawns and formal gardens.

We traded wild predators for tame egrets, peacocks, and crested cranes. Indeed the only undomesticated element in view was snow-capped Mount Kenya in the far distance.

Even the hunting had become civilized. While our friends Tommy and Duree Shevlin played golf, and enjoyed gourmet lunches and dinners, their scouts were swarming over the Serengeti in search of the great-granddaddy of all bull elephants.

Bing scorned such decadence, but I reveled in it, whether lounging on the balcony of a baronial suite, floating about the pool, luxuriating in a hot tub, or gorging on the fabulous food.

It all seemed too good to last, and of course it was. Bing dragged me off to a pigeon shoot.

After bumping along for three hours in a Land Rover, we were welcomed by our gun bearers. Mine located me behind a convenient bush, when my Swahili proved inadequate to acquaint him with the specifics about girls who can shoot only highly-cooperative birds, traveling slowly and sedately in a linear progression from right to left, with the good manners to check in at precisely two o'clock, and to meet their demise at ten on the dot.

Moreover, I seemed to have arrived at the wrong time of day. The feathered commuters were in transit from the water hole on my left to the deep forest on my right. A hundred yards away, I heard Bing taking his toll, but I prudently refrained from wasting ammunition. Sensing that he had been saddled with a retardate, my bearer waxed volubly desperate.

And then it happened. A squadron of procrastinators abandoned the forest, heading for the hills that hid the water. All were obligingly slow, steady, and undaunted by ack-ack. For one brief glorious moment before reverting to type, I got eight birds with nine shells, including two right-to-left doubles.

"M'dio!" I screamed, meaning roughly "Yeah man." And the bearer echoed delightedly M'dio."

Bing had taken thirty birds, including a Scotch triple, before quietly putting his gun away. Upon meeting him, I insisted on recounting my

Fellow miscreants at mass

exploits, despite his assurance that my shouts could have been heard for a good two miles down the valley.

Overjoyed at having saved face, the bearer backed up all my lies, vigorously pantomiming two or more birds falling with each splendid shot. Blessing his mendacious little soul, I tried to hire him permanently, but sadly linguistic difficulties again intervened.

On Sunday, August 10th, Bing and I attended 9:30 mass, held in the Kikuyu language in the village of Nanyuki. Above the altar in the Church of Christ the King stood a statue of the Divine White Monarch, magnanimously bestowing blessings on a congregation which was uniformly black.

In America, I was accustomed to muttered, tentative responses. Here they were clear and full. Unaccompanied voices rose in splendid song, and at my side Bing seemed thunderstruck.

"What is it?" I asked.

"It's the first time that I've ever heard a congregation sing in tune."

"Why don't you join them?"

Innocent of Kikuyu, Bing nonetheless harmonized his boom, boom, boom in a barbershop bass, with such enormous volume issuing from those splendid pipes that all attention gradually focused on him.

At the end of the number, heads nodded in appreciation. None of the worshipers knew of Bing Crosby, but they were natural connoisseurs of great music, and they recognized and appreciated the tribute to their people and church.

Bing couldn't escape the attention of two miscreants seated to our right. During the entire song, they had divided their solemn glances between him and the priest, while frantically kicking each other beneath the bench. Their immense eyes registered sudden dismay when my erstwhile Father O'Malley stared disapprovingly down upon them, and gravely shook his head.

But their guilt changed to mirth as Bing slowly winked, while delivering a healthy kick under the bench at my innocent self. Dear Lord, I was dealing not with the good priest of *Going My Way,* but with a seven-year-old hellion from Spokane, whose conduct hadn't improved appreciably in the intervening 58 years.

Temporarily the boys returned their attention to the mass, but of course I repaid Bing's kick with interest, and the ensuing scuffle caused the dark countenances to revolve our way once again. They gazed upon us with sad reproof, soberly shook their heads, and then winked in unison. Properly rebuked, we returned to our devotions.

When the mass ended, we rendered unto Caesar by driving our jeep directly to Star Tailors, where I purchased a much-needed pair of lightweight slacks, originally designed for Duree Shevlin, and two superbly-made copies of Pucci blouses, at a total cost of ten dollars.

We returned to the Safari Club for a last barbecue lunch on the lawn, before being whisked off to the airport for a flight to Waldena, where live the Omar people, a Galla tribe. Pitching our tent on the Thua Luga River, we resumed roughing it, to Bing's delight and my ill-concealed dismay.

The following dawn ushered in a dove and grouse shoot. Despairing of my marksmanship, I strolled up the river in search of artifacts, but discovered only two giant land snails.

By afternoon, the thermometer hovered around 105. I declined Bing's

Patients young and old

flock to Jeanne Mathews' medical clinic.

invitation to scout the country with him, and took to my bunk.

As the temperature in the tent continued to mount, I shed first my new slacks, then the Pucci shirt, and finally all but my briefs.

I spent the next hour with a copy of Time Magazine just flown in from London, hoping to catch up on world events.

Some slight noise caused me to glance up from an account of Nixon's around-the-world tour, to stare through the netting at what seemed to be an entire Omar tribe.

"Jambo," I quavered, hoping to brazen the situation out.

When my audience continued to stare silently, I feigned a return to my reading, but took care to hold the magazine at a more strategic angle. Eventually my admirers grew bored, and wandered off. Heat wave or no, I donned everything in range.

Meanwhile Bing's scouting party had just about decided that the countryside was barren of game when, emerging from some trees, they had to brake suddenly to avoid running down a kudu, two gerenuk, and a small herd of Peters' gazelle.

A slow, cautious stalk brought Bing to within a hundred yards of the herd of gazelle. He observed them for fifteen minutes, but no shots were heard. Returning to the Land Rover, he tossed his rifle to a bearer, and dismissed the entire incident with the laconic comment, "Hardly respectable."

An hour later, he and Terry initiated an intricate semicircular stalk, which brought them within twenty yards of another group of Peters' gazelle. Once again, there was no gunfire, but in its stead loud laughter.

It eventuated that Terry had turned Bing's own words back on him by designating the herd as "barely representative." Surely my heroic hunter was not the man to shoot a barely representative gazelle.

Shortly after leaving our tent the next day, we came upon a cow that had recently calved. Bing conscientiously sought out what he deemed to be the nearest cowboy, and explained the matter in his own peculiar combination of pidgin English, sign language, and what he fondly conceived to be Swahili.

Without pausing to reply, the native dashed off in the indicated direction, whereupon a bearer explained in quite authentic Swahili that the departed one wasn't a cowboy at all, but a renowned poacher.

"Well, he might have been a trifle more grateful," Bing insisted.

The whole day passed without sign of any "respectable" game. On our return to camp, we found that Terry and Jeanne had opened their own amateur medical clinic.

After a day spent treating stomach complaints, constipation, abscessed teeth, infected cuts, and strained backs, they were faced with a real emergency. One of the porters had collapsed with a stroke.

While Terry radioed the charter service in Nairobi, I tried to reassure the porter, who firmly believed that the half of his body which he could not feel was dead, so the other half must soon follow suit.

In spite of all my explanations, he remained steadfast in that opinion. Without much hope, I reported the problem to Bing, who had an ingrained distaste for all things medical.

Bing with his gazelle

Galla ladies with bracelets

Finding no alternative, my husband reluctantly agreed to give the matter his best shot.

Fixing the porter with an unwavering gaze, he declaimed slowly and pontifically, "I do not lie, and I tell you that you are not going to die. I say that you will live for many, many years."

Bing next administered an aspirin, explaining, "This great medicine will take the pain away."

Finally our shaman offered a salt tablet with the assurance, "And this wonder drug will make you well."

The sick man believed the truth that he knew Bing always told, and was immediately tranquil.

Moreover his "doctor's" prognosis proved correct. The porter was to die of old age, surrounded by great-grand-children.

I reflected that my husband was wasting his time in the entertainment world. As a physician, he could have distributed his sugar pills with the best of them.

We had exhausted our food supply, and Bing was under strong pressure to shoot something, respectable or no.

Finally he sighted some truly fine specimens of Peters' gazelle, where-upon he and Terry managed to get themselves so wrapped up in camou-flage that they looked like a bush with four legs.

Terry led the stalk, losing a tennis shoe to Bing's longer stride, while I recorded the event on film. For the better part of an hour, I watched the bush edge forward like a burly bug.

Then the front end hurled itself to the ground, permitting the backside to drop a buck with a single shot. Though urged to do so, Bing refused to fire again, and the herd moved on.

We dressed the gazelle, and hauled the meat back to camp, where we were greeted by half the Galla tribe. The animal constituted the *pièce de résistance* of a triumphal farewell dinner.

August 15th was the final day of our safari. Belatedly I realized that I had neglected to acquire gifts and take souvenir pictures for friends at home.

The first part was easy. The Galla maidens covered their arms with bracelets, which they continued to wear throughout their lives.

Indeed, viewing corpulent mamas with the same armbands that they had donned as adolescents, now all but hidden by rolls of billowing fat, I wondered how their life's blood still managed to circulate.

Be that as it may, such bracelets were in anything but short supply. My initial offer for one gave rise to a selling war, and soon I bade fair to corner the market.

Realizing that my shillings were viewed as manna from heaven, I bought on and on.

Bing put his foot down after I had accumulated some hundred bracelets, a few of which I later succeeded in bestowing on ungrateful friends and relatives.

But most of them provided a ready answer to those letters which begin: "Our church/school/club/charity is hold-ing a celebrity auction, and if you could just sent some item with special meaning for you...."

Meanwhile, back in Africa, I was fully aware that capturing rural natives on film is always a touchy business, but my shillings had made a good impression, and one mother agreed to let me photograph herself and her two children.

I'd have preferred the crew of our viking ship
to the bureaucrats at the Rome Airport.

I raced for my Rolliflex, and when several other women clustered round, I snapped them too, being very careful to make them understand the procedure.

When I ran out of film, Bing lent me his camera. Flushed with success, I threw caution to the winds, with what might well have been disastrous results.

Two young warriors let out what could be described only as war whoops, raised their spears, and prepared to charge. I screamed for Bing, who had retired for a siesta in the tent.

Out he came, clad only in khaki shorts and gold-monogrammed house slippers. Taking in the situation at a glance, he yanked the camera from my hand, thrust it upon a leaping warrior, and insisted that the African take the pictures. The delighted young Galla used up the rest of our film, shooting group portraits of Bing, me, and all the present members of his tribe.

Apparently a camera occasioned no difficulties if wielded by a local.

All in all, it would have been a delightful afternoon if Bing and I had not been out of sorts, he because he never did get his nap, and I because my champion had prudently chosen to sell me out, rather than joust for my honor.

The whole village escorted us to our handmade airstrip, and waved as we took off, with Bing, as ever, holding the plane aloft while I snored.

I was half awakened by the landing in Nairobi, only to sleep through the drive to the Norfalk Hotel, where Bing had ordered by radio a formal dinner, which included most of the civilized delicacies which I had so longed for in the Serengeti.

On Saturday, August 16th, we flew from Nairobi to Rome. We touched down at 2 AM on Sunday morning, and Bing shook me awake to inquire about our passports.

My mother had lamented that I would lose my head, were it not firmly affixed to my shoulders, so it is with great pride that I ever produce any desired object. With a flourish worthy of Blackstone, I withdrew the little green booklets from my handbag.

Oddly enough, my theatrical gesture failed to reassure Bing.

"Where," he inquired grimly, "are the yellow cards?"

Now that he mentioned it, I did recall that in far-off Burlingame Dr. Hanfling had furnished me with evidence of our recent vaccinations.

"I didn't see them when I unpacked in Nairobi," I admitted, "but I'm sure they won't be necessary."

I had tried to speak soothingly, but must have fallen short of the desired effect. "Oh my God," Bing moaned.

Certain that he was being unduly pessimistic,I focused all my charms on the nearest official.

Clad in the obligatory sweat-stained black suit, he was tiny, fat, bald, and redolent of garlic.

After listening attentively to my tale of woe, he announced benignly, "Since you have no proof of inoculation, of course you must be vaccinated."

Since sex seemed to have failed us, Bing tried a little muscle: "That's what you think," he countered resolutely. "Where's your boss?"

Sono il capo," was the discouraging reply. Drawing himself up to his full four feet eleven, our representative of millennia of bureaucracy launched into a lengthy recounting of the cases of smallpox recently discovered in remote areas of Africa.

Now You Has jazz.

Our boulevardier

May all your Christmases be white.

Irritated by the man's atrocious accent in Italian, Bing replied in polysyllabic English, explaining that the areas in question were hundreds of miles distant from those we had visited.

Refusing to be swayed by mere reason, our tormentor favored him with a superior smile, and replied that no such considerations made the slightest difference to him.

To my utter surprise, Bing then favored him with a lengthy paragraph of fluent Italian, whereupon we were both vaccinated with a vengeance.

While nursing our wounds in the hotel, I asked Bing what in the world he had said. It turned out that he didn't quite know.

Back in the Whiteman days, during a lengthy break in a recording session, Joe Venuti, greatest of all jazz violinists, had amused himself by teaching Bing an ancient Sicilian curse, which our crooner's perfect mimicry had permitted him to repeat exactly. The petty tyrant at the airport must have believed that a master of dialects had been toying with him all along.

By the time we managed to crawl into bed, it was 5 AM. For Bing, civilization brought insomnia. The Cavaliere Hilton thrones majestically above the turmoil of the Roman streets. We had chosen it for its isolation, forgetting how sound travels upward.

The din of all the Vespas in town was reflected straight into our suite. Bing had yet to doze off when the bells of Rome summoned him to early mass. After we left the church, I plied him with *espresso,* before insisting that we tour the city in the comparative quiet of a Sunday morning.

As a practicing Catholic, Bing had developed his own Sabbath ritual. He invariably proceeded directly from the altar to the first hole of the Burlingame Country Club.

Reluctantly, he followed my suggestion that we walk off our residual fevers from the redundant smallpox vaccinations, but he clearly suffered from the lack of fairways in the Eternal City.

At 11 AM on Monday, August 18th, I had an appointment with Father Heston, the American who headed the Sacred Congregation, to discuss the right of the Immaculate Heart sisters to experiment with new life styles. With Machiavellian cunning, I invited my husband to accompany me.

Overwhelmed at the thought of entertaining Bing Crosby, Father Heston proved a charming and knowledgeable cicerone, who led us on an extended tour of the Vatican, while totally ignoring both the nuns' cause and their humble petitioner.

At the risk of seeming pushy, I brought the matter up just as we took our leave. Father Heston, who at least nominally oversaw the activities of all American nuns, professed total ignorance of any problems that the sisters might have, but evinced surprise that Bing should concern himself with them.

My crooner had to admit that he too found his role to be a trifle obscure, but he did ask just who the appropriate authority might be.

With relief, Father Heston suggested Archbishop Paul Marchinkus, the Pope's right-hand man, who was subsequently to be featured in a Vatican securities scandal.

Sure enough, on the 19th we spent three hours with the bemused prelate, who had been experiencing difficulties with his putting, which he was delighted to discuss with a distinguished golfer.

A terrifying prospective acquisition

We toured the magnificent Vatican gardens, and compared the relative advantages of tapping and stroking the ball with putters of various weights, while I struggled to interject queries about woman's lot within the Church.

Both Bing and the Archbishop seemed to find my behavior mildly disruptive, but our cleric good-naturedly paid for his golf lesson with observations about the unique problems of American womanhood.

Nowhere else did females cause such trouble. Didn't they realize that the Church was a hierarchy, with a proper place for everyone, and that higher education, planned parenthood, women's liberation, equal rights, and above all wild experiments on the part of nuns, who had sworn to abandon such worldly snares for the spiritual joys of contemplation, were simply flying in the face of God's will?

Eyes cast doggedly downward, I practiced humility, but the golfer's eloquence had struck responsive chords within my husband. Abandoning his dissertation on the excessive wristiness of Marchinkus' putting stroke, he began to pose ever more penetrating questions about the duties of a Catholic wife and mother.

For my part, I had resolved that if I could abandon the premises without a double murder on my conscience, I would account the meeting a triumph. As Bing and I bade farewell to the Archbishop, and took our leave of the lovely gardens, I was minded of the fate of two such other rebels against divine interdictions:

They hand in hand with wand'ring
steps and slow
Through Eden took their solitary
way.

And even in that antediluvian paradise, it had been the little woman who had caused all the fuss.

From Rome, we drove to Porto Ercole, to relax at the home of American friends. Bing's needless vaccination had reacted violently. I dressed and bandaged it daily, but he continued to run a fever, and his macho friends added insult to injury by teasing him mercilessly about his way with customs officials.

On Thursday, August 31st, we were invited to lunch at the home of the Marchesa Lili Genni. This was the first year that Bing had succeeded in limiting me to a Spartan safari wardrobe, and I was still mindful of a gaffe in my last brush with royalty.

"Should I imitate your girl friend Grace?" I inquired. "Will slacks do?"

"They did very well for her as I recall," Bing mused, with a far-off look in his blue orbs, "but in your case I'd suggest something casual but elegant."

I dug deep into my single suitcase, and came up with Star Tailors' best, those self-same Pucci ripoffs that Duree Shevlin had rejected in Africa. Hardly elegant, but certainly casual. One out of two would have to do.

Surrounded by *la crème de la crème* of Roman society, in pearl-laden silk shifts and sophisticated white linens, Bing and I in our bush costumes were certainly outstanding, in the original sense of the word.

Taking no notice of the conventions of costume, he as ever was the belle of the ball, while I hid my face in the caviar-laced consumé.

"You theater people are so magnificently informal in everything you do," remarked our hostess into one very red ear. With nothing else to consider,

Nathaniel's missing incisors

I wondered idly whether khaki just might become the rage of the Riviera for what remained of the season.

It served us much better the following day, when we lunched on Lowell Weicher's yacht. Seated on deck beneath brilliant canopies, warmed by a bright Italian sun, and cooled by a soft sea breeze, we gazed out at the brilliant blue of the motionless Mediterranean.

Privately I counted my blessings. I become carsick at moderate speeds on mountain roads, and can endure not the slightest rocking motion on a boat. Casually I tuned in on my husband's conversation.

"I'd want something at least 80 feet long," he was insisting, "with full crew and chef, ready to cruise Italian and Grecian waters by the start of next summer. Of course it would have to have ample accommodations for the entire family. I'd be happy to let the builders charter it during the winter when we weren't using it."

Saints preserve me, another building project! Had I really dispensed so much of my youth and strength, preventing Bing from constructing dream houses in odd corners of the earth, only to fall prey to an ocean-going calamity? Something would have to be done.

It was. Throughout the rest of 1969, Bing corresponded with European shipyards, and at times it seemed to be a near thing, but at the last moment some little impediment or some small person always prevented the signing of a contract.

On Sunday, August 24th, we flew from Rome to New York City. Bing settled down with *Sports Illustrated,* and I actually managed to digest fifty pages of *The Godfather,* before lapsing into a dreamless sleep.

On Monday, Mary Morrow and I lunched at Club 21 with Malcolm McLean, who bet her a million dollars that she would be married within the year, and handed me a hundred-thousand-dollar check for Immaculate Heart College, thus preserving me from returning home empty-handed, or ever escaping Bing's ire.

That evening, we flew to San Francisco, and I unpacked in Hillsborough, while Bing drove our daughter Mary to Rising River Ranch.

They returned on Saturday, August 30th, just in time to celebrate the arrival of Nathaniel's first permanent teeth, his front incisors, which at long last were beginning to fill the void left when he had fallen off a tricycle at the age of three.

Solemnly we drank a toast to the three gloriously gap-toothed intervening years..

In further tribute to them, we held a party, and organized a ping-pong game on the dichondra side lawn. The guest of honor soon tired, and was carried in for his nap, but Harry and I fought Bing and Mary to a standstill for over two hours, after which we lived without grass for six months.

Monday, September 1st, was Labor Day. After crawling about in the garden all morning, and lunching on the terrace, I retreated to the library with my copy of *The Godfather.*

The blissful silence remained unbroken, until my three little scholars arrived.

"Whatcha readin' mommy?"

"A book," I admitted cautiously.

"Will you read it to us?"

"No. Go outside and play."

"We'll play our games right here 'till you read to us."

There's Nothing That I Haven't Sung About.

Knowing full well the noise level which my diminutive blackmailers could generate, I temporized:

"Will you be very quiet?"

"Yes, mommy."

All three arranged themselves on the big down couch. Nathaniel plopped his head into my lap and prepared for sleep, his definition of reading.

Briefly I recounted my expurgated edition of the story to date. Then I continued on page 161. The things a mother does for a moment's repose!

In the event, the arrangement proved surprisingly satisfactory. Within five minutes, all three children had nodded off, and I was deep in a jolly good story, my voice droning on because I had learned from sad experience that a sudden pause might awaken them.

Suddenly Bing's baritone thundered from the doorway: "Are you reading that book to my innocent children?"

"Uh, not really."

"Am I to deny the direct evidence of my senses?"

"Under the circumstances, I wish you would."

"None of your levity. How in the world can you explain such behavior?"

"Well, you see, the fact is that they're all asleep." I glanced hopefully over at three wide-eyed stares. "You haven't heard a word of this story, have you, children?"

"Oh yes, mommy. We think it's wonderful."

"Now I know where they learned those awful words that the teachers complained of last year."

Fathers have a fragile grasp on reality. "You've got it all wrong," I insisted truthfully. "They learn those words in school, and come home to teach them to me."

"Well I don't want to see any more of that book in this house." Bing stamped off down the hall.

So he didn't. I tucked it away in the depths of my desk, and retrieved it only when I felt perfectly secure from unlawful searches and seizures. I might have been a child again, reading by flashlight beneath the covers, after my mother thought that she had tucked me safely into bed.

School reopened on Wednesday, September 3rd. Usually Bing and I took a lively interest, but this year we'd decided that we'd rather not hear about it. He left on a hunting trip, and I read *The Godfather*.

On Monday, September 15th, Bing flew to Florida to tape *The Jackie Gleason Show*, where its host had a new song written for him: *There's Nothing That I Haven't Sung About*.

It wove in many of his greatest hits, from the beginning of his career to the most recent numbers, and it became his all-time favorite for stage shows.

It was while Bing was in Miami that I finally lost my coveted place in the duck blind. Not that I'd ever been what you might call a hit with my fellow hunters.

With my low blood pressure and minimal circulation, I was perennially frozen stiff, and not one to suffer in silence. My letter to Bing broached the subject as follows:

"I get cold chills every time I recall breaking through the ice, as I fought my way back across the rice fields, with so little sensation in my hands and feet that I couldn't climb the bank to the trailer. After you carried me inside, I stuck my feet in the oven and melted my waders. Wouldn't you prefer to take Harry with you the next time?"

Jean Brodie in St. Louis

Bing would and did. Perhaps I had been a trifle too graphic in reminding him of all the times that I had forged courageously forth, only to stumble miserably back, with him tagging sadly along behind to make sure that I arrived safely. Whatever the reason, that missive ended my days as a duck hunter. Henceforth it would be Harry who staggered behind Bing across the frozen marshes. In retrospect, one might almost suspect that I'd planned it that way.

On Sunday, September 21st, I flew to St. Louis, where I had arranged for Anita Caspary, Reverend Mother of the Immaculate Heart Nuns, to play the grownup Sandy, who narrates *The Prime of Miss Jean Brodie.*

Of course she'd had to have permission for this, and I'd secured it by blackmailing Bing into calling Cardinal McIntyre, who had assured my husband that we could have her for as long as we wished, with the sole proviso that we never return her. He wanted Bing to understand clearly that the insufferable woman was driving him and his colleagues nuts.

Alas, I never would get the hang of the Church hierarchy. It seemed that Sister Anita's theatrical career was controlled not by the good Cardinal, but by that self-same Father Heston, whom I had recently encountered in Rome.

Before we could begin our first rehearsal, he appeared in St. Louis, and denied her the right to act, think, breathe, and generally continue to serve as an annoyance to the Church. Jean Tsokos, the willowy wife of our producer, was hastily summoned from her duties in the box office to represent the adult Sandy.

We were to have a four-week run in the Falstaff theater, located in the famed Spanish Pavilion, which St. Louis had purchased at the New York World's Fair. I was well acquainted with it, for I had tried to buy it for the nuns, planning to ship it through the Panama canal, and reassemble it in Hollywood.

It was fortunate that I knew my role, since we gave our first performance on September 30th, after only six days of rehearsal.

It was a long-anticipated event. Following years of misadventures in summer stock, I was in legitimate theater, or thereabouts.

The set was superb, the cast competent, and we opened to a full house. Moreover Lois Kibbee, our director, had informed us with pride that we had union labor backstage. I wasn't quite sure what that meant, but for one accustomed to a technical staff formed of fans and cousins, it should constitute an improvement.

It didn't. To be sure, backstage all went well enough, but the light booth was located at the rear of the audience, and there sat more union labor, in the form of someone's obese grandmother, a dyed-in-the-wool science fiction fancier, whose head was buried deep in Robert Heinlein's latest during the entire performance.

To her credit, it must be added that at random intervals her right hand did flick out to punch buttons, often with spectacular effect. Twice I entered onto a scene swathed in total darkness. Thrice I was spotlighted long after I had presumably exited, while the action on stage remained obscure.

I was assured that the situation would improve, but it didn't. After our third disaster in as many nights, I sat a

With Cyril Magnin, Mr. San Francisco

non-union understudy in the booth at granny's elbow, which appendage she jiggled at appropriate moments.

With this sole modification, we mounted a surprisingly effective production. The play was sold out for its entire run, and audience response was usually enthusiastic. When the house was liberally laced with well-lubricated conventioneers, the applause swelled to levels that would have surely gladdened even a Barrymore's heart.

It was in the middle of the fourth week that my long-neglected merits seemed at last ready to receive their just reward. Into my dressing room marched a youngish playwright, profuse with excuses for his brilliant partner, a composer who had been unavoidably detained elsewhere.

My rescuer was afflicted with a slight stammer, but his message came through loud and clear. He wanted me for the lead in the upcoming Broadway production of his new musical, the weighty script of which he forthwith thrust upon me.

I fled with it to the adjacent apartment which I shared with my mother, and swallowed the manuscript whole. Sure enough, as the beleaguered heroine, I dominated the stage from beginning to end, and had all the best songs.

Truth to tell, their relationship to the rest of the text was occasionally tenuous, but wasn't that the way with every musical?

When my benefactor returned three days later, I was letter perfect and ready to sign. Just by way of making conversation, I did inquire idly about my salary.

"Anything you want," was the amazing reply.

At last reality was beginning to live up to my expectations. Nonetheless, I'd been around long enough to be a trifle surprised. "Who is financing all this?" I ventured to ask.

"Well, we haven't quite decided yet. It's such a great opportunity that we wanted to make it available to you first. Do you think that Bing will want to keep it all for himself, or to bring in Bob Hope and some of his other Hollywood friends?"

"I'll let you know," I replied glumly, my brilliant future cascading about my ears.

My author insisted that I retain a copy of the script to show to Bing. I still treasure it in a secret compartment of my desk, next to a dog-eared copy of *The Godfather,* to be resurrected on rainy days, when I invariably run through a number or two, with my fertile imagination supplying stage, orchestra, and admiring multitudes.

Meanwhile, back in reality, our would-be diva returned home to spend the next six weeks packing for Bing's trips to the duck club, and inventing excuses for her children's insufferable conduct in school.

On Wednesday, December 3rd, Immaculate Heart College sponsored a dinner in Los Angeles, in honor of their favorite Jewish regent, Cyril Magnin. "Mr. San Francisco" was to be presented with the newly-originated and hopefully one-day-to-be-coveted *Pacem in Terris* award.

I had volunteered Bing as master of ceremonies, but had somehow neglected to mention the matter to him. By the time he learned of it, he claimed to be scheduled elsewhere.

I threatened him with divine retribution, but he remained unmoved.

In the library at Hillsborough

There was nothing for it but to slip into my latest Jean Louis' creation, and play mistress of ceremonies myself.

In the grand ballroom of the Hilton Hotel in Century City I smiled at the assembled throng and announced demurely: "Bing's terribly sorry that he couldn't be with us tonight, but he sends his best wishes, and as his own further contribution to the future of Immaculate Heart College, he has delegated me to pick up the check for tonight's activities."

In the audience, our business manager nearly fell from his chair, but Bing never mentioned the donation. He knew revenge when he saw and felt it.

Christmas found Bing exhausted from rushing hither and yon across the face of the earth. My mother and I prepared a huge turkey for the staff's annual celebration, and the entire Grandstaff clan, some forty strong, descended upon the household to prepare venison, duck, and dumplings.

Short weeks before, I had lost an appendix to the surgeon's knife, and Bing was touched to see how loyally my enormous family rallied around their recuperating runt.

213

Merry Christmas to all

1970

Fortunately California's benign climate permitted year-round golf, and in early January a respite from rain and bursitis led to a veritable orgy of fairway heroics.

Critics complained that Bing merely waved his hands loosely at the ball, but his simple swing had endured the test of time, and at the advanced age of 67 he still shot in the low 70's.

His leisurely game predated carts, and he had always abominated the "mechanistic madness" which they had introduced. As a consequence, he remained one of the handful of club members who continued to hire caddies, and he understandably enjoyed vast popularity with the bag-toting tribe, whom he regularly overtipped.

This was all very well on weekends, but he discovered to his horror that several enterprising young scoundrels had been playing hooky from school on the off chance of continuing to carry his clubs on weekdays. Bing promptly shooed them back to the halls of academe, but he was then faced with the unwelcome prospect of lugging his own clubs up hill and down dale.

Meanwhile his good friend Burleigh Pattee had resolved a related problem. Unlike Bing, he had been perfectly content to roll along the fairways, majestically enthroned upon a huge electric cart, with Sparky, his favorite Labrador, happily ensconced on the seat beside him.

But their faithful dedication to this mode of transportation had led both man and dog to astounding increases in girth, which had prompted their physician and playing partner to order them to dismount expeditiously and to start hiking.

Resourcefully, Burleigh had designed a novel doggy-harness for an adapted pull-cart, and had trained his canine crony to mush upon command.

With Lawrence Wood in Cowan's watercolor

As a golfer, Bing had always been a stout traditionalist, but a single session with Pattee and partner would have convinced Jones himself that the age of the tailwagger had dawned at last.

Our hero thought of his own six Labradors, and decided that training sessions might be in order, but first there was the small matter of acquainting himself with the new lore.

"Mind if I borrow Sparky for a few rounds?" he inquired speculatively.

"Not at all. The dog knows you, and he'll obey you if I tell him to. Let me show you how to hitch him up."

Bing, Sparky, and Ferdie Stent, who had outlived one of his legs in the course of a long and colorful career, were just teeing off at Burlingame, when a pair of young hotshots from the Stanford University golf team asked if they might play along.

On the first hole, it developed that the youngsters could hit the ball out of sight, and loved to bet on their games, but were a trifle reluctant to take candy from such an eccentric brace of veterans.

By the end of the first nine, Bing and Ferdie had helpfully relieved them not only of the last remnants of remorse, but also of half the contents of their wallets.

"That's the most fantastic chipping and putting I've ever seen," one remarked. "Let's have lunch, and make it double or nothing on the second nine."

During the repast, the two sports plied the oldsters liberally with Burgundy, and of course had to down a few drams themselves to avoid seeming too obvious.

Bing had never had any tolerance for alcohol, so Sparky, the only sober mammal in sight, had to double as seeing-eye dog throughout the long, hazy afternoon.

However, aided perhaps by his newly-acquired tunnel vision, the old crooner's shots flew straighter than ever, while Ferdie, whose wooden leg had long been reputed to be hollow, continued his brilliant play around the greens, capping off another triumph by chipping in on the treacherous 18th.

The would-be hustlers sought consolation in the bar, where one of them was moved to voice what Bing later characterized as the saddest plaint ever uttered by mortal man:

"Skunked!" the embittered youth declaimed to his shot glass, the barman, and the impassive adjacent tipplers. "Skunked, and fleeced, and skunked again! Skunked by a one-legged grandfather and a drunk with a dog for a caddie!"

On Saturday, January 10th, Bing and I flew to San Antonio, whence we were driven to Woodsboro. Our host, Lawrence Wood, was the scion of an old Irish family, rich enough in tradition among the early Yankee settlers of Texas, but he remained a mere parvenu beside his wife Leonora, who traced her lineage back to Manuel Iturria, one of Hernán Cortés's stout lieutenants.

As ever, I had dreamed of a romantic idyll sans chores and children, but the enormous Victorian headboards made me feel, in a word, Victorian. I languished on my lonely pillow, and dreamed of distinguishing myself in the morrow's hunt.

The desert dawn found me dressed to the nines and ready for battle. Which was indeed fortunate, for the dry South Texas growths concealed a hitherto unheralded breed of killer quail, which

With Leonora Wood and Major Tom Armstrong

persisted in taking off straight into my face, with wild whirring sounds that completely unnerved me, and led to novel ducking maneuvers, accompanied by the random discharge of both barrels of my puny 28-gauge straight skyward.

After Bing had filled his own bag, he finally deigned to take notice of my plight, and chivalrously offered to "cover my back," if I would just make shift to face the foe.

And well it was that he did so, for, confronted with a particularly ferocious covey, I surged straight backward with a momentum which carried us both through a clump of prickly-pear cactus, and almost into the embrace of two enormous diamond-backs, closely entwined in a free-form sculpture some three feet tall.

Not one to lose my presence of mind, I made an admirably quick decision: Despite all their inherent viciousness, I definitely preferred the quail. I broke my previous record for the standing backjump.

"Aren't you going to kill them?" I hissed indignantly.

"No," Bing drawled. "The path of true love never did run smooth, but far be it from me to stand in its way. For all I know, they're happier than we are, and a lot less imperiled by their immediate environment."

A possible allusion to my recent exploits with a shotgun? I dismissed the thought as unworthy of me, and made shift to salve my wounded pride by flirting outrageously with Major Tom Armstrong of (where else?) Armstrong, Texas. There just had to be some field in which I was equipped to compete.

The following day, we were joined by Jack Cowan, a celebrated painter of sporting scenes, whose renditions of my hunting exploits are still proudly displayed on our walls, an outstanding triumph of creative art over mere mundane reality.

Weak as my shooting had been, I could at least derive some merit simply for showing up. I forfeited even this small advantage when I insisted that the Woods summon their plane to fly an extremely reluctant husband and myself to Austin, where I was scheduled to receive the University of Texas Most Distinguished Alumna Award.

At a chic luncheon, Chancellor Harry Ransom, President Gene Hackerman, and a bevy of distinguished academics totally ignored me, while tripping all over themselves with encomiums for my failed undergraduate of a husband, whose sole claim to scholastic distinction was an honorary doctorate, resulting from his donation of the funds for The Crosby Library to Gonzaga University.

"Doctor Rhythm" was assured, in no uncertain terms that Texas was ready and willing to reciprocate for more of the same.

My turn finally came with the end-of-lunch speeches, where one and all gravely disregarded my academic record, my artistic and financial contributions to their drama department, my leading roles in films, my seat on the Board of Immaculate Heart College, my sundry attempts at public service, etc., to fasten upon my sole relevant achievement, namely my marriage to Bing Crosby.

It was proudly announced that, in the entire history of the University of Texas, only two other women had received the Most Distinguished Alumna Award, namely Ima Hogg and Lady

Off to the wars

Facing the killer quail

Bird Johnson, the former for being born into wealth and power, and the latter for marrying into it.

Contrary to popular belief, there was no Ura Hogg, or she would certainly have usurped my place on the totem pole. In firm grasp of the situation at last, I thanked everyone prettily, and got the hell out of there.

Bing and the Woods clamored for an immediate retreat to Armstrong, where Major Tom awaited us, but I insisted that Robstown, where I had lived with my aunt while attending high school, was right on the way. Darkly muttering something about majorities of one, Lawrence filed a new flight plan.

Forewarned of our arrival, Aunt Frances had summoned her friends to lionize Bing, and he was immediately surrounded by a gaggle of stately matrons. Proudly I presented my roster of celebrities: Sarah Stone, who had introduced me to William Shakespeare, Beatrice Jackson, my mother advisor at Rainbow Girls, Beulah Homeyer, my piano instructor, and Fannie Magee, my Methodist Sunday School teacher.

For a moment, I feared that I remarked a soupçon of desperation in Bing's glance as he was crowded into the nearest corner, but then he had recourse to his inexhaustible repertoire of stories, while I sat back to reflect on just how many strong females it had taken to launch one diminutive Texan on the river of life.

I was awakened from my reverie by a torrent of girlish giggles. There were the very women whom I'd always considered to be the true grownups, the guiding lights of my youth, my monuments of maturity, delightedly making fools of themselves over my

husband, who in turn was glowering over their shoulders at me.

I rescued him, promising to return soon, since everyone had obviously had such a lovely time.

Lawrence Wood, who had recently purchased the Robstown National Bank, gleefully poured gasoline on troubled fires.

"Bing," he commented, "all this bub-bub-a-boo nonsense of yours is a waste of time. You can make a better living as my shill. I've picked up twelve depositors in the last half hour."

We flew due south to Armstrong, with the Gulf of Mexico on the left, fleecy clouds beneath, and a full moon above, still chuckling his vast delight at the petty strifes of man.

At 6 the following morning, after some four hours of sleep, I pried my eyes open with a huge mug of black coffee, only to spy my husband joining the menfolk in ritual drafts of *leche colorada*.

My suspicions aroused, I soon ascertained that the innocent-sounding liquid actually consisted of hot, sugared milk, liberally baptized with bourbon, rum, rye, or even Scotch, to individual whim or taste.

These roisterers were about to take up shotguns, and sally forth to assault the local fauna. And I, alas, was scheduled to join them.

Our conveyances awaited us. They consisted of topless, stretched, jeep wagoneers, the interiors covered in cowhide, jump seats on the fenders, and truck beds in lieu of trunks. Add a scoop of swacked hunters, a dollop of doomed dogs, and two terrified females, and we were off to the wars.

One of the many inconvenient features of a hunt is that, once begun,

With Freddie Prinz and Bob Hope

there is seldom a way to escape from it. But in this particular instance, the men seemed conscious only of the happy, buzzing noises in their heads.

As they abandoned their vehicles, and set off to wreak their mayhem amid the mesquite, Leonora and I slowly dropped back, and finally slid behind a hospitable bush.

No one sounded an alarm. We, at least, would survive to tell the tale.

Back we strolled to the nearest wagon, from which we removed crackers, caviar, and a magnum of champagne. Thus fueled, we perched upon the cowhide seats, and indulged in some cheery, sensible girl talk.

After an hour or two of this regimen, we began to suspect that the rugged outdoor life might have something to recommend it after all.

And the death-bound dogs? One by one they crept away from the front lines, and sneaked back to join us.

They had fed prodigiously, and were resting quietly, when their masters finally arrived to complement us on the advanced woodsmanship which had permitted us to preserve our Abercrombie and Fitch costumes in such excellent repair.

Leonora and I accepted their accolades with becoming modesty, and served refreshments.

After very nearly becoming one himself, Bing decided that he had had enough of drunken Texans. We returned to California, where he lazed through a Hollywood Palace, and then made his annual appearance at his own golf tournament.

The weather was surprisingly sunny, as we followed Bing's friend Jack Nicklaus throughout the final round, in which he posted a 65 in a valiant but vain attempt to catch up with Bert Yancey, who eventually triumphed by a stroke. Bob Rosberg and John Brodie were the Pro-Am winners.

Then Bing was off to New York, to star with Bob Hope in a benefit for the Eisenhower Hospital. Mindful of how expensive my last performance in the Big Apple had proven, he escorted Mary Morrow, radiant in simple black and millions in diamonds.

"But Kathryn is a trustee of the hospital," Mary remarked. "Shouldn't she be here?"

"Kathryn has already been to New York," was the irrefutable reply.

We spent the months of February, March, April, and May in Mexico, but we expanded our base of operations. Helen Cerda, a friend from Catalina, was the proprietress of a shop in Guadalajara, and something of an authority on Mexican artifacts, in which I was developing an interest.

She invited me to accompany her on a dig in the remote area of la Piedad, remarking cryptically that it might prove exciting.

On April 14, I was packing my tools and clothing, when Mary Morrow arrived, and Bing, despite his terror of small planes in general and ours in particular, flew to La Paz to meet her.

She arrived looking newly blonde, serene, urbane, and fashionable, whereas Bing staggered off the plane, vowing never to board it again. It seemed that he had taken it upon himself to distract Mary from the sight of our adolescent pilot's cackling as he buzzed the burros off the runway so that the plane might land, while neglecting to consider the effect that such a scene might have on his own psyche.

223

Bing breaks for second base.

Mary showed her first signs of apprehension when Bing recovered sufficiently to announce that she was about to accompany me on an archeological dig in the wilds of central Mexico.

However, since she is a model of decorum, and the good guest always accommodates her hosts, she proceeded to organize her version of a costume for an outing, starting with a broad straw hat and silk gloves.

We flew first to Guadalajara, with Bing noticeable only for his absence. There Helen Cerda met us to announce that we might wish to reboard the plane, since there had been serious trouble in la Piedad, and she couldn't vouch for our safety.

"Nonsense," I replied firmly. "We've come to dig."

"Now Kathryn," Mary admonished. "Surely Bing wouldn't want us to do anything foolish."

"How can we be sure it's foolish until we try?"

Helen drove us to la Piedad, where we stayed the night in the San Sebastian Hotel, replete with embroidered sheets, deeply carved headboards, and legions of bedbugs. The following morning, we continued by truck to Zula el Viejo.

Our arrival there developed into a triumphal procession, with the entire village turning out to stare in fascination at Mary's parasol, blonde hair, fashion sunglasses, wedgie sandals, and perfectly pedicured bright-red toenails. She enthroned herself beneath a shady tree, while I took up my trowel, and disappeared into an adjacent trench.

Hours later, I emerged to find Mary, surrounded by all the children and most of the men of the town, generously spraying the assembly with *Femme*.

Next it was the women's turn. They trekked up the hill bearing gifts for the goddess. Mary accepted an enamel pot containing a tortilla with fried egg and fiery salsa. With a twist of the wrist she prepared a neat little roll for herself, and consumed it fastidiously, but with evident enjoyment.

She nonetheless experienced difficulty in satisfying Señora Mendoza. That stout matron had brought her prize rooster, bound at the ankles, but with inch-long spurs and decidedly mobile beak, to sire fine chicks in Mary's Palm Desert establishment, which sadly lacked a chicken coop.

With genuine regret, Mary asked me to translate, while she explained the impracticability of the plan, since the rooster could not be fitted with an oxygen mask, and flying without one in the luggage compartment of an Aeronaves jet would doubtless prove injurious to his health.

At this point I improvised. Would the señora perhaps allow our flaxen-haired beauty to visit the noble bird on her very next voyage to Mexico?

"Seguro que sí," and all was well for the moment.

With the rooster, that is. Otherwise my performance remained unsatisfactory. When I marched up to Mary's tree with a tubful of shards, she murmured in obvious disappointment, "No jade yet?"

When I triumphantly presented a perfectly preserved doll's plate that I had unearthed with my own grubby little hands, she sighed, "But after all it's not gold."

It was 4 PM, and exhaustion had set in. I was handing a *cerveza* to the leader of my band of volunteer helpers. As he reached to accept it, a huge hog's

Dr. M.W. Sullivan

leg pistol crashed to earth at his feet. There was a moment of frozen silence, and then the rest of the men roared with laughter, and brandished their own guns. It was like something out of a Pedro Armendáriz ranchero movie.

"We are here to protect la Señora Crosby and her beautiful friend from evil *bandidos*," the leader explained ironically.

Slow-witted I may be, but I was nevertheless reflecting that I seemed to have enlisted as helpers the very bandits that they were ostensibly guarding us from.

It transpired that we were excavating at a *yacata,* a pyramid which had yet to be uncovered, and that the inhabitants of Zula and the environs made a tidy sum as night diggers, illegally unearthing artifacts which they then sold under the table in Guadalajara or Mexico City.

And here came a diminutive gringa, who seemed to think that with a trowel, a few bottles of beer, and a gorgeous blonde shill, she could take over their territory.

I was seriously pondering the matter, when my thoughts were interrupted by the sudden arrival of an ancient crone, on a steed worthy of Ichobad Crane.

"Thieving foreigners," she shrieked, brandishing her riding whip, "remove yourselves from my land immediately."

"Whu-what?" I stuttered resourcefully, "I was unaware that we were trespassing."

"What's happening?" Mary inquired.

When I informed her of the problem, she smiled, and asked me to translate the following:

"Gracious lady, might your valuable property be for sale, and if so, how much might I pay you for it?" And so it was that, for the tidy sum of $100, Mary Morrow purchased dubious title to ten barren acres of well nigh vertical hillside, and our lives.

I say this because I mentioned to the beldam the little matter of the *bandidos,* who had observed the entire transaction warily.

"Oh them!" she hissed contemptuously. "I'll soon rid you of those worthless scum."

Whereupon she rode full at them, laying about her with the whip, and scattering the rogues to the four winds, while warning them never to return if they valued their miserable lives.

Sighing, I continued for two more days with an otherwise uneventful if none too productive dig.

We returned to las Cruces for Bing's annual baseball and golf clinics, wherein the instruction was traditional enough, but the terrain left something to be desired. I won't burden you with all the details.

Suffice it to say that the wing-tip of our DC-3 constituted second base, and three brightly-painted oil drums, sunk at intervals in the arroyo between the hotel and the wind-sock, served as a novel driving range.

Meanwhile, to the children's dismay, I was demonstrating that it was not for nothing that I had lately obtained my teacher's certificate.

To Dr. Sullivan's programmed courses in science, math, English, and Spanish, I added my very own versions of history and social studies, in the course of which we advanced backward, until we arrived at the pre-Columbian cultures, thus providing me with all the excuse I needed to demand that my students resolve the jigsaw

With Jeanne Reynal

puzzles presented by the shards from my recent dig.

In the course of the following month, my aspiring young archeologists did indeed assemble some 40 pots, several of which might even have borne some slight resemblance to the originals.

Given time, we could have come up with a whole new culture. But Bing was waxing restless, and making noises about visiting his friends on the King Ranches in Argentina.

"Do you remember our last abortive visit?" he grinned.

Did I remember? It had been during my struggle to become a registered nurse.

I'd feigned a nervous breakdown, so that I could present a doctor's excuse, and be spirited off South America way, while my classmates proceeded with fascinating topics such as *Respiration: First ascertain that your patient is breathing. If not, further treatment is likely to prove futile.*

In my desperation to escape, I'd been tempted to submit a report reading, *No pulse, no respiration, no temperature. Patient resting quietly.*

And then the trip had been called off, and I'd had to reverse my conduct by offering what I considered proofs of my sanity, only to be viewed with deep suspicion for the rest of the program.

Now it was I who was regarding my husband with a certain lack of confidence. How many times does a girl have to make the same mistake?

Listening attentively, I had to admit that this time the project had the ring of authenticity. Jeanne Hughson, San Francisco's erstwhile deb of the year, had married Juan Reynal, a dashing international polo star, and settled down to rearing her own team in far-off Argentina. Now she was inviting us for an extended visit.

I decided to pack. Unlike Jeanne, I had espoused a good old boy, whose notion of romance was wading through swamps to spider-infested duck blinds at 4 AM. There was reason to rejoice at the prospect of a ramble across the pampas on a sunny afternoon.

We flew from San Francisco the morning of June 3rd. After a brief layover in Panama, we arrived in Buenos Aires at 6 AM.

We disembarked, blinking into the dawn's early light, to be greeted by newsmen, TV cameras, and hordes of fans. Bing was surprised at the royal welcome.

"I haven't been here since 1941," he mused. "These people must have tenacious memories."

And warm ones evidently, for the announcement of Bing's arrival crowded the World Cup soccer matches and the kidnapping of an ex-president off the front pages of the local papers.

We collapsed briefly at the Plaza Hotel, French in style, with gilt Louis XV furniture, marble bathtubs, feather beds with bolsters in lieu of pillows, a splendid view of the broad esplanade, and the Río de la Plata in the distance.

Thence we were driven to the Reynal townhouse by an armed and liveried chauffeur, who solicitously escorted us inside the door.

At the formal dinner that evening, I watched Bing chatting amiably with a bevy of glamorous señoras, and reflected that he had traded time zones, hemispheres, and environments, to plunge headlong into a civil war, and yet seemed none the worse for wear.

The following morning, we were scheduled to fly to Abolengo, one of the

Our band of hunters

King Ranch properties. The same husky chauffeur loaded us into a Mercedes, and headed for a private airport on the outskirts of the city. Wide boulevards yielded to two-lane roads, teeming with potholes, and lined with military.

We arrived safely at our Cessna 310, but we were not alone. Surrounding it was a cluster of reporters, demanding to know Bing's reaction to Buenos Aires.

Never at a loss for words, he praised the people, the architecture, the food, and the atmosphere, until one of the reporters asked if he could find nothing to criticize.

I shuddered as I heard Bing reply that he had just been made aware of one striking deficiency:

"I don't know what the government does with your tax money," he commented, "but you certainly need some freeways into the city. Your roads are a mess, and your railroad crossings have no overpasses On our trip out this morning...."

Our hosts had been awaiting us at the plane. They were now aghast.

"I thought that Bing never talked politics," Juan groaned.

"He's doesn't know that's what he's doing. You and Jeanne climb aboard, and I'll retrieve him."

I elbowed my way through the newshounds, grabbed my husband's arm and gushed, "Darling, we must be on our way. The partridges are waiting at Abolengo."

Bing's head swiveled like a Labrador catching his first scent of quail, and he fairly ran up the steps into the plane. The pilot gunned the engine, and most of the reporters retreated immediately, but one intrepid individual climbed onto the wing, and stuck his microphone into the side window.

"What now?" Bing sighed.

"Sing him a loud chorus of *Adios, Muchachos,*" I suggested.

And that was just what Bing did. Whereupon the plane started rolling, and the fearless one finally leaped off.

At 16,000 acres, *Abolengo,* our destination, was one of the three major King Ranch properties. The others were the equal-sized *Esperanza,* and the 28,000 acre *Carmen.*

True to my promise, no sooner had we arrived at *Abolengo* than we sallied forth on a trial hunt. The mechanized approach was reminiscent of Texas. Two jeeps were stationed some fifty yards apart, with a wire strung between them.

As they advanced through the grain field, the wire dragged on the ground, and partridges exploded in every direction. So did pollen. My eyes itched, my nose clogged, and my head throbbed mercilessly.

Bing, who was having the time of his life, groaned when I demanded to be taken home.

At dinner that evening, I was subjected to a eulogy of the Argentinean partridge, part of which I understood through my sniffles:

"I love the bird," Bing ruminated. "He's tough, game, fast, and flushes hard, but he does have a curious weakness.

When you get close to him, he whistles, and thus tips his mitt. You know about where he is, so you're ready when he takes off.

It's hard to explain in classical Darwinian terms, since it would seem to militate against perpetuation of the species. Kathryn, please try to control

With Juan in the field

that sneezing. The rest of us can't hear ourselves think."

Head down, I munched on my fillet, feeling my incisors grow. Would that the flesh had been raw, and baptized *carpaccio of Irish Crooner.*

After we'd retired that evening, Bing remarked that I looked dreadful, and suggested a hot water bottle.

"Tomorrow we're having a real hunt," he continued, "and Juan has arranged a barbecue. You'll have to be ready for some exciting action at the crack of dawn."

But I wasn't. I was curled up in a corner with a copy of *Nicholas and Alexandra,* experiencing the Russian revolution in imagination, and an Argentinean one from safe seclusion.

I was closeted all morning, disturbed only by sounds of distant shotgun fire, and I remained so all afternoon. After downing a bowl of soup, I fell asleep, to be wakened sometime after midnight by the noise of a house party.

Joined by a superb guitar player, Bing sang to Jeannie Reynal, *You came, I was alone, I should have known, you were temptation.*

Accompanied by the same guitar, he continued with, *I Dream of Jeannie with the Light Brown Hair, Moonlight Becomes You,* and *Wrap Your Troubles in Dreams,* before concluding with *Good Night Sweetheart,* and then dancing to *Blue Tango* on a table. He returned to my chaste pallet at 3 AM, to complain that our hosts were keeping him up.

The next day was Sunday, the 7th, and I was still sick in bed. Bing rode over to *Carmen,* while I continued to ponder the fate of the Czar, Czarina, and all their children.

On the afternoon of the 8th, I revived sufficiently to turn on my bedside radio, and tuned in on a bit of history in the making.

Four years after he had assumed power, following a military coup, President Juan Carlos Ongania was being forced to resign by the commanders-in-chief of Argentina's army, navy , and air force, who had surrounded the Pink House with tanks. The announcers seemed proud that, for the first time, the presidential guards had stood their ground, until their leader had agreed to leave peacefully.

On the 9th, a ground fog lent a romantic quality to the landscape, and incidentally rescued me by settling the pollen. Bing and I lunched at *Carmen,* and then repaired to a pasture reputed to be full of partridge.

We were met by two gauchos. Bing told them that we would not require the wire, which he viewed as unsporting, but that he would appreciate their flanking us on horseback to retrieve downed birds.

Since I am at heart a modest creature, hesitant to allude to my rare successes, I shall quote the following from the diary of my beloved:

"The day was misty, but the partridges were plentiful. I wasn't getting my gun up fast enough, and I missed a lot of birds.

Kathryn, on the other hand, was shooting spectacularly, and it wasn't long before she had me down at least ten to one.

I missed a beauty that popped up right in front of me, and she knocked it down. This is known as *wiping a fellow's eye,* and she was grinning like a jackass eating thistles.

The gauchos had never seen a woman shoot before, and they applauded each of her feats with

With gaucho retriever

enthusiastic *bravos* and *olés*, while completely ignoring me.

I finally attracted their attention by getting a few birds down, but Kathryn's streak continued, and it wasn't long before she had wiped my eye again, and again, and was beaming like a genuine little smart ass."

I hasten to deny the last allegation. I'd never be guilty of such an error, having often been warned by sensitive males that conspicuous gloating is unprincipled, unladylike, impolitic, and doubtless fattening.

We returned to Buenos Aires to stage a television show for the benefit of *Maternidad Pardo,* an obstetrical hospital which treated mothers who couldn't afford proper care.

The program was presented live, with no rehearsal, and of course in Spanish.

Given my specialization in charitable begging, I was chosen to narrate the history of the hospital, and to explain the need for donations. I also joined Bing in a series of duets, in which, as ever, he relied on me for most of the lyrics.

After the first song, he explained, in his own inimitable Mexican Spanish, "Dispensen, por favor. Caterina es muy tímida cuando canta."

I appreciated the sentiment, but felt that the message was superfluous. There was no crying need to inform the audience that I was terrified. After all, this was television. They could see it for themselves.

The show was a triumph, Bing was high as a kite, and I was collapsing in nervous exhaustion. I am told that we attended a formal dinner, and went night-clubbing thereafter, but my first recollection is of awakening on the plane, four hours into the long flight back to San Francisco.

Upon arrival, we drove to our Rising River Ranch in Northern California. On July 12th, we all attended the rodeo at McCloud.

Only then did I learn that Harry and Nathaniel were competing in the calf-riding contest.

"Not any more, they aren't," I declared categorically.

"You can't cancel their entries at the last minute," Bing insisted. "You'll make them a laughingstock.

After all, Gary, Dennis, Philip, and Lindsay all took part in rodeos at Elko. How many of them have broken bones?"

"All of them, as I recall."

"Well, some of that was from football. Give these kids their chance."

So I did, but reluctantly. Harry came out of Chute 4, giggling hysterically but holding on. He lasted his eight seconds, and won a silver belt buckle.

I had no time to savor his triumph. Nathaniel had been assigned a large, mean calf, upon which he had been sitting in his chute until both were half asleep. When the gate suddenly opened, the bovine awoke first, and dumped my youngest on his head.

Laughing, he scrambled to his feet, and raced over to assure the family spoilsport that no permanent damage had been done.

When he finally succeeded in convincing me, I counted the day a triumph. Everyone had survived.

On July 16, Bing, who still owned a share of the Pirates, took Nathaniel to Pittsburgh for the dedication of Three Rivers Stadium. Upon his return, he announced that he had made plans for another safari.

I had found life in Africa initially fascinating, and finally terrifying. Upon mature reflection, I decided that I had had enough of fleeing for my life across the Dark Continent, and pusillanimously nominated our son Harry to take his mother's place.

I therefore lack first-hand knowledge of the expedition, and am forced to have recourse to Bing's diaries, retaining his words, but condensing some three-hundred pages into the following brief narrative:

"We flew from Nairobi to the camp, and pitched our tent on a creek. The weather was cool, averaging 65 during the day, and dropping to 35 at night.

Harry's excitement combined with the usual nocturnal animal concert to preclude sleep on that first night.

On the second day, I drove into the mountains to show him the most beautiful part of Africa. I asked two Masai about potential sites for a dove shoot, but they were no help, so I cruised around until I found a water hole some fifteen feet wide.

We set up a blind by cutting down a tree, and dragging it up to the bank. Flights of sand grouse and doves appeared, and a strong wind made for sporty shooting. Harry bagged his dinner with his tiny 410.

Over the next couple of days, I introduced him to cape buffaloes, wildebeests, kongoni, impalas, Grant's gazelles, Thompson's gazelles, eland, klipspringers, dik-diks, mongoose, hyenas, jackals, wild dogs, and zebras.

He found the wild dogs to be by far the most interesting. They are black, with yellow spots and enormous Mickey-Mouse ears.

Highly intelligent and curious, they have a strong affinity for man, and repeatedly allowed Harry to walk right up to them.

I had to warn him that they remain wild animals, and rank among the most savage predators. He still wants to take one home.

At about 4:30 PM on our fourth day, we investigated a tree-hung wildebeest. It was a clear, cold, windy afternoon. We approached stealthily and circuitously, crawling to within a mile of the bait in the Land Rover, and then sneaking in on foot, being careful not to break any twigs, or step on loose rocks.

After we finally reached the blind, I peered through the spy hole, and sure enough, there was a big male leopard on a limb above the dead wildebeest, sleeping with his back toward me, and with his long tail dangling.

Since I could see only his rump and ears, I decided not to shoot, for fear that I might simply wound him.

It was over half an hour before he rose, climbed down the trunk, and started working on the bait. As he reached down, he exposed his left shoulder, offering me the shot I wanted. I sighted through the aperture, held my breath, and let fly.

He rolled out of the tree, lit on his head, and was off in a flash into the bushes. I followed, penetrated into a thicket, heard a rustling in the shadows, walked over, gun at the ready, and found Mr. Leopard, stone dead.

He was a beautiful animal, measuring over seven feet, with the long hair of cats who live at high altitudes. If one of the big five has been taken, it's traditional to sound your horn, long and loud, as you near home.

The Africans came out to meet us. I was enthroned on a chair, and carried in triumph about the camp.

Nathaniel and calf part company.

A delegation arrived from the nearest Masai village, with the request that I kill a leopardess that had taken dozens of their goats, and threatened the lives of their children. Of course I had to refuse, because it's illegal to shoot a female leopard.

On the fifth day, we amused ourselves with a group of giraffes. I headed straight for them, and drove beside them while they ran, taking splendid pictures. They seem to be barely moving, as they lope along, but it was all that my jeep could do to keep up with them.

Harry was growing impatient, and I feared that I'd been stealing his show, so when we sighted a prime buck amid a herd of kongoni, I sent him off on a stalk with a native bearer, and anxiously awaited the results.

I watched as the buck spooked and raced into the bush. For an hour, I thought they'd lost him, but then I heard a rifle shot, and the bearer returned to inform me that Harry had dropped the beast with one round from a distance of 185 yards.

I drove him back to the prize, which Harry was guarding proudly, as well he might, for it dressed out at 360 pounds, and fed our camp and the surrounding villages for a week.

On the 7th day, a guide picked up some buffalo tracks. For two hours, we followed them up a mountain ridge and into some very rough country.

When we reached the top, I sighted a buffalo, so I hid the Land Rover, insisted that Harry stay with it, and started off after the animal on foot, accompanied by two guides.

I had walked only a few hundred yards, when there was a call to lie flat, which I immediately did. Then I heard the guide sing out, "He's right over there on the far left."

I hauled out my tripod, mounted the rifle on it, and tried to sight the creature in its scope. Usually my color-blindness permits me to penetrate any sort of camouflage, but all that I could make out was a mottled gray shape in the gloom of a thicket, and I wasn't about to fire at so uncertain a target.

While I was pondering the matter, the beast spooked, and went crashing away through the brush, with me hot on his heels.

I blundered straight into the whole herd, and suddenly they were stamping and thudding all around me. It looked as if I was going to have to jumpshoot several of them with a weapon ill-suited to the purpose.

The buffalo weighs a ton, is mean and fast, and will charge anything when annoyed, which he always is. I lay as low as possible, and never did manage another shot, which suited me just fine.

After twenty minutes of this sort of diversion, I'd had just about all the fun I could stand, and I counted it a moral victory when I finally reached the Land Rover alive."

After fifteen days in Africa, Bing and Harry flew to Rome for a celebrity tour of the Vatican, including what my son denominated "the Pope's locker room," otherwise known as the Sacristy, where the Pontiff stores his robes, miters, scepters, crowns, chalices, and many of the gifts from royalty and other heads of state.

Harry was especially fond of The Sistine Chapel, with Michelangelo's painting of The Last Judgment positioned behind the altar. Amid the sinners relegated to Hell, stands the Vatican administrator who had caused

Bing's leopard

Harry and friend

On safari

the painter the most agony during his five years of back-breaking labor.

Recognizing his features among the damned, the bureaucrat petitioned the Pope to remove his face from the painting. His Eminence sympathized, but explained that, while he admitted to having some authority in Heaven and on Earth, his jurisdiction didn't extend to the Nether Regions.

Father and son toured the Vatican Gardens, attended mass at St. Peter's, and lunched in the Square of the Four Rivers, where Bing's dark glasses conspired with the beard that he was growing for *Dr. Cook's Garden,* to preserve complete anonymity.

The travelers then flew to Copenhagen, where Bing introduced his son to our Ambassador, Guilford Dudley, and to the Count and Countess Bernstorff, whose medieval castle, surrounded by a moat, fascinated the twelve-year-old.

London was next, for a rubber-neck tour, a day at the races, and an introduction to British aristocracy. Then it was time for the long flight home.

Meanwhile, back at the ranch, my father and mother were riding herd on Mary and Nathaniel. Bing never hesitated to entrust his offspring to their care, since he considered them far more adept at rearing children than their younger daughter.

In whole-hearted agreement with his evaluation, I joined my sister in a tamale safari of our own. In Mexico City, we actually took part in a *tienta,* a test of aggressiveness for young cows, to see whether they will make good mothers for fighting bulls

In our version, we held out capes for the animals to charge. Singer Julio Iglesias, who still had his wits about him, fled for his life to the accompani-

ment of catcalls from the crowd. I, on the other hand, stood my ground, paralyzed by raw terror, and was roundly applauded for my purely fictitious courage.

Returning home a week before Bing, I took Mary and Nathaniel to Disneyland, causing them to decree that I should henceforth let them live with their grandparents, appearing only at rare intervals to offer diversions.

On August 23rd, our travelers returned. Harry seemed to have grown a foot, and his father had sprouted an ugly and very scratchy beard. There was no time to get settled, because on the 29th "Dr. Cook" was off to tend his garden in Vermont.

Bing considered the role an interesting challenge. He was to portray a lovable country physician who, in the kindness of his heart, dispatched patients that were terminally ill and in unbearable pain, along with those who were simply too mean to live.

Our crooner delighted in the people of Vermont. "They're all Bill Sullivan's cousins," he reported, "with a humor as fey as the Irish, though perhaps a trifle more taciturn."

"Yesterday," he continued, "I drove through a number of small towns, and ended up hopelessly lost. Finally I coasted up to a curb, and asked an old codger standing on the corner, 'Do you know the way to Rutland?'

'Yes,' he replied, and walked on."

On September 8th, I was giving some Mexican friends a grand tour of Hollywood, when I received a message from the Crosby office to call the highway patrol.

I was informed that there had been an accident. My mother, father, and the three children were in Mercy

The changing of the guard

Placing a bet

Hospital in Redding. I was on a plane within the hour.

Upon arrival, I learned that my father had been driving along a sort of freeway, had come to a full stop, and had turned left across a lane of traffic.

Out of the shimmering noontime haze had appeared a vehicle, traveling at top speed. The driver had hit her brakes, but only those on the right side had caught, causing her car to swerve into my father's.

Had she not braked at all, or had her brakes worked properly, there would have been no accident. As it was, my father and the three little ones had cuts and bruises, whereas my mother had suffered a fractured clavicle and eight broken ribs.

The children were still in surgery, but my mother seemed to be resting quietly. With my father and sister, I sat by her bedside.

Characteristically, she was concerned only for the rest of us, and full of advice: "Take the children home as soon as possible," she counseled. "Avoid lasting psychological damage by keeping them to their normal schedule. As for you, Emery, you'll have to can all those peaches that I left soaking."

She sounded so matter of fact that I too was calm when I phoned Bing to relate that the medic who first reached the scene of the accident said he had never before seen such brave children.

"They had waited patiently," I continued, "while heavy equipment cut the wreck open so that they could be removed. Nathaniel had been asleep when the crash occurred, and he initially started to complain, but Mary hit him a lick, and he subsided.

Harry, who was the worst hurt, insisted that his siblings be attended first, so that he could sit with grandpa, who was obviously sick with guilt. Here he comes now. A nurse is wheeling him down the hall.

'Here, darling, say something to your father to let him know that you're all right.'"

Harry grabbed the phone from my hands, and chirped immediately, "Hi, Dad, how's the weather back there in Vermont, and how's the film going? Have you bagged any quail yet?"

I learned that there had been a series of fatal accidents at the same crossing, and I reflected on how lucky we were to have escaped so lightly. In a few weeks time, all this would be just a bad dream.

On Sunday, September 13th, an embolus moved to my mother's lung, and 19 seconds later she was gone.

Services were held in the tiny chapel in Burney. Flowers filled the church, and covered the ground beneath the huge pine that would mark her resting place.

I was helpless, and Bing had to make all arrangements for the family. He scheduled our flights from the ranch to San Francisco, and thence to Los Angeles, to commence work on The Crosby Christmas Show.

"You don't mean it," I objected. "The children can't possibly learn their lines, and sing, and dance. They haven't begun to heal yet."

"Remember what your mother said. We must make every effort to stick to a normal schedule. Besides, we have a formal obligation, and thousands of people depend on us."

"You mean, the show must go on?"

"In a word, *yes*. Further grieving won't help your mother, and it will harm many fine friends."

My Mother, Olive Catherine Stokely Grandstaff

Somehow we taped the program. Bing had worked much more than he wanted to in 1970, and now it was my turn. Beginning October 2, I was scheduled to be at the University of Texas in Austin, to play the lead in *The Prime of Miss Jean Brodie.* For once, Bing insisted that I participate.

The whole environment was laden with nostalgia. I was haunted by memories of my sixteen-year-old self in *Dear Brutus;* and in *Much Ado About Nothing,* when Ellie Light had an attack of appendicitis, and I had to substitute for her at the last moment.

I recalled every word of my roles as Emmy in *First Lady,*and Isabel in *The Enchanted.* Now, after the briefest of rehearsals, it was opening night once more. I had been informed that the aging Hogg auditorium needed to be replaced, and that fifty million dollars would do the trick nicely.

I made my entrance, gazed right through the fourth wall into the audience, and spied in the front row, smiling indulgently, at least twice the money still needed for the building fund. I opened my mouth, went dry, and gave the worst performance of my life.

Bing had taken advantage of my absence to escape to Canada, where he was playing his favorite role of Nimrod, with Jack and Mary Morton in Lethbridge. Determined to bag some honkers, he was experiencing scant initial success, since the wily birds fed in the middle of open fields, guarded by alert sentinels.

The moment a hunter slipped under a fence and started to work his way toward them, an alarm was sounded, and the geese took wing.

"Therefore," Bing wrote, "we decided to enlist the aid of *Big Red,* a life-sized plywood replica of a white-faced cow. True to its name, it is painted scarlet on the outside, with the occasional white spot, while inside there are leather straps at the front and back.

I put my arms through the front ones, Jack followed suit in the rear, and we headed for the geese. I was definitely a method cow, who stopped frequently to simulate grazing. I also bobbed the head up and down, while Jack continuously flicked the tail.

I approached the geese on the bias, and the sentinels gradually lost interest, but I almost blew the whole scam by roaring with laughter when I considered how ridiculous we must look.

When we arrived within 15 yards of the main gaggle, I whispered *now,* and we pulled our arms out of the straps, letting the cow fall abruptly to the ground. We each fired three times, bagging as many geese."

During my final days in Texas, my crooner called nightly. He was experiencing yet another tragedy. Remus, his all-time favorite dog, had disappeared.

Bing drove all over Hillsborough and Burlingame, and finally found the black Labrador, lying in a roadside ditch. Remus was rushed to the veterinarian, and given every possible attention, but it was much too late.

Bing had comforted me throughout the fall, and I now tried to console him by recalling what a long and happy life he had given his spoiled canine friend.

The Lab's picky eating habits would have driven anyone else to distraction. I finally coaxed a smile with the mention of Leonard Meyer's lament that he wished he could afford half the meat that dog refused.

In an attempt to end the year on a happier note, I decided to marry Mary

Remus and friend

Morrow to Dr. Sullivan. Let me admit at the outset that my interest in the affair wasn't wholly altruistic. Bing had admitted several times that if Mary had been free at the appropriate time, she would now occupy my spot.

This is not the sort of news that cements a perfect friendship between females, but I couldn't help liking Mary, who had always proved a delightful companion.

Now I grasped an opportunity to perform a good deed, and incidentally to retire a temptress who had it in her power to become my most dangerous rival.

When I communicated to Bing as much of my plan as he was old enough to understand, he seemed dumbfounded:

"I can't conceive of choosing a socialite like Mary, however beautiful, for an academic," he snorted, "and I'm not sure that I'd recommend Bill as a marriage prospect for anyone. He's by far the most self-sufficient human I've ever met."

"Aw, you've always been in love with Mary, and you can't stand the thought of a friend's snapping her up.

They'll be perfect for each other. Dr. Sullivan does nothing but make money that he has no use for, and Mary can relieve him of his burden by effortlessly spending it all."

"When you put it that way, I have to admit that you've chanced upon the perfect symbiosis."

On December 17th, Mary arrived from Las Vegas for a visit, and on the 20th I threw a dinner party, at which I subtly sat my potential victims side by side. They immediately fell into an animated conversation, and I glanced triumphantly at Bing.

"Don't gloat yet," he admonished me. "They're both highly articulate, and for the moment they're just feeding off culture shock. Neither one has ever imagined that a creature like the other could exist.

I'm reminded of the comment of an ancient Roman, when he first spied a giraffe, and stated flatly: 'There's no such animal.'"

Miffed, I tuned in on my lovebirds' tête-a-tête, initially with renewed hope, since they seemed to have hit upon a topic of mutual interest. Both had just returned from Nevada, and had found the state fascinating.

It developed, however, that Mary's sole interest lay in shopping in Las Vegas boutiques, while Dr. Sullivan was considering purchasing the place.

Since both had traveled considerably, they moved on to a discussion of modes of transportation, Mary introduced the topic of boats, and it transpired that Bill's sole experience was in racing small ones with sails, whereas to Mary the word meant luxury yachts based on the Riviera.

I sighed with relief as they turned to cars, but her taste was for vintage Rolls Royces, while he favored Ferraris for sport, and diesel trucks for heavy hauling duties.

There was no immediate end to the lively exchange, so I hoped for the best as they took up the subject of dream houses. Could I get them to agree on the construction of a love nest?

Apparently not, for Mary plumped for mansions in Palm Springs and limestone façades on Fifth Avenue, whereas Bill had constructed only sprawling ranch houses in the remote fastnesses of the Santa Clara mountain range.

Mary Morrow as a reborn brunette

The soliloquies in tandem continued, and Bing was eying me knowingly, but I refused to despair. They certainly made an attractive couple, and I thought that more privacy might help, so I invited them to join me in a luncheon at the Palace Hotel garden court, and subsequently at The Nutcracker Suite, where they not only failed to mesh, but showed not the slightest tendency to establish minimal communication on any level.

"Congratulations," Bing smirked. "I knew you had a talent for these things, but you have at long last succeeded in bringing together, or at least into close proximity, the least compatible couple in the history of mankind. I'm recommending you for a place in The Guiness Book of Records."

On December 27th, Dr. Sullivan retreated to his mountains, and Mary departed for Palm Springs, both resolutely unmarried, and strongly reinforced in their determination to remain that way permanently.

I sought solace in the reflection that it was the least of my many disappointments, in what had turned out to be my most disastrous year. I looked forward to 1971, secure in the conviction that it would have to bring my little family happier times.

Posing before our Munnings painting in Hillsborough

1971

On January 6th, Bing flew back from guest-starring on the Artie Johnson show in Los Angeles, and I drove to the San Francisco airport to pick him up. Still numb from the loss of my mother, and preoccupied with my attempts to remain at the curb long enough for him to find me without being ticketed yet again, I paid little attention to his demeanor.

But the fact was that he was strangely silent upon arrival at the car, and he remained so for the next few days. He had comforted me throughout the last few months, and it was high time for me to reciprocate, but I was still too deeply immersed in my own ills to pay much attention.

It was time for the annual Bing Crosby Pro-Am, so we spent the next week in preparations, and then followed Arnold Palmer, the galleries' favorite, in the expectation that one of his patented last-ditch charges would pull out yet another victory.

The weather was spectacular, and so were Arnold's shots, but his magic about the greens forsook him, and he had to settle for second place behind handsome young Tom Shaw. George Coleman, our long-time friend and Las Cruces neighbor, teamed up with Jackie Burke to take second place in the best-ball Pro-Am.

Then it was home to Hillsborough, and there was nothing for it but to face up to our mutual sorrows. I took it upon myself to take the first step:

"Bing, you got me through last year with that frantic *The Show Must Go On* motif. Now, for the children's sake and our own, I suggest that it's time to get on with the rest of our life."

"I agree in principal, but I fear that the children are precisely the problem."

I was nonplused. To the best of my knowledge, ever since the tragic accident, all three of our progeny had been uncharacteristically quiet, obedient, and even occasionally helpful.

Bing's first family

Dennis, Phillip, Gary, and Lindsay

"What have my little wonders done now?" I asked resignedly.

"Not yours, Dixie's," was the surprising response.

"But I thought we'd agreed to support them emotionally when permitted, and to furnish money and help when asked. They're all of age, and they were uncontrollable when they weren't. You were the one who stopped me from interfering, and insisted that it was time to acknowledge our helplessness."

"I know, and it sounded fine in theory, but now, in the face of their self-destructiveness, I just can't stick to it."

Mentally I reviewed the problem: The first time I had seen Bing staring bleakly into space in the present fashion was when we were initially engaged. Lindsay, his youngest, had been accepted at Brown. Bing had celebrated with a huge party for him and all his friends.

"Wasn't Lindsay pleased?" I had wondered aloud.

"I don't know. He didn't come."

My reminiscences continued. At the age of seven, the twins had defeathered their pet canary, and giggled at its dying squeaks.

During his army service, Phillip was at a nightclub, regaling his companions with tales from early years at Bing's Elko ranch. As a camel joined the circus act, which was part of the floor show, he shouted, "Now watch how I bulldog a steer!"

With that, he plunged down upon the animal, and snapped its neck. A fight broke out, started by animal lovers, who were all for lynching Phil, and Bing was privileged to tender apologies, to replace a deceased camel, and to redecorate the nightclub.

After leaving the army, a drunken Phillip broke his own neck in a traffic accident. He recovered, only to shove his pregnant wife Sandra downstairs in his version of a joke.

The year that we moved north to Hillsborough, he had thrown a series of wild parties at Trader Vic's, signed the checks in Bing's name, and stolen a full set of silverware from the dining room.

At Bellermine, a Jesuit preparatory school, Gary had gone out for football. Bing had proudly turned down a TV special to watch him play. In the third quarter, Gary had started a fight with a member of the opposing squad.

When his teammates sought to separate the combatants, Gary fought them off. The referee tried to intervene, and was clobbered in turn. When a group of fans booed, Bing's eldest raced up into the stands to attack them.

While completing his required military service at Fort Ord, Gary went AWOL. His father learned of it when a state police officer phoned to report that the youthful private had holed up in Bing's Pebble Beach house with a girl, a bottle, and a gun, threatening murder and suicide.

Bing abandoned a major film to fly up in a private plane, talk Gary into surrendering, and patch things up with the civilian and military authorities. It hardly seemed worthwhile, for no sooner had he enrolled his eldest in Stanford, than the drunken freshman struck a pedestrian in a crosswalk, drove on to a motel, and phoned his father for help.

Hours away, and trapped once more in the middle of a movie, Bing sent friends to Gary's rescue. It wasn't easy, because the hit-and-run driver kept repeating, "I'll bet the SOB isn't even a citizen," thus falling somewhat short of the desired feeling of remorse.

Gary and Bing

Like each of his brothers, Gary married a showgirl. Barbara was seven inches taller than he. One night he came home drunk, picked a fight, and struck her.

Towering above him, Barbara challenged, "Go ahead, Tom Thumb, hit me again. You'll have to sleep sometime!"

"And would you believe it?" she reported. "He's been docile as a lamb ever since."

The story actually made Bing laugh, but his relief was temporary. On June 3, 1961, it was a desperate lamb who once more phoned his father, demanding that he come immediately because Barbara was dead.

Bing and I raced to their valley home to find Barbara fast asleep, with a half-empty bottle of Seconal on her bedside stand, and Gary helpfully downing water glasses of vodka from the nearby bar.

Recalling my nursing training, I took her pulse, which was indeed slow, but strong and regular. I decided to let her sleep, and, since it was well past midnight, to return home for some shuteye of my own.

When I awoke the following morning, I phoned to find Barbara bright and cheery, and Gary sleeping off his drunk. This seemed to good to be true, and indeed it was.

In the afternoon, Gary awoke to chase Barbara into the bathroom. She locked herself in, threatening suicide, and of course both of the antagonists phoned Bing.

Once more we raced across Laurel Canyon to their home. Again Gary was drinking vodka, but this time he was pointing at the bathroom door.

I curled up on the floor outside, and addressed Barbara in a low voice, while Bing dragged Gary away, and tried to slow down his drinking. A glance had revealed more empty vodka bottles, but one emergency at a time, thank you.

It took 15 minutes to convince Barbara that her husband had indeed left. She then unlocked the door, walked quietly over to her bed, and murmured, "Stick around, you guys, and don't let him near me. I really need some sleep."

However, Gary had not been idle during our wild ride through the canyon. Suddenly three orderlies and a nurse rushed in, seized Barbara, crammed her into a strait jacket, and carried her off on a stretcher.

She kicked, screamed, bit, and glared at me accusingly. "You did this to me, you traitor," she howled. "You're having me put away in some hell hole."

After a few moments, she calmed down enough to laugh hysterically and to concede, "After all, it can't be any worse than living with him."

In my innocence, I had consoled myself with the reflection that nothing could outstrip this slice of life, but as they still say in the television ads, there's more....

On July 2, 1962, we had just landed in Hawaii, when Dr. Sturdevant phoned from St. John's Hospital in Santa Monica, recommending that Bing commit Lindsay to the psychiatric ward, since his wife, whom we had designated as little Barbara to distinguish her from Gary's tall dancer, feared for her life.

Bing agonized for a few minutes while he discussed the case, but he finally decided that he couldn't do it. He found the thought of imprisoning a grown son against his will reprehensible. "I couldn't stand having a relative do it to me," was how he put it.

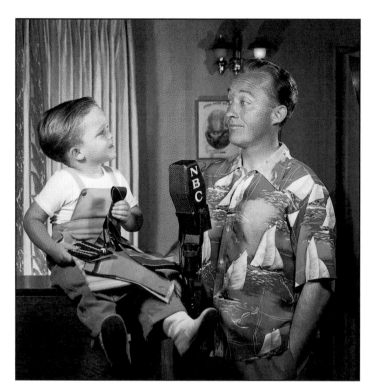

Lindsay as a tot

An older Lindsay with Elizabeth Taylor and
Margaret O'Brian

In March of 1963, little Barbara's gynecologist phoned to say that she was in the hospital. My first thought was, "Thank God that Bing is in Las Cruces, with no phone available."

The physician had taken his wife out to dinner, so it was his nine-year-old daughter who took the call, and had him paged.

In a suicide attempt, little Barbara had swallowed the contents of a bottle of sleeping pills, changed her mind immediately, and phoned her doctor. She was still in a coma at St. Joseph's Hospital in Burbank, but it was believed that her stomach had been pumped in time to save her.

I reached the hospital in forty minutes, to find that little Barbara had arrived there at the precise moment when she went into labor. She had been in her eighth month of pregnancy, and a perfect little boy had been stillborn.

When little Barbara awoke, I moved into the room with her, and asked why she had swallowed the pills.

"Lindsay screamed at me," she sobbed. "He called me fat and ugly and useless, and said he was going over to Frank Sinatra's to play with all the gorgeous broads. When he left, I just wanted to die."

I phoned Sinatra's, and found that Lindsay had left for Miami, where the four boys were scheduled to perform their nightclub act. When I finally caught up with him, I tried some screaming of my own.

"Come home," I howled into the mouthpiece. "Come home, and bury your dead son, and comfort your poor wife, and meet with Father Kaiser, and see if you can find some way to make things right with your God."

The other boys' wives were caring for his first child, David Lindsay. I sat by little Barbara's bed, while she cried her heart out, and I asked myself what had gone so wrong. How could bright, healthy, wealthy young people make such a mess of their lives?

I received a partial answer when Lindsay finally did arrive. As I escorted him up the stairs to little Barbara's room, Dr. Sturdevant interposed his bulk, and inquired, in a soothing voice, just how the lad felt.

"I don't have time to worry about that," was Lindsay's reply. "I have to visit my wife, bury my baby, and see Father Kaiser."

"Good," I approved. "You've remembered what I said."

"Oh, I don't believe you're up to that right now. Wouldn't you like to ride with me to St. John's for a thorough physical and a nice rest?"

I gaped at the doctor. Didn't he realize that it was the child who had died, and the mother who had just emerged from a coma, after surviving a suicide attempt and labor?

At long last, the real perpetrator was trying to do something right, and this was the encouragement that he received.

"But he has to plan for the funeral," I wailed.

"The housekeeper can take care of that. This boy badly needs a vacation."

I arranged for the baby's burial at the foot of Dixie's grave. Lindsay spent two weeks at St. John's, never admitting to himself or to anyone else that his child was dead, and that his own behavior had contributed to its demise.

When Bing returned from Mexico, we drove to the cemetery, knelt at the

Dennis and proud papa

foot of Dixie's grave, said a rosary, and wept for the dead child, and for all four of the lost children that Bing and Dixie had brought into the world. How had they gone so far astray, and what could I do to recall them to reality?

Back in the present, I insisted that Bing share his pain with me. "Who is it this time?" I inquired resignedly.

"It's Dennis. I never quite believed Patty when she avowed that she was divorcing him because he had neglected his three sons.

She admitted that he had never even raised his voice to her, but she left him for that one reason.

After the nightclub act broke up, I gave him a job at Bing Crosby Productions. He continued to drink until he met a secretary named Arlene, who seemed able to settle him down.

They married, and now she's pregnant. He claims that they're having money troubles because he also has to support Patty's family and Marilyn Scott's child.

He went on to say that there's no food in the house. But the cost of the liquor that he put away, while telling me all this, would have fed a dozen people for a week.

This was my first day back at work, and Arlene phoned me on the set, whimpering that last night Dennis had threatened her with a butcher knife. I find it hard to believe that he would hurt a woman, but the evidence against him is piling up.

I gave all the boys houses as good as my own, and I've been putting money into their accounts monthly for the last five years. In Dennis' case, I had prayed that a strong, steady girl like Arlene could handle him. Now I don't know what to do."

The truth was that I didn't either, but I was incapable of admitting it. What I said was, "Bing, I have a great solution: I realize that I've promised not to interfere, but you know how well I take charge of things.

Our house at 1200 Jackling is enormous. Alan Fisher and Norma have it under perfect control. I'll bring Arlene up here as soon as the baby is born. I can provide whatever nursing care is needed, and I'll be right here to straighten Dennis out in case of further trouble."

I'm not sure quite what reaction I expected, perhaps a mixture of relief and gratitude. What I got was fright. Then the look of pain was replaced by one of fierce determination.

"Kathryn," my lord and master enunciated distinctly, "you will start packing immediately, and you will leave day after tomorrow at 7 AM on the Richfield plane for Las Cruces. There you will make preparations for the children's studies this spring.

Tomorrow you will ask Bill Sullivan for more school texts. We'll all study Spanish, and you can continue with the French and German programs. It's the one field in which you demonstrate a certain talent."

Bing rose, and stomped upstairs to bed. From the landing, I heard him mutter, "Good God, if there's anything worse than sons who can do nothing, it's a wife who thinks that she can do everything."

I met with Dr. Sullivan, piled armloads of books and tapes into the car, and paused as a thought crossed my mind. Before I could lose my courage, I blurted out, "You're deep into psychology. Tell me what's wrong with Bing's kids."

Bing's boys

I was rewarded with a wide Irish grin. "Nothing that the substitution of a more stable mother figure couldn't easily cure."

I sensed a confusion of referents. "Not mine," I explained, "Dixie's."

"I've barely met them, but Bing has hinted that they cause him difficulties."

"That they do. But what is their problem? My nursing studies would indicate that all four are sociopaths, moral imbeciles, unable to interiorize the rules of society.

For unknown reasons, such creatures are born randomly, into the best and worst of families alike, but they are statistically rare. You wouldn't expect four in one brood."

"No, you certainly wouldn't. A present-day clinician would probably conclude that they represent a form of infantile imperialism, extended into adulthood.

They've always been able to gratify any whim immediately, and have never had to endure the slightest frustration. Understandably, they must consider themselves omnipotent.

From what I hear, Dixie was a loving mother, but utterly permissive. Children are rather like horses, who test the limits of a rider's tolerance. In the case of those boys, there were no constraints. They reached out for the boundaries of reality, and found none.

So we're now confronted with modern adults who resemble the Caesars of ancient Rome. They feel that they have an absolute right to get away with anything, to satisfy all their desires instantly."

"But what good does such an insight do us at this point?"

"None that I know of, but you're talking to the wrong man. As an experi-mentalist, deep into learning theory, I have no savior complex. Find yourself a clinician who wants to play God, and turn him loose."

"They've had that sort of care all their lives, and so far it has done nothing but harm."

"Well, for what it's worth, my own view is that, over a period of time, any man becomes what he's reinforced for. In the Crosby boys' case, it's been whining and grabbing, so we've had more and more of the same."

"So they now have to learn some new behavior, just as we do in your programmed courses?"

"Precisely."

"You've taught me that learning is a change in behavior, and behavior in turn is a set of responses."

"Right again."

"So somehow we have to elicit and reinforce a whole new set of competing responses?"

"No one could argue with that."

"How do we get enough control to manage it?"

"Bing will just have to stop supporting them in their viciousness, and bailing them out of all their scrapes. He must let them hit bottom, sink or swim, change or suffer severe punishment. If they have any element of rational self interest left, they'll strike out on a new course, which should then be strongly reinforced."

"Do you think there's any chance of Bing's doing that?"

"Do you?"

"Frankly no."

"I believe that you've answered your own question."

The next morning, I did indeed fly dutifully off to Las Cruces, with a cargo of Dr. Sullivan's programmed books,

261

At Pinebloom Plantation

The children remained at the ranch with Uncle Leonard.

only to hitch a ride back up to Hillsborough as soon as Bing was safely off to New York, where he taped the David Frost Show on January 21st, and then completed a conservation film on the Atlantic Salmon.

Upon his return, we fled from all our problems in a Southern pilgrimage. In Albany, Georgia, we stayed in a lovely old mansion on the Pinebloom Plantation of the brilliant founder of Rockwell Industries.

While Bing was out harrying our feathered friends, I made for the nearest telephone, and ordered Gary's wife Barbara into the breach vacated by me.

She took Arlene into her home, and made Dennis promise for the millionth time to stop drinking.

I then joined an upland game shoot, which I much preferred to a swampy duck blind. Clad in one of Bing's hats, King-Ranch chaps, and appropriate accessories, I was the cat's meow, as even Bing had to concede. Could I help it that I was born shallow?

Unfortunately, I failed to perform up to my outfit. My bag was six new varieties of wild flower and a ravenous appetite for dinner.

At the evening gathering, some guests played cards, others billiards, and only I practiced needlepoint, which Mary Morrow had suggested as a welcome predinner activity for a person who didn't drink, and had no small talk. Indeed, the clinching argument had been that a parrot with thumbs could carry it off with style.

I cocked an ear when Bing, properly urged, started telling his gentle Irish stories. Since I have no memory whatsoever for tales told offstage, each was always a fresh surprise.

After having received extreme unction on her death bed, his great aunt Kate had reached out to her husband and murmured, "Give me your hand now, George."

He complied, sobbing, "It's a hand that was never raised against you."

Whereupon Aunt Kate opened her eyes wide, sat bolt upright, and enunciated distinctly, "And it's a damn lucky thing for you too."

Dan Galbraith, whose father had lured Bing into a long-term relationship with the Pittsburgh Pirates, inquired about hunting in Nevada, on Bing's Elko ranch.

Bing recounted how he had invited Ben Hogan and Jimmy Demaret to join him there. Two of the greatest golfers who ever lived, they were a study in contrasts:

Ben was the greatest theoretician in the history of the sport, whereas happy-go-lucky Jimmy had settled as a boy for a simplified variety of hands golf, based upon a flick of his powerful forearms and wrists.

Characteristically, Ben had studied and analyzed shooting as he did everything else, and had developed into an exceptional and highly competitive marksman, while Jimmy just trailed along, needling his hunting companions at every opportunity.

Demaret had wandered off one morning, and Bing was just wondering whether his guest had managed to get lost, when he heard the report of a rifle, and headed toward the sound.

Sure enough, Jimmy emerged from behind an outcrop, and waved him over to the biggest buck ever seen in that country, a huge, twelve-point mule deer, which had been felled by a single, perfect shoulder shot.

Roger and Thea Bacon

Bing and Roger with their ducks

Inspecting Jimmy's buck with John Eacret and Ben Hogan

At lunch that day, Jimmy waxed expansive at Ben's expense. "You can practice all you please," he assured the wee iceman, "but there's just no substitute for natural talent."

"Stupid muley got a glimpse of your ugly phiz, and died of fright."

"Tell you what, I'm going to follow you around, and never even raise my rifle until you match my performance."

A man on a mission, Ben charged through the rugged foothills for the next two weeks, without ever catching sight of another buck.

Asleep and awake, he gnashed his teeth until Jimmy dubbed him "blades." He lost ten pounds, but Demaret never let up, and toward the end Bing thought he might have a murder on his hands.

Ben stopped short of homicide, but he never returned, whereas Jimmy practically lived at the ranch for some years. In his easy-going way, he was careless about details, and phenomenally absent-minded .

"We were off to the higher altitudes in search of mountain goats," Bing reminisced. "We each took two horses, and kept in touch by binocular. We rode as long as we could, walked as far as possible, and then crawled as much as we had to.

I spotted a herd, managed by a large billy. It was around the hill from Jimmy, but I waved him on, and saw him creep behind a covering boulder.

The billy left the grazing nannies, the light was good, and conditions were perfect for a shot. I saw Jimmy rear up, spooking the goats, and then walk disconsolately down the slope toward me. 'What happened?' I asked.

"I forgot my gun."

"Jimmy was capable of worse sins of omission. Driving from Elko back to Houston, his wife Red went to the ladies room during a fuel stop in Yerington. He was an hour and a half down the road, when he realized that it had become very quiet in the car.

He hardly dared return for Red, when he considered how angry she'd be. He was not disappointed."

At the end of January, we traveled to Horseshoe Plantation near Tallahassee, Florida. Our first dinner was formal, and I reached for my only possible dress, a demure little ensemble that I had worn on a Christmas show. Our hostess gazed down my décolletage and remarked dryly, "That's very fetching, my dear."

I raced for my room to find a stole, wondering whether I needed to camouflage any other portions of my anatomy. After dinner, many of the men played backgammon, a gambling game that I found incomprehensible.

I gravitated toward a group telling sporting tales, and found Bing at the center of it, recounting one at my expense:

"We took Roger and Thea Bacon to our Rising River Ranch for the opening of the duck season. She is a countess, who has made a determined effort to adjust to her husband's primitive life style.

On our first sortie, she was impeccably garbed in an Abercrombie and Fitch hunting outfit, but she tumbled into the first flooded rice paddy that we tried to cross.

'Better hurry up and change,' Roger suggested helpfully. 'The sun will be up in 17 minutes.'

Thea is 5'2" tall, and weighs 90 pounds soaking wet, which she certainly was. Kathryn hauled her back to the trailer, and returned shortly.

Bing photographed this lioness, elephant,

and cheetah.

Then my wife slid in beside me, casting about as usual for snakes and spiders, and enunciated loud and clear, 'Listen, groaner, if I ever take a header into a rice check, and you offer no more help and sympathy than Thea got, you won't have to worry about the next sunrise, or any other!'"

Next we traveled to the Lambert Ranch in my home state. After dinner, like true Texans, the men started recounting politically-incorrect stories about deviates, and demanded one from Bing, who at first demurred.

At length they coaxed the following out of him: Shortly before my father passed away, a reporter queried him about his attitude toward homosexuality. He replied as follows:

'In my grandpa's time, it was a crime. In my father's era, it was denounced. In my generation, it is fully accepted. I just hope I die before it becomes mandatory.'"

On February 5th, Bing flew to Los Angeles to perform in The Bob Hope Show. Upon his return, I noticed a lack of the usual stories about the practical jokes performed by the pair of cronies.

"Is it the boys again?" I ventured.

"I'm afraid so. As you know, when Dixie died, I relinquished my half of the inheritance to them, and threw in every additional cent that I could find at the time. Their capital is preserved in an enormous trust, and all of them have to agree on any investment.

I met with their lawyers while I was in Los Angeles. In spite of guidance from business managers, agents, accountants, and trustees, those four can't get together on anything. Each just wants to spend every bit of money he can lay his hands on.

"How are they doing?"

"As usual. Gary wants me to buy him a new home. Dennis needs to be committed. Phil was arrested again for DUI. And Lindsay has married a new girl, who insists that I straighten him out forthwith."

"How's the weather in Las Cruces?"

"What kind of weather are we having here?"

"Thirty college kids for dinner tonight, a valentine dance for fifty on Saturday, the Segovia concert, daily ballet, and a trip to study the Sullivan Reading Centers in San Jose."

"And when will the typhoon cease?"

"Around the 18th."

"See you then."

When Bing returned, he found that nothing had improved in his absence. Gary was visiting, and pressing for his new house. Even given my scant grasp of economics, his approach to financing still startled me.

"Dad," he wheedled, "don't think that I'd ever go over your head to a bank. You're the only person that I'll ever come to for money."

Understandably, Bing left for Africa on March 8th, where he first flew to a camp near Isiolo, in a valley ringed by tall cliffs. There he photographed lions, cheetahs, ostriches, hyenas, jackals, and above all a large herd of elephants.

Each time he came upon them, the latter formed a tight circle with the younger ones inside, and the big bulls and cows facing the danger. Bing drew so close that several of the cows trumpeted and charged, but he insisted that they were simply showing off for the rest of the herd. I shuddered just reading about it.

The next destination was Garba Tula, but Bing was stranded when his truck foundered in a deep animal

Stranded in Garba Tula

At camp in Benone with Ibaris

burrow, and he had to abandon most of his food and fuel.

He exhausted himself getting back into action, but he reported cheerfully that the ride was so rough that it must have shaken loose at least three of the kidney stones that had so plagued him of late.

"It was on to Benone," Bing continued, "and a camp on a river where the elephants arrived each evening to drink and bathe. I crept very close, but it was too dark for pictures, or even for headlong flight in the event that they objected to my presence.

I settled for pursuing the vulturine guinea fowl, who were strong flyers, but preferred to lead me a wild chase. They ran me ragged, leaving me too exhausted even to attempt a shot.

In this area, the natives are Somalis, descendants of the Hamites, who are mentioned in the Bible. A sixteen-year-old named Ibaris has adopted me, rides in my truck, and delights in hearing his voice on the dictaphone.

Last night he paid me the ultimate compliment with the gift of a quart of milk. He also pointed out pairs of his tribesmen, making a hundred-mile trek to the Tana River, carrying only a teapot and a handful of grain.

I love to sing duets with the African golden oriole, the first three notes of whose song are those of the ballad *All of Me*. There is also the boo-boo bird, technically known as the dueting shrike, who works in pairs and in close harmony, while I do my poor best to form a trio."

While Bing was in Africa, Gary and big Barbara visited me for a week, while they recovered from a grievous disappointment. Unable to conceive a child, they had decided to adopt a sister for Barbara's son Steve.

Since Gary was unable to pass a social worker's close scrutiny, the Crosbys opted for a private adoption. Their lawyer put them in contact with an unwed mother, purportedly desirous of finding a good home for her prospective child.

The child was born healthy, and spent a month adjusting to life with Gary and Barbara. Then there was a knock at the door. The natural mother had arrived to demand the immediate return of her daughter.

Or perhaps not. She offered to let the Crosbys keep the child temporarily for a mere $25,000 in cash.

Gary's first impulse was to pay the conniving woman, or to hurl her from the porch, but Barbara interposed herself, insisting, "Stay where you are, mam, while I fetch your daughter, and then leave here for good."

After the mother had departed with her offspring, Barbara explained to Gary, "If we'd paid her, that woman would have returned to blackmail us every couple of months. We'd never have been free of her manipulations. As it is, she's off to sell the child to some other victims, on her version of the installment plan."

When Bing returned from Africa, he applauded Barbara's decision. "She's had a hard life," he observed, "and she knows trash when she see's it. She and Gary are well out of that mess."

This time, it was the whole family who departed on April 3rd for our spring break in Las Cruces. Before preparing the necessary foods, I laid out those blessed programmed courses from Dr. Sullivan, for which Bing still insisted on taking full credit.

Springtime in Las Cruces

Then I left on the 11th for a week of cohosting the Mike Douglas Show, taking Harry along to guest star with his songs and guitar, and to meet show business talents such as Rosemary Clooney, Jimmy Dean, Joe Williams, Liza Minelli, Sammy Davis Jr., Artie Shaw, and Richard Pryor.

On the same trip, Harry also performed on the Dinah Shore Show, as a premature reward for an ordeal with a plastic surgeon, who removed still more debris from under the left eye that had been permanently blackened at the age of four by our Mexican auto accident.

Upon my return to Las Cruces, Bing chortled, "It's your turn now," and abandoned me with the children, while he fled to Los Angeles for business meetings, and for a long recording session with Henry Mancini, after which he opened the fishing season at Rising River Ranch.

Bing finally returned to Las Cruces with Dr. Sullivan, demanding that our sage assume responsibility for Mary's many failures in math.

Nothing daunted, Bill handed her a college-level trigonometry text, while remaining beside her to observe her progress, and to register approval for each correct answer.

Thus he inadvertently supplied the missing ingredient, for it transpired that our little performer had no interest in mathematics per se, but would cheerfully apply her formidable IQ to extracting praise from a noted educator, with a sole proviso: The moment he left the scene, or even permitted his attention to wander, the honeymoon was over.

Dr. Sullivan expressed bewilderment. "The program has been tested on thousands of subjects," he insisted, "and they were all sufficiently reinforced by their success, and by their immediate knowledge of results. Not one demanded a separate cheering section. I can assure you that this child is indeed different."

Little did he know. After a glance at me, Bing distracted Bill's attention by proposing a Sullivan Language School in beautiful La Paz. I longed to join its first class, and envisioned returning to Hillsborough after a few months, to astound our friends with my overwhelming fluency in Spanish.

Under the guise of science studies, I enlisted the children's help in my expeditions in search of shells, specimens of coral, and interesting rocks.

Bing's evaluation of our spring semester was duly logged in his diary: "The entryway, the terrace, and all the walls of the house resemble laboratory displays in biology and geology.

I struggle toward the front door through samples of such mineral matter as flint, quartz, geodes, and lava, and such natural history specimens as shells, corals, and innumerable fossils.

Harry has contributed various engine parts to the general chaos. He works with our mechanics on the cars and boats, and seems to have developed a knack for repairing such things, surprising in the offspring of parents whom it would be charitable to designate as helpless and hopeless."

The family returned to Hillsborough on June 4th, and on the 12th, thanks be to God and the Sullivan programmed courses, our children passed all their exams with flying colors, and promptly scattered to the four winds.

Bing took Nathaniel to Hawaii, Mary was invited to stay with friends in Guadalajara, Harry was off to our

On the patio in Las Cruces

With the Galbreaths in Canada

Rising River Ranch, and I had the first weeks to myself in many a weary year.

I took full advantage of them. Now that I had completed the Sullivan Spanish Program with reasonable results, I determined to expand my acquaintance with the romance languages by delving into the world of French.

This time, the voice on the tape was that of Eliane Burroughs, a Sorbonne graduate, who lured me from one correct answer to the next, until I was studying twelve hours a day with sheer delight, and with no trace of fatigue.

I tried to persuade my husband that we two should swear, Middlebury-style, to speak only French to each other. Unconvinced, he favored me with a wry smile, and departed posthaste for Canada, where he swore to speak such French as necessity might demand.

On June 25th, Bing returned from Canada to Columbus, Ohio, to pick up John Galbraith's executive jet for the flight to Darby Dan Farms, where he'd been invited to stay the night.

His plans were thwarted by one of the worst electrical storms in United States history. Fortunately Bing was still on the ground in Columbus when it struck, and there he remained.

The weather cleared at 9 AM on the 26th, and Bing flew with Senator Bill Saxbe of Ohio, over Montreal and Quebec to the airport at Sept-Isles, the city where the iron ore from Labrador is boat-loaded for shipment.

Thence it was on to Mingen, and up river in an eighteen-foot canoe, with an outboard motor attached to the stern.

Both Bing and the senator had great luck with the salmon, but the latter was recalled for a congressional vote, while declaring ruefully that if there were a filibuster, he'd slit his throat.

As a precaution against the vicious flies and mosquitoes, Bing recommended a hooded rain outfit, fitted tightly at wrists and ankles. He admitted reluctantly that he had been forced to run some fierce rapids lest his prey escape, and to kill a starving black bear, which had invaded the campsite in search of food.

Not the sort of news to reassure a home-bound wife, whose husband resembles an adventurous teenager, with small regard for his own safety or that of his companions. Unwilling to dwell upon the dangers to which he constantly exposed himself, I decided upon an escape of my own.

I joined my sister in a trip home to Texas. There, with our offspring well out of the way, we expatiated to relatives upon the talents of said progeny. At the end of the visit, Frances Ruth and I reviewed our claims, and decided that my nose should henceforth be slightly longer than hers.

I returned to find that Bing was off to the Bohemian Grove, an elegant boys camp for prominent males, to which he had mistakenly introduced Phil Harris.

When I asked how things had gone, Bing replied, "I can vouch only for Phil's luggage, which I guarded with my life. Its owner spent the two weeks across the river, where he'd discovered that there were ladies and libations."

Certain that I had been chosen for the task, I accompanied my sister to Washington, to explain to the power structure how to solve our nation's problems in the field of education.

We lunched with John Tower of Texas, who was acquainted with my

That giant marine when still a corporal

father, since Emery had run against him for his senate seat.

Gazing raptly at my gorgeous sister, the senator volunteered to campaign for her in any sort of election in which she might choose to run, while I tried to introduce the subject of the Sullivan programmed courses, with a sinking feeling that no one was even considering listening.

We took tea with Secretary of the Navy John Connally and his wife Nelly, who expressed surprise that Mary Morrow hadn't participated in the caravan of beauties that visited Bing's Palm Desert home on the occasion of Jack Kennedy's residence there.

"After all, she lived only fifty yards away," John smiled.

"And there she stayed," Frances Ruth assured him, while I reflected that Pierre Salinger had indeed extended a strong invitation, which Mary had flatly rejected. I reminded her of it when we joined her for a social whirl in New York.

"You needed protection and still do," I insisted self-righteously, "I told you to marry Dr. Sullivan. That giant ex-marine would never have let lotharios trouble you. I guarantee it."

"I'm sure I'd have been safe from metropolitan mashers," Mary agreed, "because he'd have spirited me off to some remote wilderness, where I'd have had to deal principally with bears and mountain lions. All things considered, I think I'll settle for run-of-the-mill urban philanderers."

I admitted defeat. It's just too much trouble to save some people. Returning home, I found an Edinborough newspaper article, describing Bing's rounds of golf with Gleneagles' professional Ian Marchbanks.

When the press queried Bing about the absence of Bob Hope, who had formerly appeared with him, my husband told the following story about an exhibition near London:

A tiny Scotsman introduced himself as Bob's caddy. "Are you an experienced one?" Hope asked.

"Aye."

"Are you prepared to advise me on the proper club for each shot?"

"Aye."

"Are you good at finding golf balls?"

"Aye."

"Well, don't just stand there. Find one, and let's get started."

After a lengthy stay in Normandy, Bing returned from Europe to perform in a dozen TV specials, and in our own annual Minute Maid Commercial.

The latter had a picnic theme with a sinister twist. Bing tossed flapjacks over a campfire, and I stirred something that represented batter against the backdrop of a huge motor home, employed to dress up the set.

When the commercial ended, the Minute Maid executives presented us with this mightiest of all recreational vehicles, thus reviving Bing's dreams of a glorious mechanized tour of Europe, wherein he and the boys golfed in the mornings and hunted in the afternoons, while Mary and I occupied ourselves with finding parking places for their monstrosity, cleaning it out, and cooking enormous meals for our weary athletes. It was enough to make any girl's heart jump for joy.

Warily I suggested a road test during the Thanksgiving holidays. I made Bing drive his magnificent home-away-from-home all the way north to our Rising River Ranch. Fortunately the weather cooperated nicely. The vehicle

Christmas 1971

was swept hither and yon by side winds, reeled and guzzled like a drunken sailor, and terrified everyone with its propane heating and cooking systems.

Unwilling to take unnecessary chances, I engaged in private financial investigations. It transpired that the whole family could live for a month in the Ritz Hotel in Paris for the cost of shipping our little darling abroad.

Momentarily convinced, Bing donated the motor home to KQED for their public television auction, presented me with a Mercedes sports car and several Faberge items as yuletide gifts, and saw to it that the children's Christmas was sheer delight.

Recording in London

1972

The practice rounds for the 1972 Bing Crosby National Pro-Am were scheduled for Monday through Wednesday, January 10-12, thus affording the contestants a chance to play each of the three tournament courses, namely Pebble Beach, Spyglass Hill, and Cypress Point.

For the first time, our entire family joined the gallery, but the presence of the children was overshadowed by another new visitor in the person of our old friend, Mary Morrow. The winner of countless beauty pageants as a brunette, and known to model occasionally as a regal blonde, she had arrived for the final practice round on Wednesday, newly transformed by the coiffeur's art into a ravishing redhead.

Bing was ready and willing to devote considerable attention to her, but he had just started to give her a tour of the three courses, when he was supplanted by the debonair French con-

tender Coco Dupont. At first sight of Mary's flaming tresses, Coco simply walked away from the 12th tee of his practice round at lovely Cypress Point, and abandoned a considerable gallery to invite her to lunch with him in the clubhouse.

"These American courses are impossible anyway," he explained through his strong Gallic accent. "Why should I torture myself in their devilish bunkers, when I can have the supreme pleasure of spending my day with you? More brie, wine, dessert?

There is an enchanting bit of headland behind the 17th tee, where one is perfectly screened from potential spectators. Let us stroll there now, to observe the sea otters sporting about in their natural state."

The former Miss Georgia laughed, and admitted that she much preferred a more civilized state, in which they might sit on the terrace, and watch his

With Coco Dupont

fellows contend with the 18th hole, as he himself should be doing after striving for the coveted invitation, and crossing the Atlantic to compete in golf's most prestigious event. "Think of your future career," she insisted.

"It is all a matter of perspective. I much prefer to think of you."

"No American golfer could imagine making such a sacrifice."

"My heart bleeds for them, but I can waste no more time on their foolishness. Let me waft you away to my chateau, where we will soon forget all this nonsense of golf."

"I fear that might be a trifle inconvenient at the moment."

"Then permit me to fail to qualify, so that I may dedicate all of my final Sunday to you."

I watched the would-be seduction in fascination, and later discussed the matter with my husband:

"Would he really renounce his one opportunity to win The Crosby for a brief interlude with Mary?" I inquired.

"Not a chance. He's a brilliant golfer, the only one I've invited from France. The four days of competition start tomorrow, and from then on he'll be all business."

With Mary in his large gallery, Coco did indeed play superbly on Thursday and Friday. A mediocre performance on Saturday would qualify him for Sunday's playoff, and Mary's virtue seemed perfectly secure.

In the event, the Frenchman's shots became more and more erratic. But he was still in grave danger of qualifying when he reached the par five 18th at Pebble, where he resourcefully dumped two shots into the Pacific, and another into a yawning trap. Emerging ecstatically with a triple bogey, he

rushed up to claim his fair Mary's hand and heart.

There were other heroics that Saturday, including a hole-in-one on the 160-yard 5th hole at Pebble Beach by Bing's amateur friend, Richard Snideman, and new course records set at both Pebble and Spyglass.

Returning to Pebble Beach on Sunday, Jack Nicklaus and Johnny Miller topped the survivors with four-under-par totals of 284, and Nicklaus won the sudden death playoff on the 15th hole, with a 25-foot uphill birdie putt. Lee Trevino and Don Schwab triumphed in the Pro-Am competition.

All this was well enough, but my attention was fixated elsewhere. I had loaned Mary my new Mercedes sports car, and she had disappeared on Saturday afternoon with it and Coco.

When she returned on Monday morning I demanded an accounting, and received only a pensive smile for my pains. As ever, I rushed to Bing for an explanation:

"Would you throw away your career for the chance at a moment's mad passion?" I queried hopefully.

"Not on your life."

"Well, obviously Coco would."

"Yes, I was wrong there."

"Are all Frenchmen like that?"

"No, I've seen both types of behavior in my time."

"For instance?"

"Well, on my side, there's the case of my friends, the young and old Counts de Bender, who shared an enthusiasm for golf.

"Their yacht was anchored off Cannes one June night, when the old Count was awakened by moonlight streaming through the porthole above his bed, and noticed that his beautiful

Essaying the role of temptress

young mistress seemed to have disappeared. Thoughtfully, he strolled over to his son's cabin, where he discovered the pair elaborately intertwined.

'There you go,' he thundered at his offspring, 'ruining your golf game again.'"

"Does that mean that Coco is a freak of nature?"

"No, there's also a tale that supports his willingness to sacrifice his entire world for love."

"Well, don't just stand there. Let me hear it."

"When I was making *Little Boy Lost* in Paris, I was approached by Claude Terrail, proprietor of the famous restaurant *Tour d'Argent*. He was an ardent movie buff, wild about getting into films, and I constituted his sole hope of achieving his dream.

I offered him a bit part, and promised him more if he worked out. It caused a shutdown, since the camera crew was made up exclusively of communists, who regarded Terrail as a major fascist collaborator.

I sneaked him off the set, and flew him to Los Angeles, where we could shoot all his scenes in Hollywood. I also threw a party for him, with some 200 guests, including my producers, my leading lady Nicole Maurey, our old friend Merle Oberon, and half the starlets in Hollywood, one of whom was my date for the evening, Mary Murphy."

(And for many another evening, and night too for that matter, I reflected glumly. I'd had my hands full with that bewitching little beauty.)

Unaware of my mute interruption, Bing continued: "The evening was off to a fine start, with perfect weather, cocktails on the terrace, light hors d'oeuvres, and a splendid dinner.

Right in the middle of it, the guest of honor excused himself. Twenty minutes later, Mary was called away to answer a phone call in the library.

She returned, with eyes even larger than normal, to whisper the following in my ear: 'Your dear friend, otherwise known as that French scum bag, just phoned me from the Beverly Wilshire Hotel, where he says he has their best suite, overflowing with champagne and caviar. Just like that, he wants me to leave you and your party, to join him for the rest of the night.'

'What did you tell him?'

'Nothing. I hung up.'"

Bing returned to our present discussion: "For Claude Terrail, that was the equivalent of Coco Dupont's behavior at The Crosby.

He knew that he was sacrificing not only my friendship, but also his sole hope of continuing his movie career, and yet he tossed it all away for the remote chance of captivating one beautiful woman."

"So the French are, after all, rather like us, some crazy in one direction, and some in another."

"That would seem to be the case, though they may be a trifle more extreme in their madness, where romantic love is concerned."

"Was there any danger of Mary's running off with her dashing young Frenchman?"

"In a word, *no*."

"Careful now. You were wrong about Coco's preferring fame and fortune to her charms."

"True, but I knew Mary for years as Bill Morrow's charming wife, and she has a very level head on her pretty shoulders. Besides, you don't know her full history.

I was doing something wrong.

"Indeed I don't. How did she ever evolve into such a detached sort of beauty?"

"You'd have to know her ex-husband Bill. He was a great writer, but his sexual adventures prevented him from ever finishing a script on time.

Bill was catnip to women, and vice versa. He put Mary through endless heartache, including the time that he left for a week in Paris and stayed three months.

Nonetheless, she remained a dutiful wife, and even after he precipitated a divorce, she nursed him through a painful and lingering death.

I believe our Mary has had quite enough of illusory passions and matrimonial snares. She'll devote the rest of her life to avoiding suffering any more of the same. Whatever the attractions of the Coco's of this world, she's ripe only for serious proposals from solid citizens."

"I remember that when she and my sister were modeling for Jean-Louis in New York, Frances had her hands full mollifying the wives, while Mary danced with all the big-time buyers."

"But the results were that Mary rejected dozens of propositions, Jean-Louis sold out his inventory, and Frances Ruth learned countless new recipes. By the way, did you know that she was the toast of the London season with Sir Charles Clore?"

"She never mentioned it to me."

"They chanced to be seated together at a Hollywood dinner. The British tycoon was so captivated by her southern charm that he invited her to spend the winter at his country house.

While he was making the overture, the princeling on Mary's right put his hand on her thigh. Remaining focused on Charles, Mary bent his highness's middle finger back until he abandoned all thoughts of lechery. Through his moans, she then gravely accepted the billionaires invitation, called our house the next day, and asked to speak with our butler, Alan Fisher.

Alan created a twenty-page primer entitled *Protocol for a Guest in London during the Season.* Jean Louis filled Mary's suitcases with evening gowns, and she spent the flight over committing to memory such gems as, "Do not approach strangers with the greeting, 'Hi y'all, I'm Mary Morrow from Tifton, Georgia.'"

After The Crosby, Mary accompanied us on a trip to the King Ranch. While the men were out hunting, she regaled their women with tales of beauty contests, life in Hollywood, and a hunt from which she had emerged with a full-length sable, designed to shield her from the deadly dampness of a duck blind.

I was doing something wrong. Bing had just had the butt of my shotgun modified and padded to prevent further bruising of my right shoulder. But the pad was definitely not made of sable, and as for the chill of a Texas autumn, long johns would have to suffice.

When we took to the field, Mary preempted the driver's seat of the drinks wagon, and complemented the hunters on their prowess. From then on, it was indeed fortunate that weapons were limited to one shotgun per macho, and that no one was actually wounded in the rush to perform heroic feats for the goddess with the crimson tresses.

Our hostess, Ila Clements, had initially dismissed Mary as a useless

Barneby Conrad's portrait of Bing and Remus

city slicker, but she now began to pay attention to her guest's performance.

"You're the best huntress I've seen in these fields," she admitted. "Tell me more about Beverly Hills."

Thenceforth Mary was surrounded by a coterie of Texas wives, eager to contrast the joys of owning one's own brand, country store, and leather chaps, with movie roles, modeling, lunches at Club 21, nightly balls, dates with celebrities, and alligator bags.

On January 22nd, Bing flew to Los Angeles to star with Bob Hope, Carol Burnett, and Pearl Bailey in a special entitled *Bing and his Friends,* and I lured Mary away, before she could sew any more seeds of domestic discord.

Returning home at the end of the month, I checked on the children's schoolwork, and began my own studies at the conveniently-located American Conservatory Theater.

I performed in scenes from *Hamlet* and *The Prime of Miss Jean Brodie,* took lessons in singing and mime, and resumed tap dancing, which I had originally abandoned in disgust at the age of eight. Anne Miller remained safe. I demonstrated only how right I'd been to quit the first time.

Bing arrived on February 7th, to invite me to join him and the children for a week in a condominium at Sugar Bowl. "Surely you jest!" was my unhesitating reply.

I was born in Southeast Texas, a stone's throw from the Gulf of Mexico, where reality is universally and engagingly flat. I had since been introduced to mountains, but I hadn't liked what I saw, and I'd felt no need to conceal my reactions.

I'm frankly terrified of heights, or of even minor elevations, and I've found it much simpler to admit the fact than to try to compensate for it.

When engaging in a hunt, it's not necessary for a woman to be a great shot. Being a good sport will suffice.

But on the slopes, individual performance is required. Somehow one has to survive a terrifying descent, only to regain the summit, and again hurl oneself suicidally into the abyss.

My offspring had inherited none of my fears, and my husband had matured amid the mountains of Washington. Fortunately he was kind enough not to ridicule my horror of heights, though he'd been known to tease me about my acting, singing, and gross domestic ineptitude.

My clutch of Crosbys spent their week at Sugar Bowl, and returned to a mother figure who refused to hear of their adventures, but insisted that her husband translate her to a gentler clime. We left for Las Cruces on Sunday, February 20th.

When in Hillsborough, I had tried, however ineptly, to direct domestic operations. In male-oriented Mexico, in spite of my superior Spanish, Bing's was the sole voice of authority.

So it was he who had to direct the cook, housemaids, gardeners, boatmen, and even our daring bush pilot. He had to order the groceries, and arrange all trips, in spite of the fact that he was even worse at it than his wife.

Bing had grown up as a poor boy, and he had retained a distaste for telling others what to do. He preferred to assume that they knew their jobs, and to let them have at it.

Chavalo relaxing and Mary fishing   Juana dispensing coffee and smiles

Our new casita

Our Mexican staff took full advantage of this weakness by feigning activity whenever they were sure that they had attracted Bing's attention, and relaxing the rest of the day.

Chavalo, a gardener and general handyman, had adopted the practice of passing by our bedroom window well before dawn, acquainting us with his industry by whistling a chorus of *Me voy lejos de ti,* and continuing on his way to the kitchen and several cups of Juana's coffee, all of which put him in the right frame of mind for a siesta.

When others began to imitate his tactics, my insomniac of a bedfellow, aware of what was coming, would close our heavy curtains against the dawn, prying eyes, and any vagrant breeze that might chance along. He had always preferred death by asphyxiation to loss of dignity.

In the interests of sleep, he cast about for a permanent solution, and found it in the adjacent banana grove, where he caused a separate bedroom to be constructed, safe from any roosters, servants, or children, who took to saluting the dawn.

I helped only once. A plumber asked me to sign a note, authorizing him to purchase any needed materials in La Paz. I was so overwhelmed at being consulted on anything that I cheerfully granted him permission to acquire some $30,000 worth of materials, which he promptly discounted to local entrepreneurs, and thus financed his translation to the United States as a man of means and influence.

His successor actually constructed an enormous tile tub. It was the size of a swimming pool, and it filled somewhat more slowly, even in the rare instances when ample water was available.

On February 29th we returned to Tinseltown, so that Bing could guest star on the Flip Wilson Show, and record with Count Basie.

Since the Count was on an extended tour, he had made his orchestral recordings in New York. Then Bing, with only his earphones and an engineer, dubbed in the vocal in Hollywood.

This was viewed as the cutting edge of technology at the time. At last Bing could record anywhere, knowing that his performance would later be cut and polished until it was ready to air.

Bing had never learned to use a typewriter. Initially he had scrawled all his correspondence in an almost illegible hand. Then he had formulated his letters for a live secretary. Now he dictated them onto tapes, which were mailed to Los Angeles to be transcribed, and thence dispatched to the far corners of the globe.

So comfortable was he with this system that he could orally compose dozens of letters an hour, and entrust them to a distant secretary, without ever desiring a second glance. He always claimed that he completed most of his work while waiting for me to get ready for our engagements.

Arriving back in Hillsborough, I was immediately confronted by an emergency. Our daughter Mary had decided to pierce her ears.

Typically, she had performed the operation in her locked bathroom, and had left behind a bloody mess. After the time-honored tradition of irate mothers, I marched to her school, and bellowed her name in a voice that interrupted recess and all other activities.

When Mary emerged cautiously from behind a pillar, I cut the thread from her lobes, handed her a tube of

Doctors Harry and Constance Buncke

penicillin ointment, and snarled, "If those ears don't heal before the weekend, you won't be performing in *Peter and the Wolf* with the Santa Cruz Symphony Orchestra."

It's always helpful to have leverage. Mary would have died, had she been denied the opportunity to participate.

Characteristically, she did manage to mutter, "I asked you what you would do if you heard that someone you loved had pierced her ears, and you said you didn't know."

"I didn't then. Now we both do."

From a silly, inconsequential mutilation, I graduated to the big time, or more accurately to the big toe.

Carl Tagler, a Redwood City fireman, enjoyed all types of woodworking. In a moment of inattention, he had removed most of his right thumb with a power saw.

Dr. Harry Buncke had been called upon to set the matter right, and incidentally to originate the field of microsurgery. My tribe had already contributed heavily to his extensive experience.

I'll cite just one example: When Nathaniel had refused to relinquish his shady spot beneath the lone tree at the Cary Nursery School, the proprietor's son, irate at such lack of respect, had tossed the brick that split the scalp that released the blood that smeared the face of the howling child who was rushed to the office of the plastic surgeon who repaired the damage.

Any one of the Crosby children could give Dr. Buncke all the references he might possibly need. This circumstance combined with my nurse's training to afford me a unique opportunity to observe the history-making surgical procedure.

Carl Tagler's preoperative status was summarized as follows: "Loss of the proximal and distal phalanx of the right thumb, severely compromising the function of the hand. Pulp-to-pulp pinch, key pinch, and chuck pinch also lost. Moreover opposition and grasp are severely limited."

I reflected that it might also have been noted that an occupation had been lost, since Tagler was no longer in condition to climb a fireman's ladder.

Continuing in surgeon's jargon, "On a four-fingered hand, a great-toe transplant was performed to restore a thumb amputated through the metacarpophalangeal joint, with reconstruction thereof, using the articular surface of the proximal end of the proximal phalanx of the great toe."

What I actually saw on March 9th was Dr. Buncke, heading one team of surgeons who cautiously removed Tagler's right big toe, and directing another group who opened the scarred portion of the right hand to insert and secure the toe, and thus make of it a new thumb.

The second team worked with veins and arteries so tiny as to defy belief. Dr. Buncke's caution to his colleagues emphasized the delicacy of the procedure: "We must maintain continuous circulation, where even two joined platelets can suffice to obstruct the blood flow."

As I left Franklin Hospital, I pondered the miracles of modern science. If my daughter persisted in her present tendencies, she might become a celebrated surgeon. For the moment, her ears healed rapidly, and she won wide acclaim in *Peter and the Wolf*.

On March 23rd, all five Crosbys made their spring leap to Las Cruces,

In Acapulco

Borrachita Me Voy

where I taught them to paint on the lovely orange scallop shells called *catarinas.* We printed lyrics from Bing's songs on the bottom half of the open bivalves, and appropriate pictures on the top half.

Irving Berlin telegraphed his delight with his yuletide scene, which was captioned *May all your Christmases be White,* and included an enclosed card reading, "Made at Casa Crosby by loving if often reluctant hands."

For two weeks, I devoted twelve hours a day to the Sullivan German program. It posed oral stimuli demanding spoken responses, visual stimuli requiring written responses, oral stimuli with written responses, written stimuli with spoken responses, etc.

Oral responses were checked against the voice on the tape; Written answers were revealed by pulling down a slider.

If mine matched, I was delighted. If it didn't, I could correct myself instantly, with no one the wiser.

The rest of the family continued with the Sullivan Spanish program. Harry and Mary raced ahead, in a mad scramble to outdo each other, while Bing made shift to keep up with the lagging Nathaniel.

In April we traveled to Acapulco, where I played tennis with the great Don Budge, and Bing golfed at Tres Vidas all day, and indeed most of the night, since the fairways were brilliantly lighted.

April 8th found us in Guadalajara, where we were invited to join in a picnic and colombari. "Fine," I agreed gamely. "By the way, what's a colombari?"

"Well, a colombófilo is a pigeon fancier. The event is named for the leading participants, who are skilled in removing a couple of key feathers so that a bird's flight will be erratic.

The tosser stands in a circle ten feet in diameter, whirls like a discus thrower, and releases a pigeon. The shooter must down his quarry within a surrounding circle of perhaps forty feet."

"Ah yes, I remember something like that at the King Ranch. Who is the local expert?"

"Pepe Hernández. He has tossed up more birds, and taken more pellets, than any other man alive."

After a surfeit of food and drink, Bing joined several other picnickers in snapping off shots at the careening birds. I was relieved to see that he did no more damage than they.

All the pigeons flew happily off to regrow their plumage, while roosting on the roof of the barn, and devouring the grain from the fields.

Back home in Las Cruces, I inaugurated "science field trips," which consisted of night-time sallies, carrying black lights that made the scorpions glow in the dark.

We used long-handled cooking spoons, and dumped the little critters into glass jars with perforated lids, before mailing them off in special tubes to Dr. Stanke at a research laboratory in Tempe, Arizona.

Said containers were labeled *May be Opened for Postal Inspection,* and the children delighted in imagining the look on the face of whatever bureaucrat took us at our word.

Of course the object of the game was to determine just how poisonous the local species were. Long before we received a report, we had proven in our flesh that their sting was less than lethal, for we had each been struck various times.

At sea with Cindy

Our favorites were the little straw-colored scorpion who lived in the date palms, and the giant hairy one whose sting was very painful but far from deadly.

Not desiring even these for household pets, we learned to patch up the chinks and crannies in our stone wall, to shake out our clothing before hanging it up, and to throw back the sheets for inspection before retiring.

I also put our scuba equipment to good use, leading my troops on daily explorations beneath the waves.

North of Cerralvo, near Bird Rock, we discovered a giant murex with her own maternity ward. This beautiful shell mother inched serenely along, depositing a sort of honeycomb for her tiny offspring.

Her complete dedication to the task made me vow never again to collect living specimens. I exhausted several scuba tanks, floating above her ledge and watching respectfully.

My ill-considered decision to change Bing's torn pillowcase involved me in a much more frantic aspect of maternity. For background, it must be known that my diminutive Labrador retriever came into season each time we flew to Las Cruces.

As long as she remained in my dressing room, she seemed quite content, though Bing and I certainly weren't, since we had to listen to our neighbor's giant Irish setters howling as they patrolled the yard throughout the night.

I stuffed Cindy with Clorets, which lent her tongue a becoming shade of green, but failed to dissuade the male dogs. We were coping, though just barely, when I unaccountably waxed domestic.

Cindy followed along on my walk to the laundry room, and as I rummaged about in a locker, she seized her opportunity to nose open the door that was customarily left cracked against the steam which Juana's operations generated, and to make her break for life, freedom, romance!

Cindy disappeared into the brush. In our isolated environment, the countryside was alive with coyotes, who serenaded us nightly. I screamed hysterically for my four-footed friend.

The children arrived to inquire why mother had gone round the bend this time. Finally even Bing strolled up.

"Cindy's gone," I sobbed. "We have to find her before the coyotes do."

We raced up and down the driveway, calling the dog's name. Not that this behavior was particularly appropriate, but it beat tripping through the surrounding cacti in the dead of night.

When I paused to gulp some air, Bing tried to soothe me: "Even if the coyotes do get to her," he explained, "there have been numerous cases of dogs having coyote pups without serious problems."

Somehow this reflection failed to reassure me, so he tried again: "A coyote has to mince around and court for at least five minutes, and if two or more arrive, there'll be a fight over Cindy. She can just sit back, play female, and enjoy the fuss."

"Thanks a lot," I snarled, "but I think I need a new therapist."

I had wild visions of my beloved pet being gang-raped by hordes of sex-crazed coyotes, and then torn to shreds.

Sobbing uncontrollably as I stumbled through the night, I failed to notice the black blob that dogged my heels,

Fishing season opens at Rising River.

until the children brought her to my attention.

I carried Cindy into the house, and inspected her for the marks of fangs. Then I demanded that my husband hold her in the tub while I administered a strong vinegar douche.

Bing was laughing so hard that he was of little use. Finally he gasped, "Just what do you think this is going to accomplish?"

"It will relieve my anxiety, that's what. It's my very own version of canine birth control. If you have any better ideas, I'd be delighted to hear them right now. More help and less criticism would be highly appreciated.

Cindy never did give birth to a coyote, though I worried about her for some weeks, distracting myself with swimming lessons for Nathaniel, who finally mastered a jackknife into the Rodriguez's pool.

He really did show some aptitude for aquatic sports, as well he might. To be sure, I was no great shakes as a swimmer, but Bing had won ten medals in his initial meet.

On May 4th, the whole family returned to California, Bing for the opening of the trout season at Rising River Ranch, and I to attempt to pacify the Hillsborough school officials, after the children's annual absence from their jurisdiction.

Obviously I couldn't be in both places at once, so I was spared the frustration of lashing the river to a fleecy froth in my futile attempts at fly casting, and Bing was saved from the sight of my dragging big lunkers to the bank with my spinning rig, after I reverted to type.

"Don't you realize that fly-fishing is a fine art?" he had inquired. "For trout,

this is the best stretch of river in California, perhaps in the world, and you persist in sullying it with the tactics of a market supplier."

"Would you prefer fried or broiled?"

From the ranch, Bing went on to New York, where he was installed in the Golf Hall of Fame, and thence to Las Cruces until the end of the month.

He was staying out of the way while I tried to organize our one big bash of the year, a dinner dance in honor of Angie Reynal, Bing's goddaughter, the off-spring of Juan and Jeanne Reynal.

The groom was Dick Theriot, who was later to head the San Francisco Chronicle. He and his bride were beautiful young people, who contrived to make most of the preparations for the event comparatively easy for an awkward party giver.

Mary Morrow flew north to create the decorations, my sister organized the ceremony, Alan Fisher planned the menu and the music, while I hung around, wringing my hands, and later taking undeserved bows. Bing danced with all the ladies, and forgot to complain, although the festivities lasted until 4 AM.

Dame Margot Fonteyn and Karl Musil were performing in Cupertino. The whole family went to watch them in *Swan Lake,* and the next day they came to lunch.

I was amazed at Margot's appetite, and frankly envious of the amount she managed to consume. She explained that a major ballet is the caloric equivalent of running five miles.

I hated to see the visit end, and as a matter of fact, it didn't. The dancers rented car broke down, and we drove them back to the huge Cupertino auditorium, staying to watch them perform

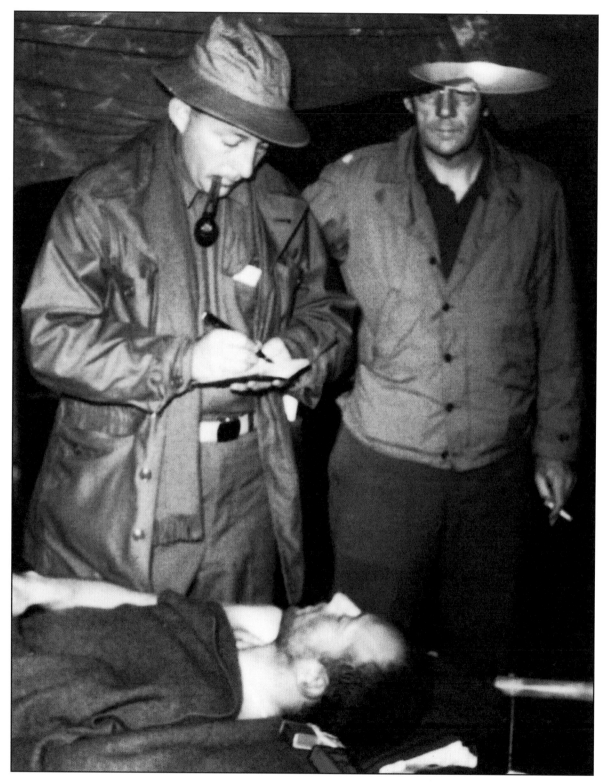

Taking names in a World War II field hospital

in *Romeo and Juliet*. After the show ended, we chauffeured Karl and Margot back to Hillsborough, to dine and pick up their car.

A further discussion of the quantities she consumed led the ballerina to reminiscences of her European tours during World War II: "All food was in short supply," she recalled, "and there were days when we had none at all.

We often had no place to stay, no piano for music, and no level wooden floor on which to dance. Every night we had to adapt the choreography to the circumstances."

"It was a lot easier being a singer," Bing decided. "All I needed for a stage was the back of a truck, or even the top of a tank. With a guitar player and a mike, and often without, I was ready to perform in the front lines.

Of course they had better facilities in the hospitals, where I could take down names, and dedicate songs to individuals when I returned to do my radio show. The worst part was trying to cheer up the blind and crippled young men."

I felt a sudden chill. Dame Margot was married to a South-American politician of great charm and sway. While exercising his power, he'd been shot in the back and paralyzed.

I timidly asked how she and Tito Arias managed now. In the twinkling of an eye, she was transformed from her girlhood in World War II to the mature woman that she had become.

Flashing her inimitable smile, she assured me, "We do everything that we ever did. It just takes a little longer."

Bing hastened to lighten the moment by recurring to war stories: "A singer's superior mobility did have its disadvantages," he admitted. "One day,

my driver and I were visiting some forward units. For what seemed like a long time, we drove past burned-out buildings, disabled tanks, and abandoned artillery.

Suddenly I noticed some unfamiliar uniforms, ducking down amid the ruins. Very quietly, I asked my companion, 'Do you have a map?'

'Yes, sir.'

'Well pull over into those shadows, and let's check our position.'

He did, we did, and at least one of us turned very cold. We were some ten miles behind enemy lines.

We wheeled our vehicle about, and advanced to the rear, doubtless setting a new European record for rutted road racing.

GIs who wrote from prison camps said their guards loved to listen to my songs, and called me *der Bingle*. I was nonetheless of the opinion that, since the Germans possessed all my records, they had no crying need for my person.

A month later, I was in Paris with General Eisenhower. Since I was soon to return to The States, I asked if there were anything I could send him.

As a boy, Ike had lived in Texas. With a faraway look in his eye, he replied, 'The thing that I miss most over here is grits. Do you think you could mail me a box?'

I reached home safe and sound, and sent off the desired package immediately. Since parcels often took months to arrive in Europe, I also mentioned the general's craving on my radio show.

Three weeks had passed when I received a special-delivery message from the war department:

'Help! Call off the grits! They have arrived by the ton, plain, boiled, fried, raw, and with gravy. Many thanks, but

299

Our trencherman

Mary as a budding Annie Oakley

the sheer volume of them is interfering with our transport. Best regards, Ike.'"

Dame Margot smiled vaguely. "That is a charming story," she conceded, "but what in the world are grits?"

As the sole local authority on all things below the Mason-Dixon line, I felt called upon for a tutorial: "Corn is processed to remove the skin and the grain," I explained grandly, "and then coarse-ground.

Grits are the soul of the Confederacy. I could never have attained my present imposing stature without them."

"When Phil Harris and I were in Atlanta for the Masters," Bing added, "we breakfasted at our hotel's coffee shop. Phil ordered ham and eggs.

'Sorry, sir, we can't do ham and eggs,' replied the pretty young waitress.

'You mean you don't have any eggs?'

'Yes, sir, we have eggs all right.'

'Well, what about the ham?'

'We have plenty of ham.'

'Then why can't I have all the ham and eggs I want?'

''Cause we ain't got no grits.'"

On July 30th, Bing took daughter Mary, nephew Bill Meyer, and wife Kathryn to Europe, en route to Africa.

Bill was a 220-pound linebacker for the Oregon Ducks, who looked like an overgrown kewpie doll. Almost immediately, we became aware that feeding him might present a problem.

On our first night in London, Bing had reservations at the Savoy Grill, where the maître d'hôtel approached our table with a two-tiered tea trolley full of hors d'oeuvres.

After Mary, Bing, and I had each chosen one, he turned to Bill, who cheerfully swept the entire top layer onto his plate.

The glorified waiter turned pale, but he gamely stood his ground, inquiring as to whether anyone would care to select from the second level.

"Oh, do I get that too?" gushed Bill in obvious relief.

While Bing watched in delight, Bill consumed all the hors d'oeuvres and several portions of Beef Wellington, before demolishing three desserts.

No eyebrow was raised in the august salon, but as Bing smoked his Dunhill cigar, an ancient waiter eased over to our table and murmured, "What a delight it is to have you with us, Mr. Crosby, and it's a special pleasure to attend to your young friend.

My goodness, I haven't seen dining like that since the time of good King Edward VII. Ah, but there were true trenchermen in those glorious bygone days. I never thought to meet their match again. It has been a privilege, sir, a rare privilege indeed."

In response to our queries, Bill admitted modestly that he was hardly a prodigy at the groaning board. "You should see some of those 300-pound linemen tuck it in," he added enthusiastically, and proceeded to describe his coaches' habit of halting the bus at post-game buffets, where the team consumed everything in the place.

"We can stop only one time at each smorgasbord," he grinned. "After that, the proprietors bribe the coaches to patronize the competition."

On Thursday, August 3rd, Bing managed to sneak us into the Tutankhamen Exhibit, before the Royal Museum opened for the day.

I was horrified to discover that we were to be guided through in a small party with the Duke of Marlborough, followed closely by another which

With the priest from Garissa

included, among other members of the nobility, Her Royal Highness, Princess Margaret.

Sure enough, a lady in waiting from the latter group arrived with a message for Bing. Overwhelmed by the prospect of immediate ejection, I shuddered as he opened it and nodded gamely to the noble dame.

"Have we been discovered?" I hissed into his ear.

"I'm afraid so."

"Will we be escorted to the door?"

"I don't see why. The Princess has just invited us to join her party. Cheer up. I'm certain that you'll like her."

Once again I had failed to grasp the basics of carrying off my role as Mrs. Bing Crosby, but as my husband had assured me, Margaret was a delight.

On Friday, August 4th, we flew to Nairobi, and thence to our first camp at Garissa.

Since I had expressed sundry reservations about this new trip to the Dark Continent, Bing had agreed to spare me some of the shooting, and to proceed with another aspect of my African education.

Kneeling by the riverbank, he uncovered the shells of enormous land snails, and started teaching me to read the African newspaper constituted by its sands.

"Let's begin with the most visible signs, and work on down," he suggested. "Of course these huge round prints are elephant tracks."

"And these brown cannon balls must be elephant droppings."

"So far so good. Now tell me what the big pugs with the claw marks are."

"Lion tracks. No other cat could be so large."

"And the hoof prints to the right?"

"They're large and deep. Some kind of big ungulate. How about a family of zebra?"

"Not too bad. They were made by a couple of giraffes."

"I'm getting the knack of it. Give me a real test."

"All right, smarty pants, let's go to the other extreme: What are these?"

Bing pointed to myriad tiny punctures in the sand.

"Worm holes?" I ventured dubiously.

"Not exactly." Those are the tracks of dik-dik, the rabbit-sized antelope. See where they've dug down into the sand, in search of the tiny bulbous plants that constitute their food."

"OK, I surrender. I'm not quite ready to function as a guide."

Bing persisted, teaching me to recognize the tracks of dove, vulturine guinea fowl, and finally the perfectly heart-shaped prints of a water buck. Suspecting a sensory overload, he then graciously excused me from class for the rest of the day.

Cruising along beside some flat-topped acacias, we encountered a local game warden.

"Ken," Bing inquired, "would it be possible to take a lion? I don't want to shoot anything except a bird or two, but I have a young nephew along on his first safari, and we've seen pug marks everywhere."

"Not a bad idea. We've been over-protective, and the lions have become a nuisance. They've killed twelve people already this year."

I was appalled. "How could such a thing happen?" I demanded.

Bing explained the matter to his dimwitted little consort: "The Somalis let their children herd the goats far from the villages, carrying only a bowl

The Emporer's Waltz revisited

for milk and a stick. Wandering lions prefer the taste of young child to that of goat or calf."

I couldn't wait to return to camp and alert Bill, who however expressed regret. "Just today I saw three superb males. I could have hit them with a rock. Now that I have permission to shoot, I'll bet I never see another."

He was right too. There was no dearth of wild life. Wart hogs, giraffes, and hippopotami played in the river just below our camp, where Mary shot a man-eating crocodile. We discovered leopards and cheetahs galore, but nary another lion.

On August 20th, Bill had to return to Oregon for football camp, but Bing treated Mary and me to a surprise trip to the shellers' paradise of the Seychelle Islands.

There he contented himself with sitting in the shade, and identifying the specimens that his daughter and I retrieved from the very edge of the living coral reef.

He first warned us against the potentially lethal conus geographicus which Mary had just uncovered, and then urged us to collect more of the colorful cowries which, he explained, have served as legal tender in many jurisdictions.

"Hey," I remonstrated, "who's supposed to be the shell expert here?"

"I guess you are, but you'll have to do more to protect your turf. That big cone shell projects a poison which could have cost us a daughter, and by the way, what are you now doing with that lime juice?"

"It reduces the sting of coral."

"Right, and it also removes sunscreen. Either way, you seem destined to burn."

"OK, so I'll join you in the shade. By the way, what's that you're eating?"

"It's a coconut called *coco de mer* that's famed as an aphrodisiac because it's shaped like a woman's buttocks. Here, try a slice."

I did, and sure enough either it, or the paradise of the Seychelles, seemed to have the advertised effect. It was not without a certain regret that we moved on to the Munich Olympics.

We first stayed *in einem sehr gemütlichen Gasthaus,* where the Tyrolean hats, Lederhosen, and lavishly decorated beer steins convinced us that we had finally discovered the festive Germany of the *Emperor's Waltz.*

In fact, the whole inn was so like a movie set that Bing was reminded of a film in which he, clad in a similar costume, had romanced a lovely Joan Fontaine:

"Once, when I had been unavoidably detained on a golf course, Billy Wilder, our director, assembled the entire cast in full makeup, seated on stools, chins on fists, with full lights blazing, to await my entrance.

For a moment, I almost regretted my tardiness, but then I reflected that I'd returned in triumph as the winner of a five-dollar bet."

Willy-nilly, Bing began to hum *eine kleine Nachtmusik,* while our Schnitzel was being prepared.

He had quite forgotten that he was traveling incognito. The honest burghers cast about for the source of the sound, focused on Bing, pierced the thin disguise of dark glasses, and mobbed our table.

It cost us two hours of autographs before we could move on to our hotel, the *Bayerischer Hof,* where we were greeted on arrival by ten-year-old

Watching the equestrian

and track and field events

Nathaniel Patrick Crosby, fresh from his first solo transatlantic trip.

We checked in, and repaired immediately to the games, where Bing was delighted with the design of the stadium, the superb organization, and the spectacular Russian gymnasts, among whom fifteen-year-old Olga Korbut reigned supreme.

Together, the four Crosbys enjoyed the equestrian events, but on the days which commenced with track and field, Mary and I attended the excellent ballet classes, more to practice our German than to progress in the dance.

Then Bing and Mary, who were both strong swimmers, left for the pool to watch their betters perform, while I escorted my son to the Olympic Village.

We were surprised to find a huge crowd outside it, and a contingent of the handsome German police, in their powder-blue uniforms, guarding the gates.

There was much shouting and gesticulating, and some of the fans were actually crying.

I sought out the guard in the fanciest uniform, and requested permission to enter in my precise schoolgirl Hochdeutch. Perhaps I'd best preface further proceedings with a confession:

The truth is that I am a parrot. I can reproduce sounds almost exactly, a faculty which affords native speakers of French, Spanish, German, and Russian a false impression of my fluency. Particularly in the latter two highly-inflected tongues, I often experience difficulty in interpreting their replies.

In this case, the guard overwhelmed me with a flood of highly-emotional Bavarian, of which I understood not a word. Nothing daunted, I stated decisively that the chief physician in charge of the American athletes had invited me to interview him in his office at 10 AM.

My new friend replied with a long harangue, which obviously ended in a question.

Jawohl! I retorted emphatically. Whereupon he shook his head, but finally shrugged his shoulders, and allowed Nathaniel and me to pass.

Hand in hand, we strolled through strangely empty streets, looking for the USA emblem. At last we found it on a portal, entered, and walked along a darkened corridor.

A door burst open, and an American officer rushed out, only to pause in amazement and ask, "How in hell did you get in here?"

"In German. Everyone seemed to be milling around outside, but I explained that you were expecting us, and the guard finally stepped aside and let us into the Village."

"Didn't the idiot tell you what danger you'd be in?"

"Perhaps. I wasn't too clear as to what he was trying to say."

"For a time, the major just stared in disbelief. Then he led me into his office, and pointed out the window. "Look closely at the building across the courtyard," he insisted.

I obeyed orders, but had to admit that I saw nothing unusual.

"Then perhaps I'd better tell you that you're staring at Building 31, which houses the Hong Kong, Uruguayan, and Israeli teams.

At 4:30 this morning, Arab commandos scaled the wire fence that surrounds the compound. They broke into the Israeli quarters, killed the wrestling coach and a weight lifter, and

Bill Holden, Grace Kelly, and Bing in *The Country Girl*

seized nine other athletes as hostages, whom they're holding in that building right now."

In the next room, I could hear a secretary crying into a phone: "You have to intercept the Palestinian dancers. Radio their plane. Tell them the festival has been canceled, and they must turn back immediately."

Feeling abashed, I asked if there were any way in which I could assist.

"I don't see how. We're all helpless at the moment,"

"Then I guess I'd better get my son out of here."

"I agree," snapped the major, too ironically for my taste. "We'll sneak you out, and have my driver take you back to the Bayerischer Hof."

As we left the compound, Nathaniel spied Chancellor Willy Brandt's helicopter. "He'll fix things, mom," my son announced confidently.

But even Brandt couldn't. Shortly before midnight, we watched on television as a gun battle at the airport took the lives of the nine hostages, five of the commandos, and a German policeman.

The 1972 Olympics had been spoiled for the Crosbys, as for most of the world. All four of us flew to London, where we dropped off Bing, and headed straight home to Hillsborough.

The rest of 1972 savored of anticlimax. Bing wrote from the birthplace of golf at St. Andrews that the organizing committee was providing police protection for every move he made, on or off the beautiful old course.

The Scottish Daily Express of September 14 commented, "Bing came quietly into Scotland for Friday's inauguration of a new golf tournament at St. Andrews.

The Old Groaner's generosity has ensured that there will be a Bing Crosby Cup to compete for in the years to come."

Bing returned to California for the Minute Maid commercial on November 1st, and for our annual family event, the Christmas Show, on the 24th through the 27th.

While the children and I rehearsed, he was subjected to a series of interviews, some of which I returned in time to eavesdrop on.

He began with a hilarious parody of Gary Cooper's laconic presentation speech, after Bing had won the Oscar for *Going My Way.*

He then described the sufferings of George Seaton in writing the screenplay for *The Country Girl,* and while directing the picture.

"At one point, Bill Holden had a long and difficult soliloquy which caused him grave difficulties because it involved considerable movement, close involvement with props, and having to hit his marks exactly for the lighting.

During two days of takes, Bill kept blowing his lines. On the third, he got all the way down to the last sentence, before losing his composure again.

He raced up and down the set, throwing props around, and bemoaning his ineptitude. Finally he jumped out a conveniently open window.

There was a moment of stunned silence. Then Seaton turned to the nearest camera man, and asked hopefully, "Did you pan with him?"

With Harry and Mary in Rome

1973

On Wednesday, January 3rd, some 3M executives actually inveigled Bing into joining them in a business meeting at Carmel, but by Friday the 5th, he was off with Harry to the Marysville Duck Club.

Deeply involved in sundry nefarious schemes of my own, I had refused to accompany them. The Director of ACT and I had an appointment with Monseigneur Rowe, to request his permission to use the impressive new San Francisco Cathedral as the stage for a novel cycle of passion plays.

I was to represent Mary Magdalene. The way I was feeling at the moment, it would be typecasting.

I phoned Aunt Phyllis DeYoung Tucker, doyenne of San Francisco society, to ask how to approach the Monseigneur, and was informed that it made no difference. No matter what arguments I advanced, his answer would be *no*.

When I summoned up the temerity to ask *why*, I learned that he would be disinclined to introduce street riffraff, in the form of actors, into his lovely new church. I felt that my persuasive powers could deal with this, so I confronted the cleric, and sure enough was rewarded with an immediate and unambiguous *no*.

I did obtain a bit part in the ACT production of *Cyrano de Bergerac,* and I was still at it on Monday, January 22, when Bing left for Pebble Beach.

On Wednesday, January 24th, the 3M people flew me down there, but I was able to remain only through Friday afternoon, because I had a performance of Cyrano that night, in a role so

Hunting quail in Texas

Still puffing on the old pipe

small that Bing suggested sardonically, "Why don't you just phone it in?"

Thus it was that I missed all the excitement of the sudden-death playoff, which Jack Nicklaus won from Ray Floyd and Orville Moody by holing a twelve-foot birdie putt.

It was Jack's third Crosby crown, and his third straight win at Pebble Beach in thirteen months, a string which included the 1972 U. S. Open. His triumph came only because "the Ole Sarge," Orville Moody, had squandered a five-stroke lead in the blustery winds of the final day at Pebble Beach.

Meanwhile developer Bill Satterfield had staged some fairway heroics of his own to win the Maurie Luxford trophy for the amateur who helped his pro the most, and to earn the Pro-Am trophy for himself and Lanny Wadkins.

With the tournament behind him, Bing left for Texas with Phil Harris to look for quail. Having found them, he returned home to discover me in the hospital with our son Harry, who had all the signs of a hot appendix.

The white counts showed that the virus had subsided, so there was no surgery; but Bing was gratified to find me maternally hovering. He much preferred domesticity to my wasting time in what he termed the bush leagues at ACT.

On Friday, February 16h, Bing took the children skiing, and then to visit at a friend's plantation in the East. Meanwhile I sought a shot of penicillin to relieve nagging flu symptoms.

I finished rehearsal at about three, and stopped by Dr. Hanfling's office on the way home. His nurse administered the injection, and there was an immediate buzzing in my ears, while black fingers converged over my eyes. As I collapsed into darkness, a voice from my nurse's training kept repeating *anaphylactic shock.*

Through the noise of a million bees, I could hear Dr. Hanfling's voice calling for adrenalin. There was a jab, and I anticipated an instantaneous recovery.

It didn't come. In fact, things grew worse. Another tiny jab, and I was gone completely.

I recovered consciousness just as I was being dragged to the back room, where there was provision for an IV, a shock to the heart, or a tracheotomy. The threat of such extreme measures seemed to revive me. The adrenalin and Benadryl finally worked, and I returned to the land of the living.

I spent the rest of the afternoon in EEGs and EKGs. Then the nurse drove me home. She was preparing me a cup of tea, when Bing sauntered into the breakfast room, and asked if he might join us. Extenuated, I just sat, unable to reply.

Bing focused on my face, and was startled at my wan visage. "What's the matter?" he asked. "You're looking as white as a sheet."

I found my voice: "This is nothing. If you think I'm pale, you should have seen my doctor an hour or so ago."

Assuming that I was essaying a joke, Bing smiled, and started to reply in kind, when the nurse snapped unceremoniously, "Kathryn has just had an anaphylactic shock, which was very nearly fatal.

Watch her closely tonight and tomorrow. If there's any problem at all, call Dr. Hanfling immediately, and rush her to the emergency room."

With his hands shaking, Bing tried to light his pipe. "That may be what caused the whole problem," my care-

Where all doglegs curve to the right   Christmas in March at Sun Valley

At Sehoy plantation with Margaret McLean

taker continued. "Our tests show that Mrs. Crosby is extremely allergic to tobacco."

With a gulp, Bing dropped his pipe, never to light it in my presence again. When the nurse left, he tried to distract me with tales of his junket back East, where he and our sons had visited Malcolm and Margaret McLean's Sehoy plantation in Alabama.

"As you know, Malcolm has a booming banana ball. Typically, instead of taking lessons to cure it, he has built his own golf course to accommodate it.

"All doglegs curve to the right. The boys learned to fade their shots, and had a grand time."

Bing put his arm around me, and guided me upstairs. Always cold, I slid into a bunny suit and tennis socks, and he rubbed my back. Some experiences seem worth risking death for.

Throughout the next four days, Bing watched over my every move. When he was certain that I would live, he left for Vera Cruz, while I considered feigning another crisis.

We'd experienced difficulties in finding real snow for our Christmas shows when we taped them in the fall, so Bing decided to take advantage of the abundance of it to be found in Sun Valley in March. We arrived there on the 15th.

My versatile confidante, Bridget Brennan, managed a condominium in which I lazed around, while Bing and the children gamboled about in the snow with Connie Stevens, Michael Landon, and John Byner.

After the program was safely stored away, the children were allowed time off for good behavior.

They opted to stay with their father, skating and skiing, while their spoilsport of a mother flew home to Hillsborough.

Upon our arrival, Bridget requested shyly that I apply my nurse's training to an examination of her stomach.

Bridget was a five-foot, hundred-pound bundle of energy, who had been with us for 11 years, caring for all three children, and singlehandedly rearing Nathaniel. She had always dressed in loose blouses, and I had noticed no recent change.

Now she raised a sort of smock, to reveal a hideously-protruding abdomen. Even with my unpracticed hands, I could feel a swollen liver and a severely distended spleen. I phoned her doctor, and scheduled a biopsy for the following morning.

I drove Bridget to the hospital, and sat with her while we awaited the results. As I had feared, the diagnosis was cancer, which had metastasized to a point where the primary site couldn't be determined. Not that it mattered at the stage which the tumors had now reached.

I had to leave Bridget for a performance in town that evening, but I returned to her bedside at midnight. "Mrs. Crosby," she murmured, "I don't like being alone in the hospital."

I stayed the night, obtained her release in the morning, and drove her home. At least my training had taught me to recognize a hopeless case when I saw one. There was no point in prolonging clinical tortures.

We attended at her bedside, Bing to tell Irish stories, Harry to play his guitar, and Nathaniel, the most faithful of all, to watch TV and chat. Meanwhile I visited the best shops in San Franscisco to purchase the prettiest robes and nighties that I could find.

Bridget caring for Nathaniel

By April 1st, Bing could stand it no longer. He was unable to endure any form of sickness, least of all that of close friends. He left for Las Cruces via Guadalajara, resolved to remain there as long as necessary.

On April 6th, I wrote him concerning our daughter Mary: "She just isn't functioning optimally in the Hillsborough educational system.

Please explore the Mexico City convent schools, where she might at least gain an oral command of Spanish and French. It will offer a splendid opportunity for you to spend more time in your beloved Mexico."

Resentfully, Bing returned from Las Cruces on April 12th, vowing to take Mary to lunch and straighten her out. I'd have been more optimistic if there hadn't been so many meals with Gary, Dennis, and Phillip, all designed to reshape their lives.

Meanwhile Bridget was receiving injections of the pyrimidine antagonist 5-fluorouracil, but they made her very sick, and no change was detected in the tumor, so I requested that they be discontinued, and took to sleeping in the room with her.

On Monday, April 23rd, as our Easter vacation ended, Bing forced himself to sit all day with Bridget, and the two conversed as if she were in perfect health:

"Well, Bridie girl, I'm away to Las Cruces for some heavy fishing."

"Of course you are. I hope it will be better this year. Those Japanese long liners have been taking everything in the water. Each one hauls 250 tons a week to the mother ship to be ground into sausage meat."

"I guess we can't blame them for striving to satisfy their hunger, when all we want to do is play."

"The fishermen at José del Cabo did. They eliminated the lighthouse, built a bonfire on the beach, and guided the mother tanker in to nestle amid the rocks. That was what I call real people-to-people diplomacy."

By this time Bridget was laughing until the tears flowed. She continued, "Since the children won't be going to Mexico this spring, I won't care to either. You'll need to give Juana and Chevalo their instructions, and they'll have to keep the place up without the benefit of my direction."

"But you'll be there next year to see that they all toe the line."

"I surely will."

Bing kissed Bridget's forehead, she gave him a hug, and he left her forever. When Norma arrived five minutes later with a cold drink, the patient was sobbing uncontrollably.

"Now I know that I'm dying," she wailed. "Mr. Crosby was just here, joking, and talking about my future. That means I'm surely dead. He's Irish, and he can tell."

Bing left for Mexico on the 24th, and Bridget's liver failed on the 25th. We all sat with her until she finally breathed her last, at 2:40 AM on the 26th.

Bridget's rosary and funeral were held at Our Lady of Angels Church, where Harry and Nathaniel served as pallbearers. Her body was shipped back to Nenagh, where she was buried on the family farm in a grave that I arranged to have bordered and filled with the wild roses that she had loved so much.

Our boat captain
playing with a
tame seal

Another seal on the beach at Matancitas

Bing returned May 8th for trout fishing at our Rising River Ranch, and on the 24th we two flew back to Las Cruces, fighting tooth and nail over the scrabble board all the way.

Sans children, it was a time for embroidery, shelling, gardening, and long tranquil walks. It seemed too good to be true, and indeed so it proved, as Bing first invited Phil Harris to join us, and then insisted on visiting Fernando Albarrán in effervescent Guadalajara.

Fernando threw a welcoming dinner party for Bing, who insisted sternly, "At 7 PM we must sit down to eat. Not a moment later."

"But of course," Fernando grinned.

The guests started assembling at 8; we sat down to dinner at 9; the Guadalajara Symphony Orchestra arrived at 10; Fernando's brother brought his mariachis at 11; and the singing, dancing, and laughing continued until 5 AM.

As ever, Bing had been the life of the party, contributing a dozen boleros, and dancing with every señora in sight. So of course he complained of the late hour, and I solemnly agreed with him.

We flew to Matancitas, on the Pacific Coast. It is the Mexican version of Cannery Row, and the excellent air strip is for the tuna scouts.

These are small planes which radio back the position of large schools of fish, so that the tuna boats may converge with their nets. This was hardly Bing's type of fishing, but he did enjoy flying off with the spotters, and then feeding the local seals, who were practically tame, and like us enjoyed the abundance of marine nutrients.

On Sunday, June 3rd, we returned to Hillsborough. The bad news from civilization was that Mary, despite her supposedly astronomical IQ, was making a hash of her schoolwork. Her mentors seemed disposed to promote her, with the sole proviso that she resume her studies elsewhere. It was time for a change.

On July 17th, Mary and I left for Mexico City, where we visited Vallarta, a very chic school attended by the most fashionable young ladies, and then Regina, an academic powerhouse that my daughter inexplicably adopted as her own. Within a day, we had also uncovered an excellent ballet school.

From then on, Mary took over. Like Saint Paul, she was a fisher of men, and in this case her victim was my would-be architect's son, Javier Sordo.

She had always been a night bird, and as such she was wholly out of sync with Casa Crosby. The boys, Bing, and I were almost always in bed by ten. Her lights burned until 2 AM, and any attempt to modify her schedule was met with furious resistance.

Now she had discovered her country and her people. Fellow adolescents' birthday parties began at midnight, and seldom ended before dawn. She and Javier became an item, and never missed a dance.

Malena's sister Teri had daughters of her own. She would take Mary into her house for the year, and in exchange we would take her daughter Marité to live with us in Hillsborough.

For the time being, I flew Mary, Javier, and a group of their young friends up to our Rising River Ranch, where they spent their days horseback riding. They found that they had to saddle their own mounts, clean out the stalls, and in general do all the dirty work. My daughter was unimpressed. She decided that she much preferred the Latin way.

Can we be friends?

On Thursday, August 23rd, we flew back to Mexico, where Mary passed her entrance exam for the ballet with flying colors. With typical machismo, the Mexican authorities had demanded that Bing authorize his wholly-owned wife and daughter to leave the country.

I have the permit in hand as I write. It reads as follows: "I, Harry L. Crosby Jr., head of household, herewith grant limited permission to my wife, Kathryn Crosby, and to my daughter, Mary Crosby, to leave the United States and enter Mexico for recreational, social, and educational purposes. Notarized August 21, 1973."

The deed was done. I bequeathed my only daughter to the mercies of Mexico, and took Marité home with me.

On September 7th, Bing departed for Africa. I had begged off on the shaky grounds that the whole continent continued to terrify me.

On September 28th, Bing wrote from his camp at Isiolo that he was enjoying watching and photographing lions and elephants:

"I could have spit on Simba many times, but he simply regarded me with such regal disdain that the exchange could easily have gone the other way. I'm off to Tanzania now to perform on the new American Sportsman show, provisionally yclept *The Life of the Cheetah.*"

Bing returned on October 12th to help me entertain Lord Egremont's daughter Carlyn, who was now the very image of her beautiful Irish mother. He could stay only nine days, because Phil Harris had arrived to lure him off to Canada, in pursuit of the sharp-tailed grouse.

On November 9th, Bing arrived home via Los Angeles, Alabama, and North Carolina. The following day, Mary joined us from Mexico, and her father was delighted to watch her jabbering away in Spanish with Marité.

On Monday, November 12th, a forest of orange trees arrived, and I filled our garden with them for the annual Minute Maid commercial.

But then San Francisco's ugly winter weather took over, preventing us from filming for two more days. We finally finished to our satisfaction on Wednesday, and Mary had to depart immediately for her school in far-off Mexico City.

On November 22, Bob Hope's daughter Nora gave birth to a baby girl. He and Dolores flew north to join us for Thanksgiving dinner.

Bing and Bob were at their best, trading quips and practical jokes. I found myself caught up in a mad movie, which might well have been entitled *The Road To Hillsborough.*

I became the object of one of their more elaborate pranks. For most of his career, Bob had been planning his dream house, versions of which he had shown to Bing at every opportunity.

He had brought a scale model with him, which my husband solemnly presented to me as the 30,000 square foot mega-residence into which he intended to move me.

Even after I'd finally penetrated the deception, Bing pointed out that an adjacent mountaintop in Palm Springs was still available, and suggested that we start looking at designs for a mansion worthy of the site. He himself had always been so crazy about huge houses that I hesitated to doubt him.

The Crosby and Grandstaff clans arrived on December 22nd. On the next day, I started my enormous pot au feu,

Just before the discovery of the tumor

throwing in all the geese and ducks that Bing had contributed to our freezer. We had 33 relatives for Christmas dinner.

It was a glorious holiday season, seemingly too good to last. Sure enough, Bing woke me with his coughing on the night of the 28th, and by the morning of the 29th I obviously had a sick husband on my hands.

Assuming my Nurse Jane Fuzzy Wuzzy role, I attacked immediately:

"Do you have chest pain?"

"Some."

"Any other discomfort?"

"In my neck and shoulders."

"Breathe deeply."

Bing did, and erupted into a fit of coughing. "Is this torment really necessary?" he inquired glumly.

"Yes. Now breathe rapidly and shallowly."

"That's all I've been doing for the last day or so."

"Fine, you have pleurisy. I'll drive you to Dr. Hanfling's office."

Fortunately for his health and safety, the good doctor agreed with my diagnosis. I took Bing home, administered various analgesics, wrapped his chest in elastic bandages, and made him cough against a pillow which I held against him. All the while, the ungrateful wretch insisted that he much preferred the pleurisy.

Sleeping by his side, or trying to, I noticed in the early hours of December 31st that Bing was having great difficulty breathing. By breakfast time, he was coughing up blood.

I regarded him narrowly, said, "I'll get you a cup of tea," strode into the pantry, closed the door, and streaked off to his den to phone Dr. Hanfling.

"Bing's coughing up blood," I related. "He's breathless, and he looks feverish, with shiny eyes, pink nail beds, and cracked lips, though he hasn't been outdoors in days."

"He needs to come to the hospital immediately. Shall I send you an ambulance?"

"No, let's not waste the time. I'll bring him to you right now."

I grabbed a robe, pajamas, and Bing, whom I steered down the hall with my arm around his back, just as he had so often helped me. He seemed strangely relaxed and smiling on the way to the hospital, and I wondered whether he was delirious.

I spent all day there with him, while he underwent a series of X-rays. It was unnerving to see the man who had always been so wholly in command of his world and mine, lying on a gurney, in one of those hideous short night-gowns, and freezing, because of course the doctors and nurses always set the temperature to suit themselves, and they continually move about fast enough to remain reasonably comfortable in an Alaskan winter.

I found my ailing husband a blanket, and stood by helplessly, trying to stifle a presentiment that I was participating in a rehearsal of worse things to come.

I spent that protracted last night of the year at Bing's bedside. It was not my happiest New Years Eve.

Aging rapidly during a testing time

1974

New Years Day passed in a welter of demeaning tests. By the end of it, Bing's physicians still had no notion of what ailed him, and he himself seemed fully determined to die, rather than continue with such a sorry life.

Nonetheless, he insisted that Mary, Nathaniel and I attend the opening parties for his annual golf tournament, and try to keep his friends from becoming too upset.

This was necessary because Bing had never missed a day in the 33 preceding Crosby Pro-Ams, and we had no idea of how the officials, players, and public would react to his absence.

On January 2nd, Mary and I held the fort as best we could at Pebble Beach. We then left Nathaniel to serve as our source of news, and returned to Bing's bedside.

On the 4th, Mary was scheduled to leave for her school in Mexico. She refused to abandon her father until Bing finally ordered her to go, and she departed in tears to board her plane.

The newspapers got hold of the story, and thousands of letters poured in. Bing dictated his reply in terms of a form letter:

"With all these encouraging wishes and prayers, I just have to get well. Many thanks, Bing Crosby."

But he still wasn't improving, and his physicians remained baffled. They had tested for everything from tuberculosis to leprosy, without a trace of a positive result.

Of course there was always the lurking fear of cancer, but no one could conceive of a tumor's progressing so rapidly. On the afternoon of the 5th, I insisted that I be granted a look at the latest X-rays. They revealed startling growth in a neoplasm that was about to impinge on the esophagus.

Interviewing Johnny Miller for the Kathryn Crosby Show

That night, Dr. Hanfling came to my house. "I understand that you have examined Bing's X-rays," he began.

"Yes, there's been an enormous change in the six days that he's spent in the hospital. What was just a shadow on the plate is now a life-threatening tumor. Does any sort of pulmonary cancer grow that fast?"

"Not in my experience."

"If there's a chance that its an infection, shouldn't we start the antibiotics again?"

"Yes. We interrupted them for diagnostic purposes. I'll ask that they be reinstated immediately."

Meanwhile bulletins were flying back and forth, to and from Pebble Beach. Thousands of golf fans seemed as interested in Bing's health as in the tournament. Meanwhile he was more concerned with their situation than with his own survival.

Never had the tournament needed him more. For the first and last time, it had been scheduled for New Year's week. Historically it had rained only four times on January 3rd in the last twenty years.

In the event, statistics were of no avail. Usually held somewhere between the middle of January and the beginning of February, The Crosby was famous for its foul weather, but this time the roof fell in. Play was washed out on Thursday, the opening day, and it was suspended on Saturday, to allow the hail to melt off the fairways.

Bing had always found it easy to make decisions. Never had his leadership been more in demand, as officials dithered while the rain persisted for five days, reducing the 72-hole event to 54 holes, all played under the most trying conditions.

While Nathaniel furnished his father with hourly bulletins from the fairways, Johnny Miller proved to be a great mudder. His final 208 was four strokes ahead of Grier Jones, and he teamed up with his friend, Locke De Bretteville, to win the Pro-Am Division.

Throughout the entire ordeal, the Crosby fans were incredibly faithful, and Bing's intense involvement was literally keeping him alive. From outside his hospital room, I could hear him roaring with laughter at the news that the heavy snows, blocking highway 17 at Santa Cruz, were preventing the arrival of both fans and reporters.

Meanwhile Bing had survived an embolus that had originated in his left leg, and a team of doctors had settled for a tentative diagnosis of smoker's cancer, a conclusion which I had resolutely refused to accept.

Unable to make any major contributions, I had been giving Bing daily bed baths. Now I discovered a tub down the hall, and escorted him to it, noting the difficulty that he was experiencing in traversing the forty yards of corridor. His health had deteriorated at a phenomenal rate during the last weeks.

It was a new feeling to be able to care for Bing, who had always been as independent as a mountain cat, but he said no word about the diagnosis, which was essentially a death sentence.

In spite of express orders to the contrary, thirteen-year-old Mary returned from Mexico on the 12th, to accompany her father as he endured a bronchoscopy. The mercurial growth of the tumor was unchecked. Only an immediate surgical intervention offered any hope of saving the patient's life.

On Sunday, January 13th, the three children and I said our goodbyes,

Meeting Joe E. Lewis

and Bing was wheeled into the operating room, smiling cheerfully.

The children were impressed with their father's courage, but I remained dubious. Were the burdens of his life really so grave that he could abandon them this lightly? And if so, where did that leave me?

I had asked to assist, but Bing had forbidden it. We all waited outside for four hours, and received the following report in the middle of the afternoon:

"The upper lobe of the left lung was successfully removed, and a grapefruit-sized neoplasm was pealed away from the pleura. If it had burst, it might well have drowned the patient. We are awaiting a report from pathology."

The lab's diagnosis was a surprise. The tumor had resulted from a fungus infection, which Bing might well have brought back from Africa. In his case, the invasion site had been the lungs, and he would have died within days if he had received only the prescribed treatment with sulfadiazine.

Worldwide, only 77 cases similar to Bing's had been reported. Patients treated with antibiotics plus surgery had a reasonably good prognosis. The neoplasm seldom returned.

On Sunday, January 27th, I drove Bing home to Hillsborough, and he began a long, slow recuperation. It's a terrible thing that I'm about to admit, but there is small evidence of a conscience in my family, and whatever minuscule portion I inherited, I strangled while yet in my crib, like the infant Hercules with the serpents.

So here is the honest truth: I now had my man where I wanted him. He could no longer escape me on hunting, fishing, and golfing expeditions. At long last, he was really all mine.

I took full advantage of my opportunity by showering Bing with attentions. I bathed him, and toweled him dry. I shaved him, and cut his nails. I dressed and undressed him, and I made him confess that he liked it. He really was in a weakened condition.

Prior to Bing's illness, I had been in rehearsal for *Broadway*, a play which concerned a speakeasy of the 1930s, and Pearl, a sleazy little gun moll who is also a very bad tap dancer. Under it all, I had a heart of gold, but I was determined to avenge the murder of my hoodlum lover.

In the course of my research for the role, I'd read every book I could lay my hands on about the '30s, including Joe E. Lewis's biography. Sitting in the library with Bing, I remarked, "It now seems amazing that thugs could simply drop by and cut a man's throat, and even more incredible that he lived. You show-business types must have been rather exposed."

Bing thought that one over, and apparently concluded that I was finally ready to emerge from the cotton fields. He replied, "I watched Joe work the night before they cut him up. I was staying at the Commonwealth; he was at the Rienzi, across the street.

Those were wild times when the over-burdened police didn't seem to care about minor offenses. To control mean drunks, almost any bartender had recourse to the Mickey Finn."

"Did anything frightening ever happen to you?"

"Not like what hit Joe, but one night a very attractive young man, who looked like a choirboy, or at worst a halfback from Yale, brought an armload of flowers backstage. He had curly hair and pronounced dimples, and he

Back at work

introduced himself as Jack McGurn. 'I really liked your show tonight,' he remarked.

'Thank you. We had an appreciative house. It's always easy to sing for a group like that.'

'I understand that you're something of a golfer.'

'Not really, but I'm usually ready for a game.'

'I'd like to invite you to play with me tomorrow.'

'What time?'

'My boys will pick you up at 7.'

That got my attention, but by this time I seemed to be committed. I wasn't eager to rise at 7, but I was even less inclined to thwart my new friend's wishes.

Sure enough, a couple of hoods were at my door at the crack of dawn. They drove me to a municipal course on the outskirts of town.

We teed off at 8:30, and played 18 holes, closely followed by the same two thugs, who were actually carrying violin cases under their arms.

I was so busy peering behind trees for potential ambushes that Jack won both nines. With the best will in the world, I paid off our five-dollar bet."

"Jack McGurn," I mused. "Didn't he have something to do with the St. Valentine's Day Massacre?"

"Among others, but that was his most famous job. He put together the team while Al Capone was in Florida, establishing an alibi.

McGurn planned carefully. He chose Fred 'Killer' Burke as the leader, and James Ray as his assistant. He added three more of his friends, and two members of Detroit's Purple Gang.

Then he had a bootlegger lure Moran's men to the garage where they were to be gunned down.

Like Capone, McGurn wanted to be far from the scene of the crime, so he took his girl friend to a hotel, and made sure that they were seen by a number of witnesses. He afterwards married her, so that she couldn't change her mind, and testify against her husband.

He seemed amazed that a simple business matter could have brought him such notoriety. He expressed his consternation during several subsequent golf matches, and he even introduced me to Louise Rolfe, 'the blonde alibi,' who had assured the police that he couldn't have participated in the slaughter, because he had spent the entire morning in bed with her."

"What eventually happened to your dear friend Jack?"

"About seven years later, an associate mowed him down in a bowling alley. We all have our little weaknesses, and sports were evidently his."

I solemnly considered this instance of human frailty, and then ventured forth on a new tack: "You worked late nights in those days. How did an insomniac like you ever get to sleep?"

"I hiked. After my show, while the Rhythm Boys were out on the town, I'd walk all over whatever city we were playing in. I'd go in one direction until I'd used up my excess energy, and then turn back.

By the time I reached my hotel, I was usually exhausted, and I'd come to know part of a metropolis. I could still draw you a map of midtown New York, Chicago, or Philadelphia, as they were in the early thirties."

At least he no longer smoked around me.

"Well, you're back into hiking now. We'll increase the number and length of our walks each day."

We started in the driveway in front of the house, skipping the slight decline that led to the main gate, and gradually working up to a mile a day. Evenings we spent long hours in front of the fireplace, and I continued to play nurse.

I reveled in every minute of it. At last I had a husband who was just weak enough not to be able to get away. For a bachelor-type fellow, who had never felt comfortable with girls, Bing was at his most accessible.

He even confessed to lingering doubts as to the complete removal of the tumor, admitting that he continued to feel twinges from it.

"That's where the nerves were cut, after the tumor had impinged on them."

"So the doctor said. How do you know that they got it all?"

"I visited the pathology lab. Your lung was pink, which means that it was sterile, as a result of all the antibiotics that they'd pumped into you. That huge tumor was still in one piece, perfectly encapsulated."

"But I still hurt."

"I know, darling, but remember that they removed a rib, and left you with a bias-cut incision."

"I seem to remember a nurse's saying the same thing about my kidney scars. Would you mind telling me what it means?"

"As I understand it, the best way to cut is in the direction of the muscle growth. Next best is at a ninety degree angle. Diagonally across is the worst.

It leaves you maximally weakened, and with the greatest possible number of cut nerves, just reawakening to express their displeasure at what's been done to them. Nevertheless, they will all heal. It will just take a bit longer.

"So my nurse guarantees that I'm really over the hump?"

"Absolutely."

"And she'd lie only when it suited her sinister purpose?"

"Right again."

"That certainly is reassuring."

I kept to myself the fact that, in the unlikely event of a recurrence, Nocardia can appear in the brain, liver, or pancreas. For the time being, my patient had enough to contend with.

Bing was having trouble swallowing the sulfadiazine tablets, designed to protect him from just such a relapse. I obtained a pestle and mortar to grind them up for him.

I also consulted regularly with Dr. McLaughlin, our renowned pulmonary expert. "May I assume that you've advised Bing to give up all smoking?" I inquired.

My advisor favored me with a helpless look. "How can I conscientiously do that? He knows perfectly well that I'm a lifelong chain smoker, without a prayer of kicking the habit."

It was the old story of "Do as I say, not as I do."

Lacking an alternative, I personally undertook to eliminate my husband's reliance on the weed by scaring the living daylights out of him.

"All my friends smoke," he objected. "They won't accept my ill health as an excuse, and I'd be ashamed to advance it anyway."

"I'll be the fall guy. Tell your buddies that you're tired of carrying a pipe and all its ancillary equipment around, and that I've forbidden you to spill any more tobacco on my floors."

"Surely I wouldn't be guilty of that."

Mary and Juana serve liquid ice cream.

With the Hearsts and Marité

"Just daily. While you're about it, you may also relate that I won't have you falling asleep with a cigar in your mouth after dinner."

"Have I done that?"

"Just nightly."

"At least I'll no longer have to worry about continuously fiddling with pipe cleaners, or about burning more holes in my shirts and trousers."

"Exactly."

I never did learn which of my arguments had proved conclusive, but for whatever reason, Bing never smoked either pipe or cigars again.

The pain continued, preventing sleep, and I had to inject Novocain along the incision line to relieve the stress on the awakening nerves.

I had worked not wisely but well. By April, Bing was surprisingly mobile. He left on the 5th, for his first trip since the January 13th lung surgery.

With Mary and Nathaniel, he spent Easter vacation in Las Cruces, while I stayed behind to perform in three on-going plays in San Francisco.

In spite of all my precautions, it seemed that I had lost him again. I just might have to come up with some other affliction.

Mary's heartthrob, Javier Sordo, visited in Las Cruces for a week, and then asked Bing to plead with his father for an extension of the vacation.

Our crooner was shocked when Juan replied simply, "Tell my son to come home."

Bing called me on our ship-to-shore radio to complain of such unreasonable treatment: "Juan has managed to make both his son and our daughter perfectly miserable," he concluded. "How can any father be so insensitive to his child's needs?"

"Daddies do complicate matters. Maybe Juan has a bad lung. We'll have to check."

This was a low blow, but it did make Bing reflect on the times when he had played the autocratic father. He sighed, and decided to forgive Juan.

I include the following excerpts from Bing's diary of the trip: "From San Francisco, I flew in the Falcon jet to La Paz, and thence by DC-3 to Las Cruces. I spent 14 days there in superb weather.

Each morning, I walked the three-mile round trip to the club, and played tennis while I was there. The whole Hearst family, minus the kidnapped Patty of course, is visiting Desi Arnaz.

It's their first respite since the event, and they've been gradually recuperating in spite of reporters and an attendant FBI agent, who turns out to be a decent sort.

He needed to keep up on the latest news, so I tuned in on the Armed Forces Network which, as it transpired, was just describing Patty's participation in the Hibernia Bank holdup.

That was the end of the Hearsts' vacation. I got onto the ship-to-shore phone, and arranged their immediate transportation back to Hillsborough. Of course the Hibernia Bank is owned by good friends of the family, an ironical twist which the news hounds have fortunately yet to uncover.

Harry has 25 scorpions in a mason jar, which he plans to transport back to school for a biology paper. They may occasion certain difficulties with customs upon our return.

He has also been busy with his guitar. Last night a guest at the hotel gave him $120 for playing a number upon request.

Easter in Las Cruces

The new house in San Ysidro

I've made him donate it to the nearest charitable fund. I won't have anyone running around here complaining that the eldest Crosby kid clipped him. One strolling player in the family is quite enough."

Ouch! Little did Bing know what dire plots were brewing in his minor thespian's mind. He returned to Hillsborough on the 19th, rested for 10 days, and departed for Guadalajara on May 1st.

His health continued to improve. A trifle fast for my taste, since he had recurred to his perennial theme of acquiring houses. I neglected to mention that he had been presented with one on the fairway at the *Bosques de San Ysidro* Country Club.

From it, he wrote as follows: "I like this house well enough, except for the severe traffic problems in the early morning and late afternoon, which can only worsen as development continues. I've been looking at some choice lots, and drawing plans for a more spacious and functional residence."

I shuddered, and hoped against hope that something would distract Bing's attention before I found myself in the position of having to furnish yet another Mexican home.

Apparently my prayers were answered, for I received his next communication from Las Cruces, and it mentioned only his continued furnishing of the house there that we already owned.

But I had relaxed too soon. On May 23rd a letter arrived, remarking cryptically that Bing had abandoned all thought of purchasing the house near the Albarráns, since they insisted on much too fast a social whirl, in which he was hard put not to participate.

He had, however, been looking at properties in Mazatlán and in Manzanillo, the coastal town where Patino, the Bolivian tin king, had constructed the fairy-tale development that he'd christened *Las Hadas*.

Bing was scheduled to arrive home on the 15th of June. At that time, it seemed that my only hope would be to break both his legs. I considered various approaches to the operation.

Meanwhile, back at the ranch, I was busily concluding certain small matters of my own. On May 31st I had contracted with San Francisco's KPIX for a new half-hour, five-day-a-week, *Kathryn Crosby Show,* to which I was to dedicate much of my next three years. Sure enough, Bing's strolling player was at it again.

When he returned in mid-June, I insisted on a full complement of X-rays and blood tests. The results were perfect.

Bing celebrated by scheduling an immediate trip to the new house in Guadalajara, but this time I was ready for him.

I had finished all my plays, and had postponed the advent of my TV show. When Bing left on June 22nd, he had not only two sons but a smiling wife amid his impedimenta.

I received my first surprise when I arrived at our new golf-course home at San Ysidro. The little Spanish-colonial hacienda had already been completely decorated.

Ana Cecilia Albarrán had played my role to perfection, something that I'd never yet been accused of doing. She had added hand-woven curtains to hand-carved headboards, achieving a folksy effect that even I found rather endearing.

Recording a *Hollywood Palace*

Bing himself had not been idle. He had ordered a sofa, rugs, armchairs, a dining-room table, and a set of porch furniture that permitted us to breakfast in full view of the first nine. It remained only for me to hie myself off to Tlaquepaque, in search of a brace of lamps. Then I settled down to enjoy the greenery, so different from the desert of Las Cruces.

I suggested that our son Harry, who hadn't been applying himself in school of late, might benefit from a year or two with the Jesuits at the *Instituto de Ciencias*.

Bing loved the idea. It took him ten minutes to get Harry fully matriculated, while I reflected morosely on the weeks of effort that it had cost me to perform the same feat for his sister.

But it all came to naught, for it transpired that our fifteen-year-old son would have to live with the Albarráns in the midst of a hectic social whirl.

So, on second thought, Bing reluctantly undid his arrangements in Mexico, and enrolled our first-born in Bellermine, a Santa Clara prep school that his first four boys had attended, in hopes that the lad might be subjected to the same salutary Jesuit discipline that he would have encountered in Guadalajara.

Meanwhile Bing and Harry remained in Mexico, while I returned with Nathaniel to Hillsborough on July 6th. I would enroll him in sports camp, and Mary in summer school.

Bing had to return to Los Angeles on July 26th for various rehearsals. He brought Harry back with him, and I drove the boy down to Santa Clara to finalize his enrollment.

He would spend his last two high-school years driving well over 100 miles a day, to and from classes, with six of his friends from our area.

He would earn his secondary diploma, which was doubtless good, but forget his guitar and his golf, which was definitely bad.

On August 2nd, Bing traveled to Los Angeles to record a *Hollywood Palace* with Bob Hope and Pearl Bailey.

He returned on the 3rd, first to find his wife missing, and then to locate her by turning on his TV set. I had indeed launched *The Kathryn Crosby Show*.

In a reversion to my nursing-school days, I woke Bing every morning at five as I scurried off to tape the day's performance. On the other hand, I no longer troubled him evenings with my relentless energy.

After dinner, there was no need to ask how he might amuse his driven spouse. Exhausted, she just sat on the library sofa, panted softly, and watched TV through glazed eyes.

Bing adopted the role of critic. "Darling, if you say *wonderful* one more time, your entire audience is going to barf with me."

"Agreed."

"While you're about it, you might also delete *splendid* and *marvelous* from your vocabulary.'

"Roger."

"And don't wrinkle your forehead so much. We know that you're doing your best to simulate profound thought. Just don't remind us of it so often."

"Sorry."

Ann Miller, my zingy young producer, catered to Bing, and flirted with him shamelessly. As a consequence, my recording schedule enjoyed considerable flexibility.

After I got the hang of it, I'd often tape three shows a day, until I had

He'd have preferred to travel by bicycle.

accumulated sufficient inventory to permit me to accompany my husband on his frequent excursions.

On November 3rd, we were off to Los Angeles to tape The Crosby Christmas Show. Once there, I had a fiendishly clever inspiration:

Our presentation had an abundance of talent, including Karen Valentine, Mac Davis, Randy McDougall, Nanette Fabray, Dr. Lee Salk, Joe Wambaugh of *Blue Knight* fame, and director Bob Finkel. It also boasted a staff of superb technicians.

Between setups, all these wonderful people had nothing at all to do. I proposed to fill this gap by taping interviews for my own show, thus securing contributions from celebrities who, in the normal run of things, would never have dreamed of dignifying my modest production with their presence.

It worked like a charm. I decided that I was wasted on show business. Indeed, I felt almost devious enough to have succeeded in politics or the law.

On November 25th, the entire family flew to a ranch some 70 miles south of San Francisco, to shoot our Minute Maid commercial amid genuine orange groves, using time photography to portray the process by which the fruit achieved juicy maturity.

The script called for Bing to fly above the trees in a tiny plane, while another of like size flew wingtip to wingtip with it.

The doors were removed from both planes. Bing sat petrified in the cockpit of one, while a photographer hung by a strap from the other.

The latter's instructions were simplicity itself. Addressing a participant always terrified of flight, and now winging his way just inches above a forest of trees, the cheery camera man shouted, "Action, Mr. Crosby. Just look nice and cool!"

That evening, I had to lure Bing into the plane for our return flight to Hillsborough, and to support him on his exit. He was moaning that he would never leave the ground again, no matter what the circumstances.

The Minute Maid executives had flown back with us, and Bing next revealed his own devious nature, as they joined him in a plot against his resident schemer.

It chanced that November 25th was not only the date of our annual commercial, but also my very own birthday, a circumstance which had slipped my mind in the midst of all the surrounding tumult.

Our butler, Alan Fisher, warned me to remain upstairs, because plumbers were repairing a series of fixtures. "You might hear a bit of noise," he added. "Pay no attention to it."

When I finally descended the stairs, a scowling Bing awaited me. "Take a look at the mess those repairman have made in our living room," he growled. "The whole thing will have to be refinished tomorrow."

He swung open the door, and there were 60 people awaiting my arrival. Hermione Gingold started the singing with *Second Hand Rose,* and Beverly Sills, who normally refused to participate in popular songs, hummed along until Bing chimed in, and then soared far above us all. It was my most elaborate birthday party of all time.

On Saturday, December 21st, Bing flew his wife and family down to Las Cruces for Christmas. Unable to carry presents or decorations, I bundled up all the Christmas cards we'd received,

Ho! Ho! Ho! Merry Christmas

and used plenty of ribbon and scotch tape to attach them to the laurels which surrounded the house.

Unfortunately my display attracted the only rain of the year, which left it in rather grim repair. The downpour also brought with it an unusual cold spell, for which we were totally unprepared.

Bing gathered dry wood, and I heaped the fireplace with it. Just in time, for the generator at the hotel failed, depriving us first of our electric lights, then of our hot water, and finally of the cold water too, since it supplied the power for the pumps.

Resourcefully, I wrapped the turkey in foil, placed it breast-up in the roaster, and laid the pan on the coals. The white meat emerged marginally edible, but the bottom half of the bird was reduced to charcoal. Somehow I'd neglected to set the fireplace on *simmer*.

With the warmth of the burning wood, and the light of propane lanterns, we carried on. We worked a jigsaw puzzle, and took turns reading *Great Expectations* aloud.

We welcomed the daylight with long walks along the beach. Bing seemed delighted to have recovered sufficiently to keep pace, once again, with his consort and brood, and we were equally grateful to have him still with us for yet another Crosby Christmas.

At Cypress Point

1975

On January 5th, the family flew from Las Cruces to San Francisco. Waiting for Bing were several thousand letters, one of them from Monaco:

"Dear Bing, we enjoyed the family photo on your Christmas card. Our children are certainly growing up. In a couple of weeks, Carolyn will be 18. She is studying political science in Paris, where I am spending much of my time with her.

I'll be at our apartment there, 32 Avenue Foche, 553-41-12, the first week in February, and I'll return home on the 8th.

Right here in Monaco, we have one of the best ballet teachers in Europe, Marika Beso Brasova.

Nuryev and many other top dancers study with her.

She's a delightful person and a good friend. I can recommend her to you without reservation.

Of course there is also Rozelle Hightower in Cannes. She is highly competent, and has a deservedly successful school there. It would, however, be easier for me to find a responsible French-speaking family for your Mary to live with right here in Monaco.

Please give me a call when you are next in Europe, and we can discuss the matter at length. Much love, Grace."

Evidently Bing had blushed to inform me that he had been furthering our daughter's educational plans via the old-girl-friend network, but by the same token he was unaware that Mary had refused to spend the next academic year living with friends of Dr. Sullivan in Paris.

To compensate for his absence from his tournament the preceding year, Bing left early for Pebble Beach. On Monday, January 20th, I received the following note:

George C. Scott

Jack Nicklaus

Glen Campbell

Vic Damone

Interviewing for The Kathryn Crosby Show

"Kathryn, I need your help. I've arranged for a private plane to pick you up at noon on Wednesday at Butler Aviation. Plan to spend all of Thursday at Cypress Point."

Not one to waste such an opportunity, I canceled the scheduled flight, and drove with my camera crew to Pebble Beach. On the very first day, I interviewed actor George C. Scott, couturier Oleg Cassini, golfer of golfers Jack Nicklaus, and singers Glen Campbell and Vic Damone, for my own *Kathryn Crosby Show*.

At last I had a real role at The Crosby, in addition, of course, to having a fire going and the tea hot, when Bing returned, weary and half-frozen, to Cypress Point.

The relationship proved to be symbiotic. It was as if Liza Doolittle had been transformed into a consort battleship. While Bing was furnishing his commentary in the tower, I was interviewing the contestants at the end of their round.

They actually felt flattered, so it was another way for Bing to thank them for their participation, and for me to learn the difference between a tee and a green. I found myself taking golf lessons from Jack Nicklaus and his peers, and glorying in every delicious minute of it.

When we were both free, I galleried with Bing, who was joying in his ability to walk the fairways once more. At last we were sharing in his magnificent enterprise. It had taken me only 18 years to uncover a niche that I could fill without causing embarrassment.

The first three days of the tournament were played under unusual conditions, namely bright sunlight. On Sunday, The Crosby reverted to its old tricks. Not that we had a snowstorm, but wild winds buffeted the players, and dried out the greens until they resembled concrete.

The scores skyrocketed. Johnny Pott, the 1968 Crosby winner, carded an 86. Orville Moody, former U.S. Open champion, handed in an 87.

I had been following Johnny Miller, reasoning that anyone who could win in the mud of the preceding year could probably triumph under any conditions.

This line of thought proved tantamount to the childhood one which leads a diminutive culprit to head for the nearest paved road, when running from farmers, enraged at his depredations in their orchards. True enough, he can make better time on the highway, but so alas can they.

The fastest runner this time proved to be forty-four-year-old Gene Littler. He won by four strokes over Hubert Green, who had actually shot a 69 on that last blustery day.

Littler was some 20 years older than most of his opponents, and recovering from cancer surgery. Needless to say, his was perhaps the most popular victory in the history of the tournament. The Pro-Am winners were Bruce Devlin and Jacky Lee, who carded an amazing 260 under the very difficult conditions.

On January 29th, Bing flew off to La Paz, Las Cruces, Los Planes, Matancitas, and Guadalajara, dogged by rotten weather all the way. I shan't delineate his aerial disasters, Terrified as he was of flying, they flattened him for a time, and almost finished me.

While my husband wrestled with the elements, I had fortunately elected to continue work on my television show. When Teddy Kennedy stopped off

With Senator Edward Kennedy

Columbo was written for Bing.

in San Francisco, he gave me an exclusive, and I must admit to a certain smug satisfaction when reporters from our nation's leading periodicals were forced to remain outside in the corridor, while the senator and I discussed family matters.

Without my even asking, he revealed to our audience that he had no intention of running in the forthcoming presidential election, a scoop that any one of the hard news boys would have cheerfully killed for.

Peter Falk appeared on the show to thank Bing and me for *Columbo*. In my case, his gratitude was misplaced, since I'd been unaware that the show had been written for Bing, and that the role had been offered to Falk only after my crooner had turned it down.

"Your raincoat's dirty enough to be Bing's," was all I could come up with.

"Yeah, that's what everybody says, but I still think he'd have done a better job of getting away with it. There are actually certain critics who still refer to Columbo as a slob. It's hardly worth performing for some people."

On February 16th, Bing was sufficiently recovered from his Mexican flights to head on to London for a recording session. From there, he wrote to inform me that he was presently working with a forty-two-man band in an excellent recording facility.

"They've furnished security, a Rolls, and chauffeurs," he continued. "You'd think that I'd arrived here to star in a major film.

I'm taking long walks daily, and feel fine, except for the lingering cough. A full course of tetracycline afforded no appreciable results, but an inhalant offers temporary relief. I'm sure I'd sing better without the malady, but the folks at the studio have persisted in being complimentary.

I'll be home around the end of the month, after a stopoff in New York to see a couple of shows."

How dare he visit The Great White Way without me? I was, however, delighted to hear that his recording was going well. He had been so afraid that his loss of half a lung would deprive him of his singing voice.

He arrived March 1st, right on schedule, having completed the album *That's What Life Is All About,* and he actually remained at home, commenting on my TV shows, until the 16th, when he departed for the Bing Crosby LPGA golf tournament in Guadalajara.

Bing met the girls at their plane, escorted them to a bull fight at which they were the guests of honor, and ministered to their needs, when most of them fell deathly ill at the sight of an arena full of gore.

He threw an all-night party for them, at which he sang and Harry played the guitar. He then phoned, over a crackling connection, to inform me in awed tones that the LPGA girls could easily outhit most men.

I tried to sound properly awestruck, while biting my tongue and gritting my teeth.

"When are you and my daughter coming down?" Bing finally bethought himself to inquire.

"We're going to check out the University of Texas over the weekend, so I suppose it will be late on Sunday. See you then."

"You'll have missed all the action. The tournament will end that day."

"Well, I'm certain that the women golfers won't miss me too much. I'll wager that they prefer to be with you."

Bing's LPGA golfers

"Do you really think so?"

"Mmmhmm."

I was really being too harsh on both Bing and his bevy of beauties. Up until this time, the LPGA tour had been a hand-to-mouth affair. The girls were in the same position that the men had occupied, when Bing rescued them by inventing the pro-am format.

In fact, the ladies were so short on money that many a talented golfer had been forced to abandon the tour in the interests of eating. All carried their clothes in the covers of their golf bags, and many picked up their only food at convenient grocery stores.

They were thrilled to be in the limelight with Bing, and ready to try any sort of promotional stunt to launch their careers.

At the bar across the street, several demonstrated their prowess on the piano, one played the guitar, and they all sang, doubtless elevating the Mexican taste for rock and soul to a new level.

Bing continued his panegyric as follows: "Many took advantage of San Ysidro's fine stable of horses, and Jane Blalock rode in the grand parade at one of the festivals at the Plaza de Toros.

The girls danced, they shopped for the incredible bargains in Guadalajara and in Tlaquepaque, and they certainly proved more decorative on the course than their male counterparts.

They were also remarkably good sports. Though playing head-to-head to scrape out a bare living, they seemed to realize that they were all in the same boat. They complimented each other constantly, and helped out whenever they could.

There was lots of good-natured kidding and horseplay. Two or three girls were dunked in the pool every evening, fully dressed, and they were constantly making dates with admirers under a friend's name, and delighting in the confusion that resulted.

But they can play golf. There isn't an unorthodox swing among them, and many of them scored par or better off the men's tees.

Sue Roberts, who won our initial event, was two under par for the entire 54-hole tournament. Twice she reached the green in two on the 570 yard 11th hole.

All in all, I have the same feeling that I had when I launched The Crosby, namely that of being in at the beginning of something big."

I arrived in Guadalajara with Mary on March 23rd, and spent an entire week there, feeding Bing from the markets, and encouraging him to get some rest, after all the excitement of the LPGA tournament.

I returned to Hillsborough on March 31st, and picked Bing and Harry up at the airport when they arrived on April 4th. For the first time, Bing played golf with me at Burlingame.

Predictably, he laughed a lot, but he also actually deigned to give me a few tips, before departing once again for Las Cruces.

He returned April 29th. I had taped enough *Kathryn Crosby Shows* to permit me to leave with him on May 3rd for the Kentucky Derby, where our friends, John and Dorothy Galbraith, had entered two horses.

I placed bets on both *Prince Thou Art* and *Sylvan Place,* and was furious when I lost, but our hosts weren't the least upset. They had too many years of experience to be discouraged by the results of a single race.

351

Vintage song and dance men

From Louisville, we flew back with them to Columbus, and thence to Darby Dan Farm, where I examined their many trophies, and watched the horses *breezing,* which is to say taking their morning constitutional around the track.

John's plane, *Little Current,* then flew us off to New York City, and thence back to San Francisco, where I interviewed Nanette Fabray, Donald Sutherland, Clint Eastwood, and F. Lee Bailey for my forthcoming TV shows.

Having been turned down flat on his plans to pack fifteen-year-old Mary off to Monaco, Bing decided to send her to the University of Texas. She was delighted, and left immediately.

Bing then recorded a beautiful Mexican album, *Bingo el Viejo,* in which I corrected some vestiges of gringo accent.

On June 19th, Bing, Harry, and Nathaniel left for Austin, Texas, "to check up on sister." They approved of her professors and her living situation, but wondered why she was running up accounts at clubs named *Somewhere* and *Nighthawk.*

A trifle disturbed myself, I nonetheless tried to reassure Bing by insisting, "Darling, that's just an integral part of a Texas girl's education."

"I see," Bing drawled, but he obviously remained unconvinced.

On June 30th, Bing and the two boys flew to England for a golf tour, stopping off for lessons from Claude Harmon at Winged Foot. When the famed pro tried to change Nathaniel's stance in the bunker, our cocky son replied, "Sorry, I always play my sand shots this way."

I received frequent letters that told me more than I cared to know about the pitch-and-run shots necessary to avoid bouncing over the hard English greens, and about the legendary pros with whom my contingent played.

I was perturbed to receive a phone call from Turnberry, informing me that Nathaniel was missing, only to be reassured by a subsequent message to the effect that he had been discovered practicing putting on the 18th green at midnight.

But it was Harry who achieved the initial acclaim, when his team tied for the lead, and was declared cowinner of the event—a big thrill for a boy in his first public effort.

There followed descriptions of the play on fabled courses, whose names figure prominently in the history of golf: Dalmahoy, Gleneagles, Muirfield, and finally St. Andrews, where Nathaniel shot a surprising first-round 75 on the Old Course.

Then it was off to watch a number of the same people against whom the Crosbys had just competed play in the British Open at Carnoustie.

Our group cheered Tom Watson's gallant win in a playoff against Jack Newton, and then departed for Royal Birkdale, where they golfed with David Marsh, former British champion and captain of the Walker Cup team.

Bing spent a week making an album with Fred Astaire, while Harry assisted in the control room, where he learned to read scores and pick takes.

Harry continued to work with Fred, while his father performed on a series of radio and TV shows, and he then joined Bing in a round of golf with Roger Wethered, doubtless the greatest British golfer of all time.

Bing and Nathaniel next traveled to Bremen for a pro-am in connection

Father and son harmonize.

with the German Open. Nathaniel carried his team to a second place finish, and was awarded a beautiful silver trophy from his father, who had been asked to present the prizes.

On July 27th, I flew to England to join my family. As I've mentioned previously in the case of our Minute-Maid motorhome, Bing had proposed that we tour the country in a camper. Evidently he had repressed his experiences with that monstrosity, because he still thought it a great idea.

As he'd put it originally, "I'll play golf every morning, and spend every afternoon at the races, while you and the children enjoy the camper. Doesn't that sound like fun?"

Just how does a semi-liberated female answer a question like that? Suffice it to say that I settled for staying in the best hotels, and for accompanying Bing to the races at Goodwood.

Dan Galbraith's horse, *Hail to the Pirates,* was running in the feature race, and I recouped my losses from the Kentucky Derby when he won by a neck. In the absence of the owner, Bing was asked to receive the trophy.

That night, we attended a barbecue with the popular young Prince of Wales. He chatted with us for about an hour, exuded charm, and seemed as unaware as we were of the stormy days that awaited him.

When we parted, Bing patted Charles on the shoulder, and wished him the best of luck. Suddenly struck by a premonition, the Prince replied, "Thanks very much. You know, I'm sure I'll need it."

Our children, at least, acted like loyal subjects, who were delighted to spend the next day swimming with His Royal Highness, while Bing and I re-paired to Petworth House. There I wandered through countless rooms of paintings and statuary, while my Philistine husband found nothing better to do than to hit golf balls on the thousand acres of greensward, with a gallery no less, who assured him that it was the first time that the lawns had ever seen such usage.

It was there that we first met Sara St. George, a nineteen-year-old, who had lost an arm and the use of a leg in a waterskiing accident.

Courageously, she was completing her law studies, and contemplating the future as if nothing the least serious had happened.

While the men played golf, I made a serious effort to attend every play and ballet in London and Paris. In the latter city, Bing took us all to the Moulin Rouge, where my sons were exposed to the topless Apache dancers in the company of their parents, and only their father seemed embarrassed.

July 24th found us taking tea in an enchanting shooting lodge in Ripon. As I gazed about the table, I realized, to my horror, that every man, woman, and child present was smoking.

Sportingly, I raced upstairs, threw myself across a bed, covered my head with a pillow, and bawled. Half an hour later, Bing arrived to announce that it was dinner time.

"I can't stand to sit at table with those awful people."

"You're speaking of half the aristocracy of England. Most of the world's socialites would be thrilled to be here."

"I'll cheerfully yield my place. Your lords and ladies are trying to kill me."

"How's that?"

"Don't pretend not to have noticed. A shot a week has kept me out of the

The drivers from the village

With Lady Bostock

Marooned with loader

hospital so far, but there isn't enough serum in the world to protect me from the poisons they're spewing into the air. Even the women are sucking on enormous fat cigars!"

"I guess I hadn't reacted because I'd been gratefully inhaling the second-hand smoke. Personally I've quit, but I can't be held accountable for others' contributions."

"Oh yes you can. If you're in no great hurry to become a widower, put an end to that tobacco orgy right now."

"Don't be unreasonable."

"I will if it's unreasonable to die of anaphylactic shock. I seriously doubt that Northern England boasts the appropriate equipment to bring me safely out of it."

"OK, OK, wash away your tears, and I'll take care of the problem."

And bless him, that's just what he did, returning five minutes later to inform me that there would be no smoking in the dining room, or in a special room that had been designated for cocktails sans cigars.

Reassured, I put on my face, and we descended to dinner.

We supped on regional delights, and none of the guests manifested open hostility. I was about to express my gratitude for their ultimate sacrifice, when I noticed that a broad wave of discomfort was spreading throughout the room.

I'm a failed actress, and I know an exit cue when I see one. I thanked our hosts demurely, declared that I really was too tired to await dessert, and excused myself.

Everyone expressed concern and regret, inquired anxiously as to whether I absolutely must retire, and wished me a fond good night. Before I had reached the bottom of the stairs, the cigarette lighters were in full play.

The morrow's grouse shoot was a true adventure. Not a happy one, but an adventure nonetheless. I was pleased to see that Bing experienced similar difficulties.

Our problem lay not in the grouse, which were cooperative enough, but in the layout. We shot from individual butts, semi-circular stone walls about eight feet wide, set in a line some twenty yards apart.

In mine stood my loader, in knee socks, knickers, starched shirt, tie, shooting jacket, and Sherlock Holmes hat. All this would have elicited only a smile, had he not placed himself in front of me on my right, while Lady Bostock knelt up forward with her Labrador retriever, blocking my view on the left.

With my peripheral vision beset on both sides, I could fire only straight forward, but there another problem presented itself.

The birds were driven toward us by children from the village. The former represented difficult targets, but the latter were hard to miss.

I complained to my loader, who admitted blithely that the lads had all taken a few pellets from time to time.

"How about you and dear Lady Bostock?"

"The same."

"Well, I'm not about to weight you down with any more lead," I promised, breaking my weapon, and retreating over the back of the butt, where I met Bing, engaged in a similar withdrawal.

"It reminds me of the days when we were encouraged to throw baseballs at human heads in seedy carnivals," he remarked, "while the beefy proprietors assured us that the targets enjoyed

With Leonora Wood and Lord Swinton

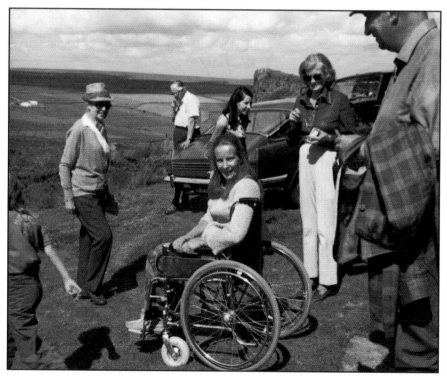

Courageous Lady Swinton

their work. The class system is still alive and well in rural England."

We viewed the other side of the coin when we stopped off for five days at Swinton Hall, one of the truly stately homes of England. Bing was particularly taken by its proprietress, who was startlingly beautiful.

Sue Swinton had been a renowned equestrienne in her youth. Weeks before her wedding, while riding to hounds, she had suffered an accident. Her horse had fallen, rolled over on her, and fractured her spine.

She had offered to break her engagement, but Lord Swinton had refused to consider so much as delaying the wedding. She became his wife, and later a member of parliament, sitting in the House of Lords.

In her wheelchair, she swept us throughout the magnificent home that had been owned by her husband's family for countless generations. We were the last guests to enjoy it. After our week's visit, the Swintons would have to dispose of it.

Estates were taxed at 110%, a rate which was simply extortionate, so their proprietors were given the choice of ripping the roofs off, or of disposing of their mansions. Rather than desecrate their ancestral home, the Swintons had chosen to abandon it.

I left on the 29th, the very night of the final dinner at Swinton Hall. Bing and I took a last walk through the endless rooms, bidding farewell to the antique furniture, the lovely porcelain, and the treasured portraits, all of which were to go under the ivory hammer.

Originally the country house had been sustained by the Swintons' tenant farmers, who owed a percentage of their crops to the landowner.

Now they paid no rents, so the proprietors had shouldered all the expenses of the estate as long as they possibly could.

One unjust system had been replaced by another, and the ancient structure was forfeit. Bing stayed on at that last party until 5 AM, singing a fond farewell to Swinton Hall.

My husband returned home on September 8th, and it occurred to me that I had been overlooking a splendid resource for my show. I brought my camera crew home to wire the house for sound.

Sure enough, on October 16th *The Kathryn Crosby Show* was taped at 1200 Jackling. My guests of honor were Mike Douglas, and, oddly enough, a certain Bing Crosby.

The latter leaned on our Erard, the same piano on which he had feigned performing for Grace Kelly in *High Society*. Of course Bing had no idea of how to play a piano. The keyboards that he fingered in his movies were blanks, unconnected to strings, so that he could run his hands over them smoothly, while the deceitful camera showed chiefly closeups of his face.

In any event, guess who it was that he was privileged to sing with this time? After all, it was my show.

Meanwhile Mike Douglas was muttering in my ear, "I can't believe that I'm here in this house, performing with a show business legend."

The taping came to a successful end, and the legend was off to the duck club, Las Cruces, and Guadalajara. He returned on November 2nd, and on the 13th the whole family traveled to Los Angeles for our annual Christmas Show, and then for the Minute Maid Commercial.

With Astaire and Hope

On Monday, December 22nd, I presented the Christmas version of *The Kathryn Crosby Show* at KPIX. Then my crew followed me down to Laguna Honda, where we taped another Crosby family presentation.

After a Christmas dinner at home, with some thirty Grandstaffs and Crosbys attending, Bing drove me to an empty golf course at Cypress point, where we had the place to ourselves for a glorious long weekend.

There were sand traps for two, birdies for him, and bogies for me, pines, miniature deer, sea lions, pounding surf, and tea in the old clubhouse before a roaring fire.

Indeed the only drawback was that we were not immortal. I for one was perfectly prepared to enjoy such scenes and such a life forever.

Waterford trophies for the Bing Crosby Pro-Am

1976

In Hollywood, on January 9th, I dined with Pat Crowley, formerly a girl friend of Bing's and fellow starlet of mine, now safely married to Ed Hookstratton. Old values die hard. "You got that great part in *Forever Female* that I tested for at Paramount," I reminded her indignantly.

"Indeed I did," she sighed. "But you got the man."

Back in Hillsborough on the 15th, Sara St. George gave us a new chess set. The board was black glass with blue butterflies, and the men were black and white onyx.

"That's the most beautiful sight I've ever seen," Bing beamed, "and I don't even play chess. We'll have to set up the library to showcase it."

For the first and last time, he actually helped me to rearrange furniture. The sideboard that had always stood in front of the Russell watercolor was relegated to the attic, and hurrah,

I could now open the picture frame to reveal the television set, without clambering on top of a large and superfluous piece of furniture.

For ten long years, the drill had been to stand on the little red footstool, step from it onto the sideboard, reach up to open the picture frame, and, since this was well before remote control, to twirl frantically at the dials. The installation of the chess set had somehow reminded us that all this behavior was susceptible of modification.

The whole family spent from Wednesday the 21st through Monday the 26th at Bing's golf tournament. We followed his friend Jack Nicklaus, as he eked out a one-stroke lead going into the final round. And then the unthinkable happened.

The greatest golfer of his time began to play like a week-end duffer. He sprayed shots all over the course, three-putted green after green, and

Bing was captivated by Virginia Cocknell's southern charm.

shot a nine-over-par 45 on the back side at Pebble Beach, ending up with an 82 for the day, and in a five-way tie for 18th in the standings.

Unable to endure the spectacle of a great champion going down to defeat, Nathaniel slipped away to cheer his buddy Ben Crenshaw on to victory. The latter had shown enormous promise as a teenager, and had won his first tour event, the Texas Open, but had done nothing much since. Suddenly he was back in the thick of things.

Young Ben shot a three-under par 69 on the final day at Pebble Beach. He finished with a seven-under-par total of 281, two shots ahead of second-place Mike Morley.

In the Pro-Am Division, fifty-one-year-old Dee Keaton, chairman of the board of Charter Oil Company, chipped and putted in a fashion that even the pros applauded, and carried his teammate, professional Hale Irwin, to a one-stroke victory.

The weather had cooperated, with four of the warmest, sunniest days in the history of the tournament. Unfortunately the dry spell was to continue all year, baking the courses to a cinder.

A charming Texan named Virginia Cockrell had been coaxing Bing to do a benefit for the Houston Symphony. In all truth, he had informed her that he didn't have an act. With the exception of a couple of minor benefits for local causes, he hadn't performed individually live since his early days with Paul Whiteman.

Bing had occasionally obliged such friends as Bob Hope, Dean Martin, and Frank Sinatra, by appearing on their shows to sing a few songs, but he hadn't even considered offering a whole program on his own.

However the 1976 Clambake had featured Joey Bushkin and his quartet, weaving together medleys of the old songs. Bing had hummed along with the group, singing a few bars of each number, and the resultant applause had been thunderous.

Encouraged by it, he headed for Houston, where he was informed that he would go on at 10 PM. Dismayed, he turned to me and insisted, "That's past my bedtime."

I exposed him to a dollop of Southern charm from some very determined socialites, and he reluctantly agreed to play his part. For backup, he had only his family, headed by a wife short on talent but always long on enthusiasm, if granted any sort of opportunity to perform anywhere.

Bing entered to his theme song, *The Blue of the Night,* and continued with *The Pleasure of Your Company,* and *Send in the Clowns.* The family chipped in with *Sing,* and I contributed a solo parody of *You've Come a Long Way from St. Louis,* in the form of *You've Come a Ways from West Columbia.*

It wasn't precisely a classic, but my friends and relatives loved it. So there!

Together, Bing and I sang *My Cup Runneth Over* and *I Love to Dance.* He and Harry offered their rendition of *You've Got a Friend* and *A Simple Melody,* and our crooner then exited with a solo Crosby medley.

His encore was *That's What Life is All About,* with a second exit to *The Blue of the Night.* He was so encouraged by his fans that he found himself caught up in the benefit business.

On March 4, I joined him in Los Angeles, where he was working on a TV special with Liza Minelli. We took long walks around Westwood Village, and he

Bing and Phil at Las Cruces

described the sleepy little place that it had been when he first arrived, with no noise or smog, and the scent of orange blossoms everywhere.

On March 17th, we performed in another live benefit with Rosemary Clooney at the Chandler Pavilion. Then Bing flew off to Canada, Texas, and finally Las Cruces, where he was met by our son Harry and Phil Harris, who were becoming fast friends.

Bing described the sequel as follows: "On the first day that we didn't shoot, in spite of my protestations, Phil and Harry decided to go fishing in a stormy sea. Off Saltita, they lost the transmission on their outboard.

The motor ran as well as ever, but they couldn't throw it into gear, so they were at the mercy of the pounding surf. Harry jumped overboard, and tried to prevent the boat from capsizing, but a big wave caught it, and over it went, dumping the Indian into the water beside him.

Phil suffered a sharp blow to the head from the wave-tossed boat, and his windbreaker was blown over his eyes. Harry caught hold of him, dragged him to a depth where they could both touch bottom, guided him to shore, tried to resuscitate him, and finally left him with a water bottle that had floated in from the boat.

Harry ran all the way home for our pickup truck, and drove to find help. With a big, fast boat, he and its crew reached Saltitas in 45 minutes.

There was the outboard, beaten to pieces, and the bottle of water, still lying on the beach, but there was no sign of Harris.

They searched half the night with flashlights before they found Phil sitting on a small hill, incoherent, and with no notion of how he'd arrived there. They drove him home, and it was three days before I could get any food into him, but I administered enough codeine to guarantee a couple of nights sleep.

He didn't even have an appetite for booze, which will give you some idea of the shape he was in. At present, he seems to have recovered whatever wits he originally possessed."

On June 2nd, we presented yet another charity concert, with Flip Wilson and Rosemary Clooney, at the Masonic Auditorium in San Francisco. From my perspective, the high point was my very rough impersonation of Rita Hayworth performing a fandango, while Bing raised his eyebrows and sang *In a Little Spanish Town*.

On June 14th, the entire family left for London, flying over the pole by way of Seattle. On our stop there, Bing led us outside, gulped in a deep breath of the scents of home, and enjoined us, "Inhale and remember. This is what air should smell like."

In London, we were whisked through customs, bedraggled, but warmly welcomed by the press, who filled the airport. Bing hadn't slept, of course, but then, it was hard to tell when he was awake at the best of times. Fortunately I had supervised a successful change from his old golfing sweater to a sports coat.

His arthritis made it painful for him to carry the luggage, and he wouldn't permit my taking over, so the children shouldered our suitcases, while Bing bore the brunt of the interviews.

On June 15th, we all watched Julie Andrews at the Palladium, in the one-woman show that she would take to Las Vegas. Then we returned to our flower-filled Green Street flat, and

Surveying the marquee at The Palladium

began to unpack. Bing shook his head as an entire set of Jane Austen came to light. Finally he ventured, "Don't they have her in England? I was under the impression that she had lived here."

"I know, but these musty old tomes take me back to New York at the turn of the century. I'm supposed to be reading them to get into my role as *The Heiress.*"

Bing nodded solemnly. "And just what is my old friend, *Tristram Shandy,* doing in the group?"

"She'd have read him too, but she'd have felt too nervous to put her knowledge to any use. Catherine Sloper is a version of me when you make me feel inferior."

"And just when might that be?" Bing guffawed.

It was no time for soul-baring. I was on the carpet for 200 pounds of overweight luggage. "When you sit there in your tweeds and brogans, looking like a page out of *Country Life,*" I replied. "Come on, help me to unpack these trunks."

"I'd just adore to," he purred, "and I'm positively devastated that I can't. Sadly I have an unavoidable engagement at Sunningdale. Mustn't be tardy off the first tee you know. It's extremely bad form in merry old England."

Bing strode off whistling. He had escaped a boring task. I fell to my books humming. I had avoided some well-merited censure.

While I worked, I recalled how I'd met my heiress, Catherine Sloper: Sir William Murray had approached Bing at Glen Eagles. He was a lord, of course, but in Scotland they still insist that they're called lairds.

He asked Bing to assist in financing the Ochtertyre Theatre, located in the Laird's castle at Crieff. Bing had modestly declined to perform in a benefit, but he had generously volunteered the services of his actress wife, who had, after all, played a lass from Edinburgh in *The Prime of Miss Jean Brodie.*

Crieff, as it chanced, was only thirty miles away. I pictured myself as Mary Queen of Scots in a regal castle. Her denouement was uninspiring, but surely a winsome modern lass couldn't be beheaded for overacting.

On Monday evening, June 21st, we opened at the London Palladium. The reception was tumultuous. The police had to form a cordon along an alley to permit us access to the stage door. Our dressing room was a riot of flowers.

Bing decided that he would act as MC, walk onto stage alone, greet the audience, and then introduce his little troupe. But he had reckoned without his public, who wouldn't let him speak for ten long minutes.

Then he was so choked up that he found speech difficult, so he sang. He'd never experienced any difficulty there.

He had accepted a performance at the Palladium in thanks for the letters and gifts he'd received after his lung operation, and as an ultimate test of his powers.

He'd made so many movies and TV specials that he'd almost forgotten what the response of a huge, live audience could be like.

At intermission, he was hearkening back to World War II, and trembling with excitement. His mind had been full of memories as he sang *The Pleasure of Your Company.*

Our three children awaited their cue to *Sing.* They were still too young to experience stage fright, but they stood in awe of their father, whom they saw

With His Royal Highness

Performing for Prince Philip's charities at the Paladium

clearly for the first time as someone other than "Dad."

The next days found London in the throes of a rare heat wave, and our butler and his wife generated their own whirlwind in our apartment. Before entering our employ, they had worked for Elizabeth and Prince Philip. Now they had been invited to visit Her Majesty in her private chambers.

A week earlier, Bing had chatted cozily with Elizabeth at Ascot, while neglecting to introduce his wife. When I had confronted him with the oversight, he had first appeared perplexed, and had finally inquired, "What should I have said? Perhaps something like, 'Hold it, Queenie, I know my wife would like to exchange cake recipes with you. Just stand right here while I mosey over and fetch her.'"

I had resolved at the time not to leave my husband, but to stand by him and sulk for the rest of his life. Ten minutes later, we had both received an invitation to join Her Majesty in the royal enclosure.

"No thanks," Bing had demurred. "I've already spoken with Elizabeth, and with the Queen Mother too. We don't wish to impose further."

"What do you mean we, Buckwheat?" I demanded indignantly. "That invitation was directed to both of us."

On the 29th, Bing was made a citizen of London by the Town Council, and he received gracious praise from the Lord Mayor, who cited both his World War II contributions and his present charitable efforts.

At 5:30 PM on July 1st, three outrageously long limousines picked us all up, and drove us slowly to the palace. I sat on a jump seat, while Bing murmured, "I've always hated this sort of formal thing. I should have said no while I had the chance"

"It would have been your last word on earth," I assured him solemnly.

He nonetheless lamented his fate all the way to Buckingham Palace, where Prince Philip was at the door to take my hand and lead us in.

I entered the formal reception room, and was so busily engaged in admiring furnishings and portraits that I failed to notice the hush when a small woman in a pale summer frock floated in.

I was recalled to the here and now when she walked up and presented herself. It seemed that her given name was Elizabeth.

I suppose that I should have curtsied, but I was temporarily paralyzed by the bright blue eyes. I sent urgent telepathic pleas for aid to my husband, but he was occupied on the other side of the room, discussing Philip's golf game.

Fortunately Rosie Clooney was at hand, and she initiated a homey little chat about children. I expressed my admiration for Princess Ann's horsemanship, but Her Majesty replied that she found it frightening, making me recall British editorials inquiring how the daughter had presumed to terrify her mother so.

Chastened, I let my mouth run on to other subjects: the drought, the gardens, our nightly work at the Palladium, Bing's fragile health, his love of horses and field sports. The Queen's tranquil smile was unhurried, and her interest seemed completely focused. We constituted an island of calm in the grand room.

After some thirty minutes, two gentlemen moved in beside Elizabeth. One glanced significantly at his watch, and inquired about my children's

A duet with Ted Rogers at the Gaity

schooling in America. The other asked Rosie about her latest album.

Her Majesty eased from the room without a farewell, since that would have put an end to the party. With my Texas background, I flashed onto cutting horses. The Queen's retainers had gently eased her from the herd.

Bing and Philip were photographed as they strode out to our car. On the way home, the crooner complained that with all the chatter he had doubtless ruined his voice for the night's performance. I inquired as to whether he thought that my strangling him then and there would substantially improve its range.

Saturday night, July 3rd, was our final show at the Palladium. All its predecessors had enjoyed standing ovations, but this one went on and on. Bing remained on stage, proud and a little embarrassed, and waved a last farewell to his loyal British fans.

We began rehearsals immediately with Jackie Gleason and Bernadette Peters for our Christmas Show, which was to be shot at Lord Grade's Elstree studios. We recorded on the 8th, 9th, and 10th, and except for a continuing heat wave, all went smoothly.

London is ill-prepared for high temperatures. Like San Francisco, it relies on its fogs and frequent rains. Bing and Jackie stifled in their Santa Claus outfits, and the accompanying snowflakes looked like the Styrofoam that they were.

Nonetheless, the old troopers finished taping a polished show, and we flew to Dublin on July 11th, only to find Rosie Clooney standing in the rain in front of the staid old Gresham Hotel.

"Just what do you think you're doing?" I inquired.

"We've had a bomb scare. Just as I was settling down for a nap, someone screamed 'Everybody out,' and I was happy to oblige."

On the 12th, we performed with Ted Rogers in the ancient Gaity Theatre. During intermission, Peter O'toole appeared backstage to greet us, to introduce several of his "brothers," and to congratulate Ted on his timely political witticisms.

The latter's smile remained fixed. After the visitors had departed, he informed us that we had just hosted the Executive Branch of the IRA.

"How nice that they're enjoying the show," Bing reassured him.

On July 14th, we flew to Edinburgh, where we were met by the Scottish press, and by a kilted Sir William Murray, the 11th Baronet of Ochtertyre, who dispatched us in a black limousine to his ancestral castle.

My early familiarity with *The Boy's King Arthur,* followed by healthy doses of Sir Walter Scott's novels and poems, had acquainted me with the outward appearance of a Scottish castle. I awaited turrets, pennants, a broad moat, and troops of heralds signaling our arrival.

Always sick as a dog in the back of a limousine, I nonetheless raised my head to a back window when the glorified hearse came to a halt. An algae-filled tarn, surrounded by barbed wire, greeted my dyspeptic gaze.

As I rotated my head slowly, my eyes chanced upon the remains of a warehouse.

"There's been some mistake," I gulped. "We're looking for the castle of Sir William Murray."

"This is it," grinned the uniformed driver maliciously.

Shooting our Christmas Show with Bernadette Peters and Jackie Gleason

"Just deposit the boys and me up the road at Glen Eagles," Bing instructed him.

"Wait just one minute!" I yowled. "Aren't you even coming in?"

"No thanks. We'll grab a bite at the club. Bye now."

"Stop! Is this where you came with the baronet?"

"God no. I've never seen this dump before. What ever possessed you to perform here?"

The three grinning males dumped Mary and me in the middle of nowhere, and were whisked off to the first tee. We'd have been standing there yet, had not our butler and his wife mysteriously appeared, and carried our bags into the tumble-down warehouse, curiously yclept castle.

"Just what are you doing here?" I wondered.

"Our holiday was a bust, so we thought we'd make you comfortable."

The first floor of the warehouse was innocent of furniture. Nevertheless, I collapsed there while Norma served tea, and recounted the recent history of Ochtertyre Castle.

For thirty years, it had served as a fourth-class girls school, and as such it had gone bankrupt. Sir William had returned from his wanderings, resolved to make a pub and theatre out of it.

I demanded to see the latter. Instead of the envisioned 18th century jewel, I found a basement gymnasium bestrewn with copious distinctly 20th century garbage.

I marched through a dungeon, past the vast piles of junk that were doubtless designed to simulate a pub, down a long tunnel to the main hall, up an interminable winding stairway, and into the room that Bing and I were destined to occupy. I saw two tall windows, one broken, two cot beds, with deep troughs in the center from thirty years of girlish pillow fights, a tiny oil lamp, a fireplace crammed with junk, a chest of drawers with all the handles missing, and a sink with rusty water leaking continuously from its sole functioning faucet.

I climbed into the nearest cot, pulled its frayed covers over my head, and cried, and cried.

Bing arrived at 5 PM, feeling benevolent. He'd inaugurated the Bing Crosby Cup, had a good round, and seen to it that the boys were stroking the ball beautifully. It took him a while to sense that I was in somewhat worse shape.

"What's the matter? Your eyes are all puffy."

"Come with me."

We walked to the gymnasium, where he surveyed the crumpled coffee containers, candy and gum wrappers, and ubiquitous dust bunnies from the last disastrous attempt at drama.

"Wow!' was his sole comment.

"Didn't you check this place out before you volunteered my services?"

"No, but Sir William guaranteed that no expense would be spared."

"I think the expense is going to be yours. Now, for God's sake, have at it."

In his favor, I must admit that he did, between rounds of course. But he might as well have been Nero, striving to command the ocean tides. For my part, I assembled a cast of sorts, and began rehearsals.

They lasted until Saturday, July 31st, when we opened to a fortunately meager audience.

We gave a performance a day through Sunday the 14th, when we

A new tournament in old Scotland

Johnny Miller, Burt Lancaster, Jackie Stewart, and Tony Jacklin

mercifully moved the show to a real theater in Edinburgh for the last two weeks.

I won't trouble you with the details, largely because I can't stand to recall them. Suffice it to say that, for the entire period, each day of my diary contains the one word *Agony*.

Those were weeks that weren't worth living, let alone writing about. It was the worst and most humiliating performance of my life, and, for anyone familiar with even a sampling of my previous theatrical disasters, that should suffice.

Bing and the boys arrived back from golf tournaments in Germany on August 20th, and *The Heiress* closed on the 21st, with all three sitting in the audience, and comprising most of it. Thus inspired, the cast and I pulled ourselves together for one final effort, the least horrible of our run.

Bing observed me quizzically. "Were they all that bad?" he wondered.

"Worse," I confided somberly. "Infinitely and ineffably worse."

Tactfully Bing asked no more questions but I was recovering enough to query him about Germany.

This brought a smile. "Harry was our hero," he assured me. "He played with Seve Ballesteros, and didn't even notice that the other golfers were taking preferred lies. His only interest lay in outdriving all the pros."

"And did he?"

"Of course. He's presently the longest hitter in the game, and his team would have won by a mile, if he had paid any attention to his rights. As it was, they came in second."

Still the only family member not flushed with victory, I returned to Hillsborough to prepare the house for Bing. He returned on September 14th, just in time for duck season, and favored me with a cheerful nod as he exited by the back door, complete with dogs and guns.

After a weekend at the duck club, he confided that duty called him south of the border. I dearly hope that my accompanying black thoughts didn't precipitate the sequel, which he described as follows:

"On my way to Los Angeles, to present the concert for the Thalians, I decided to stop off in La Paz for a week of dove shooting.

It was raining when I arrived. By the time I hit the highway, a stiff breeze was blowing, and the potholes were full of water.

I ran into Louis Benoit, who was fresh from Las Cruces in a mangled jeep. He described the road ahead as impassable.

Chevalo was certain that we could get through, but I made a good decision for once, and turned back to La Paz.

By the time I reached the El Presidente Hotel, I had to fight my way to the entrance through gale-force winds. I checked in, and lay down for a brief nap, only to be awakened by a bellboy, who announced that all guests were to assemble in the banquet hall on the ground floor.

The room had large bay windows with a view of the beach, and they began bending visibly, so we had to move into a windowless basement with strong wooden doors.

We lay down on blankets, and prepared to wait out the storm, but minutes later there was an explosion, as the windows gave way in the banquet hall. The locked-and-bolted doors to our room burst open,

Performing with Mary in *The Heiress*

scattering the guests about the floor, with much screaming and numerous cries of pain.

We were again evacuated, this time to the discotheque, a true subterranean bomb shelter, completely encased by walls of solid concrete. We were served sandwiches and coffee, and remained for seven hours, until we could hear that the wind, which had blown at over 100 miles an hour, was perceptibly diminishing.

The staff began determining which of the guest rooms were still suitable for occupancy. The hotel had lost its electricity, water, telephones, and 60% of its windows. I was escorted back to my room by flashlight at 2 AM.

I turned the key in the lock, stepped aside, and kicked the door open. A blast swept through it, and I peeked around the frame to see that all the windows had been blown out.

When the gale subsided, I gathered my luggage, sought refuge in a safer room, and finally managed about four hours of sleep.

The morrow dawned absolutely calm, and I started to consider my escape. The mile and a half to the highway was a sea of mud. No one could drive in or out. Even if I managed to reach the airport, it would be closed for lack of power.

By early afternoon, the road had started to dry out, and I rented a jeep, whose four-wheel drive managed to carry me as far as the highway to La Paz, where Hughes Air West had a working telephone.

I called Aeroméxico, and was informed that they'd know by the next morning whether the flight for Los Angeles could take off.

Our own strip at las Cruces was under five feet of muddy water.

La Paz looked as if it had been hit by a thousand-plane raid. Many buildings had been flattened, and those still standing had lost their windows.

Most trees were down, and the roads had been washed out by the deluge of water from the mountains. Hundreds of cars and many houses were completely buried.

The dam above the city had burst, and the resulting flood had swept the shacks at the edge of town into the nearby gorges. Many persons who had made the mistake of trying to flee from the torrent would have been better off remaining where they were, and hanging onto something.

Big boats were beached all along the coast, several right in front of the hotel. The death toll was over a thousand, and we had an immediate mass burial of seven hundred people, to avoid an ensuing plague. The President has flown up from Mexico City to attempt to assess the damage."

Bing finally did escape the scene of the hurricane, to present his Thalians Concert in Los Angeles. October 14th found him in Las Vegas, at the behest of a priest who had been celebrating mass in a restaurant that was about to become a topless bar. Bing had to agree that Father Ben badly needed a new church.

On November 25th, the entire family flew to Las Vegas, stayed at The Aladdin, rehearsed for an hour, and performed on the 26th and 27th. As might have been expected, ours was not a polished production.

I asked Bing what we were doing there and why.

Moonlight Becomes You.

"It's for a worthy cause. Father Ben will have his church, and the show will serve as a rehearsal for Broadway."

"For what?"

"Did I forget to tell you? We'll have just time to change our clothes before taking off on the 30th."

"Where will we stay on such short notice?"

"With a friend of Mary's."

We took our hostess to dinner. On the way home, in spite of Bing's protestations, she insisted that we stop off at a discoteque.

There the molten Latin rhythms were irresistible. Bing performed rumbas, sambas, and tangos, first with me, and then with Mary and her friend, until the wee hours.

The following morning, I was greeted by a halibut stare over the rims of the Ben Franklins. Fortunately the doorbell rang before I could be held accountable for the previous evening's activities.

Bing answered it, to reveal Father Eugene O'Brien of Fordham Prep, a nun who turned out to be his sister, and four of his honor students, eager to thank cinema's Father O'Malley for the benefit which he was about to perform for their school.

While Mary and I fled upstairs to change out of our bathrobes, my sometime altar boy, for once at a loss for words, slumped into a brocaded chair, closed his blood-shot eyes, and held his unshaven cheeks in his shaking hands.

Ted Rogers flew in from London, as did Rosemary Clooney from Dallas. We opened on December 6th at the Avery Fisher Hall. The acoustics were magnificent, and despite my fears, we were passable ourselves.

On the 7th, we moved to the Uris Theater, where our nightly performances went smoothly enough until the 15th, when Rosie's sore throat made her miss the show.

I was rushed in to fill the gap, and sang *Slow Boat to China* in a duet with Bing. I was ready and willing to volunteer for more, but he wouldn't trust me with Rosie's solos.

Fortunately, after Bing's medley, no one asked for his money back. We completed our last show on Sunday, December 19th.

On the 20th, we flew back to Hillsborough, and on the 21st, we gave our annual benefit at the Laguna Honda Hospital, and collapsed in exhaustion during the following week.

Our true Christmas celebration had taken place when we did the yuletide show in England in July. We had then rejoiced in Bing's return to full form. Such dates were special, and our private holidays were often observed more casually, if at all.

The celebrated sixteenth at Cypress Point

1977

It had taken me some time to discover where celebrities were to be found in abundance, but I had finally lucked out in 1976. I've never been one to quit when I'm winning. The week of January 16th, I moved *The Kathryn Crosby Show* to Pebble Beach, in the company of KPIX's sports commentator, Wayne Walker, and my producer, Ann Miller.

On Monday the 17th, I interviewed Dennis the Menace's creator, Hank Ketchum, and on Tuesday it was Jim Garner, Charles Schultz of Peanuts fame, Admiral Alan Shepherd, and baseball player Rollie Fingers.

I continued on Tuesday with Clint and Maggie Eastwood, Arnold Palmer, Johnny Bench, and last-but-not-least the sponsor himself, Bing Crosby. We stood on the 16th tee at Cypress Point, while I quizzed him about the 11 holes-in-one that he had made, not the least of them of them on that very same spectacular hole.

For the first time, he described his delight in hitting the tiny green, and watching the ball roll into the cup.

He chortled as he recalled Stuart Haldorn's reaction. An arthritic practical joker, who followed celebrity foursomes from the club porch with his binoculars, Haldorn had made his way to a telephone.

By the time Bing's foursome had finished the last two holes, the clubhouse was overflowing with members, ready and willing to drink any number of celebratory toasts on the crooner's tab. He admitted that he'd never had a more appreciative or thirstier public.

"It took months of work to pay for that one feat," Bing admitted. "I made it a point to keep subsequent holes-in-one strictly private."

"Do try not to make any more of them," I counseled. "You could bankrupt the lot of us."

I left Bing only to follow fifteen-year-old Nathaniel, who was appearing

In 1939, Babe Didrickson was the first woman to play as a Pro in The Crosby.

Nancy Lopez and Marianne Bretton appeared as amateurs in 1977.

Family guests on The Kathryn Crosby Show

in the tournament for the first time, as the amateur partner of Tom Kite.

As usual, Bing was busy acting as commentator in the TV tower facing the 18th green, but this time he permitted me to join him there, and to watch him demonstrate his enormous erudition and love of the game.

He had known its stars personally, all the way back to Bobby Jones, and he overflowed with anecdotes and statistics, while listening to an input of the play throughout the golf course from a tiny button in one ear.

I tried to master the technique at my own Honda tournament months later, and had to abandon the device immediately, while I was still relatively sane. I found it devilishly unnatural to say one thing while listening to another.

For the first time ever, the Crosby weather was perfect all four days. As a consequence, the gallery was the largest in the history of golf, and the scoring was phenomenal.

Tom Watson won by a single stroke, smashing by four the tournament record, set by Billy Casper in 1958. Tony Jacklin and Lee Elder, the second and third place finishers, also bettered the old mark.

As the first former president to play in the Crosby, Gerald Ford partnered Arnold Palmer. Leonard Thompson and James Vickers won the Pro-Am, while Hale Irwin and Dee Keaton, the 1976 winners, tied for second place.

I was delighted to see a favorite project of mine bear fruit, as two lady amateurs finally made the clambake a co-ed affair.

Pushing my luck, I invited Bing to guest star on my TV show on January 25th, adding the inducement that I'd include a segment in which son Harry prepared one of the trout they'd caught, and generally demonstrated his skills as a gourmet cook..

Surprisingly, Bing consented to an interview, and sang several songs from his latest album, *Bingo el Viejo*. I was delighted at such condescension, but couldn't escape a sneaking premonition that he might be falling prey to a serious illness.

While Bing and I were on stage, and every camera man, floor man, engineer and guard had joined the audience in rapt attention, Harry stood at the rear of the studio, some 20 feet back, banging pots and pans, chopping onions, mincing parsley, and filling the air with billowing clouds of pepper, as his father tried his best to finish a song. Ours was a family of egomaniacal actors, in which each member concentrated solely on his own performance.

On February 15th, we flew off to Miami, to perform for a week at the Deauville Hotel. When I wasn't part of the act, I stood at the side of the stage, and watched the mature Bing weave his spell.

There seemed to be no separation between him and his audience. His songs were personal stories, shared with a group of intimate friends.

We were staying at the Cricket Club, too far from a golf course to make commuting practical, so I had Bing to myself all day every day. But then a nasty dollop of reality intruded upon my dream world.

The script arrived for Bing's next special, which was to represent a filmed version of the Crosby family's stage show. I read with approval the solo numbers for Mary and me, and Harry's duet with Bing. Then I turned back to my introduction.

The duet from *High Society*

I hated it so much that for once I neglected to copy it into my diaries, but as I recall, it went something like this: "I want to introduce a performer who has become my favorite leading lady. Why? Because she's the only one I can get to work free."

Then I would enter, all coquettish smiles, and Bing would compliment me on every aspect of my expensive costume, hairdo, jewelry, and shoes.

I would reply that I'd just had to have all of them them for the show, and he would conclude, "Did I say free? For this price I could have had The Mormon Tabernacle Choir."

At which point I would riposte sexily, "Ah yes, but they won't cook your breakfast."

Of course it was just a spoof, but we'd had dozens of similar ones, and I was tired of serving as joke material. Matters didn't improve when I examined the song that we were to sing.

It concerned a domestic battle with a chorus of, *You're too fat and old and ugly*. I hadn't had a good knock-down fight with Bing in our 20 years of marriage. Why should I have deprived myself of such exquisite pleasure offstage, only to simulate a quarrel in public?

I sought out my husband. "How about a duet such as ˆ*Well, Did You Ever....?* I suggested. "After all, I look a bit like Frank."

"Sorry, he's cuter."

"True, but I've had quite enough." I exited in frustration.

In brief, my sense of humor had deserted me. I had never been a woman's libber, largely because I had chosen a career in which my sex had been on a parity with men. Now I, who had always earned a comfortable living, was being presented as a manipulating sexpot, who would sell her soul for a new pair of shoes. I studied the entire script, determined that my role was peripheral, and informed Bing that I had no intention of realizing it.

In spite of my previous warning, he looked up from his newspaper in surprise: "But you've been playing much the same role in our specials for the past 15 years."

"True, but I'm sick of it. I didn't abandon a movie and stage career for this sort of simpering nonsense."

Bing never negotiated with anyone, so I was certain that I had uttered the final word on the matter. To my surprise, he was back the next day.

"I've reread the script, and you've got a point. For the grown woman that you've almost become, that's a shallow presentation."

Always the dig. But I was in a mood not to notice. "What shall we do about it?" I inquired.

"You're rumored to have a way with a pen. How about writing your own introduction?"

"I can adlib it right now. I'm identified with the Kathryn Crosby Honda Civic Golf Tournament, which makes me the only sponsor on the women's tour who has her name in front of the product."

"Suits me," affirmed the individualist who had initiated the pro-am format. "Now if you'd only practice!"

We headed for rehearsals in Los Angeles, where I rejected a series of designs for frilly frocks in favor of my ten-year-old opera gown from *The Guardsman*. To my mind, it fit the theme of our duet to *Everything Old is New Again*.

I sat in the darkened auditorium, and watched the show come together.

Singing *Ten-Ten Tennessee with Harry*

Everything Old Is New Again.

There were several exciting moments, occasioned by the lowering of the center section of the stage.

During an early rehearsal, a messenger, starting across with a suggested script change for Bing, had to be tackled before he stepped off into the void. On the morning of the final shoot, a camera man backed over the edge.

"He broke the only fish-eye lens on the West Coast," lamented the producer. I noticed that the unfortunate victim had also fractured a leg and shattered his collarbone.

A network vice president arrived to inform me that my opening had been rejected as too commercial.

"Bob Hope's introduction refers to Texaco six times."

"I'm sure that will be changed."

"Fine. Suppose you explain the problem to my husband."

"I did, and he told me to get myself another crooner. I had hoped that you might prove more receptive."

"Well, I'm not."

On March 3rd, we presented our show. Hope retained his references to Texaco, and my introduction went as planned. We sang our duet, and Bob introduced Bing's closing medley as a straightforward tribute to his old friend.

The medley lasted 30 minutes. At its conclusion, Bing said farewell from the center of the stage, while the section behind him, which held the Joey Bushkin Quartet, silently descended 25 feet into the basement.

Bing bowed, stepped backwards out of the lights, and disappeared into the void. Whirling in midair, he grasped a handful of drapery, which ripped free, but slowed and deflected his fall.

Just missing the quartet's drums, which would have cut him in two, he landed on his left hip on the concrete floor. By the time I reached him, he was trying to rise.

Had he not broken his fall, his spine would have been shattered, leaving him permanently paralyzed. I shoved my coat beneath his head.

I gazed into his eyes. The pupils were the same size. I told him to wiggle his fingers, and then his toes.

One shoe had been torn off, and I saw a hole in the heel of Bing's red sock. It took a moment to realize that this was not merely his customary contempt for the dress code, but the consequence of a contact with the wall on his way down to the basement.

I glanced about, seeking help. Bob Hope was seated on a piano bench, holding his head in his hands. Pearl Bailey was sobbing in the background.

Medics arrived with a stretcher. As we left the auditorium, Bing began humming, *Off we go, into the wild blue yonder,* and I feared for his mental state as I stumbled along beside him in my high heels.

At Hunting Memorial Hospital, he was carried in one door while I was dispatched to another.

A nurse invited me to sit in the waiting room. Striving for the necessary calm, I announced firmly, "Miss, I'm a registered nurse, with experience in the emergency room. I'd be happy to assist your physicians with their tests, or if they insist, I'll just watch, but I must be with Bing."

She eyed me appraisingly, checking for the hysteria that I was trying to suppress. I passed muster, and was admitted to the examining room, where Bing seized my hand.

"Welcome to the post-show party, Babbette!" he smiled.

Enjoying the last rehearsal

I positioned him for a series of X-rays, Miraculously they revealed an intact spine, and no fractured limbs. The physician who read them decided, "You are a very lucky man, Mr. Crosby. You may go home now."

"But I can't walk."

"Then we'll keep you here for observation."

I sat by Bing's bedside until dawn, when he finally lapsed into a drug-induced sleep. At 7:30, a supervisor and twenty nursing students passed by on rounds. Each carried a pad and pencil.

For notes? No, for autographs! I rose like a cobra, and confronted the supervisor, who spun on her heel, and herded her charges out as silently as I had prescribed.

When Bing awoke, a blood clot on his hip had swollen to a point where he could no longer wiggle his toes. But by Saturday, March 5th, he managed to walk a few painful steps.

Bing's days consisted of alternate periods of therapy and rest. I spent them with him in the hospital. By Monday, March 21st, I was prepared to move him north to Hillsborough.

I had arranged for an air ambulance with an accompanying doctor, but Bing knew that he wasn't ready to go home. He was drugged, hallucinating, and depressed, and he didn't want me to continue seeing him in state.

He therefore insisted that he stay in Los Angeles, while I flew off on the 22nd to sponsor my golf tournament. As soon as I was gone, he called in his doctors, summoned the air ambulance that I had contacted, and flew to San Francisco, where he was met by Dr. Sotohall, an old friend, and an outstanding orthopedist.

I returned from my tournament to remain at Bing's bedside in Peninsula Hospital until 10:30 AM on April 5th, when he agreed to let me drive him to our Hillsborough home.

His nurse readied a wheelchair, in which to push him out to the car.

But in my presence, he still refused to be coddled. A friend had sent him a fancy, carved cane. "Just for show," he grinned, brandishing it, and starting for the door on foot.

I remained by his side, ready to catch him if he faltered. It was a walk back from death. At the entrance, he cheerily saluted a large group of waiting friends with his new cane.

Once home, he managed his first afternoon nap without medication. He was on the mend!

On April 10th, he insisted that I take Mary to Dallas for our scheduled performance in *The Latest Mrs. Adams*. I had wanted to cancel, but Bing had decided that it would be a great experience for his daughter, and, in any event, he was heartily sick of my hovering over him.

Bing wrote from Hillsborough: "Congratulations on the good reviews. You've succeeded in putting on a physical comedy in the round with one week's rehearsal.

For Mary, it will be worth two years of ACT. As for me, I'm walking better, and sleeping well in my new hospital-type bed."

On May 14, Bing took advantage of my absence to accompany Harry to Las Cruces, knowing full well that it was much too early in his convalescence. I could think of nothing else, so I proceeded to give a series of perfectly dreadful performances.

Golfing with the new men's champion

Watching Mary in *The Latest Mrs. Adams*

On May 23rd, Bing wrote that the new boat, which Harry had bought, was very fast, but a trifle hard on his ruptured disk. Unfortunately its radio was no good in Mexico, so they couldn't call for any needed help. He insisted that he was healing satisfactorily, except for continuing leg cramps.

The Latest Mrs. Adams moved on to Columbus. Bing and Harry joined us there on June 23rd. At the end of the performance, I normally made a curtain speech and signed autographs. That night I simply introduced Bing.

He received an instantaneous standing ovation, wound his way up to the spotlight, said a few words, and had to retreat to my dressing room to quiet the applause.

For the first time since his accident, Bing was able to play 18 holes. We managed it together at Blacklick, the local municipal course.

On June 26th, Bing left for San Francisco. The next day, Mary and I flew to Indianapolis for a five-week engagement.

I phoned home twice daily. In the morning, Bing was recovering in body and spirit, and full of plans for forthcoming tours of England, Australia, New Zealand, and Japan.

By nightfall, he was often depressed. The fatigue of a day's living had taken its heavy toll.

On the evening of July 9th, Bing phoned me to announce that it was the happiest day of his life. I awaited news of a miraculous cure, but it transpired that, at the age of fifteen, Nathaniel had just won the men's championship at the Burlingame Country Club.

With renewed vigor, Bing gave a concert in Concord, undaunted by a power failure, which left him stranded on a blacked-out stage, nursing the audience along for twenty minutes until the lights came back on.

I completed my last performance on August 21st, and flew home on the 22nd, to spend a few precious hours with Bing, before he left for a benefit in Oslo, en route to England.

When I arrived, he was closeted with Dr. Sullivan. Upon news of my advent, he rushed out delightedly to welcome me.

On the other hand, the normally imperturbable ex-marine passed me by without a greeting, looking as if he'd just been confronted by a legion of ghosts.

It was many years later that I learned that Bing had told him the following: "I feel fine now, but I've had unmistakable signs that I'm going soon. Promise me to take care of Kathryn and the children."

"But I'm just an academic, and anything but a financial wizard, as you well know."

"Yes, but I trust you."

"You can't die. Everyone here needs you, myself included."

"Sorry, but this is one thing that I can't control. Will you promise?"

"Of course, but I find this inconceivable. Please don't go."

"I'll do my best, but I rather doubt that we'll meet again on this green planet. Good luck, Bill. You'll need it."

And Bing had come out grinning, while Dr. Sullivan stumbled off without a word to his mountain hideaway.

Bing and Harry left for the airport two hours later. I followed on the 27th, with Mary and Nathaniel. In London, we found father and son firmly established in the same little flat that we'd occupied previously.

Back in London

We began rehearsal for the Christmas Show. The weather was benign, the production smooth. All of life took on a golden quality

Bing grew so comfortable that on September 4th he joined Nathaniel in a golf tournament. On the 5th, we began filming the final version of our show, which was scheduled to wrap up on the 9th. Incredibly we finished early.

On the 10th, we drove Mary and Nathaniel to the airport for their return to school. The farewells weren't complicated. This family was always taking off in various directions, only to come together again shortly.

Bing assured Mary that he'd see her at ACT in a couple of weeks, and promised to play Sunningdale with Nathaniel the following year.

In the event, it was I who next played with Bing at Sunningdale, after mass at Westminster Cathedral. He seemed to be at the height of his game, swinging smoothly, driving well, and chipping and putting superbly.

He chuckled at my difficulties, as my best drives failed to carry over the formidable stretches of rough that awaited each tee shot . Under his tutelage, I finally improved to a point where I succeeded in reaching a couple of fairways.

On the 12th, 13th, and 14th, Bing recorded an album in the mornings, and in the afternoons we rehearsed a new show, with which we opened at Preston on the 22nd.

Bing stunned the audience by walking onto the stage alone, delivering an upbeat *Feels Good, Feels Right,* and proceeding to discuss his 50 years in show business. As he explained, he'd come a long way since he first sang *Ben Bolt, One Fleeting Hour,* and *I Have a Dog Named Rover* at the Parish Hall in Spokane.

On September 26th, we opened at the Palladium in London, for two weeks of a show a night. With that much singing, there were no matinees, since Bing could hardly have sent in a substitute. We had plenty of time for golf, and for slow walks around the neighborhood.

On October 6th, at my insistence, Bing saw a neurologist about his continuing back pains.

On the following morning, I received a phone call: "Mrs. Crosby, in the course of a routine check, I found that your husband has alarmingly high blood pressure. It's not my field, so I'm sending a colleague to your house. He should be there within the hour."

I explained the matter to Bing, who laughed and said, "No cause for alarm. That neurosurgeon hadn't taken a patient's blood pressure in years. He could hardly get the cuff on."

The physician arrived, checked Bing's pressure three times, and decided that it was a perfectly normal 125/80. We shared a laugh over the neurosurgeon's lack of experience with sphygmomanometers.

Our lease expired on the flat, and Sara St. George offered us Claridge House, very close to the Palladium. We simply dumped our bags anywhere. Our attention was fixed on closing night, and there seemed to be no point in unpacking, only to repack everything in two more days.

We weren't interested in cooking either, so Bing took me to dinner at Claridge's, just around the corner. He greeted the doorman by name, and treated me to a glass of wine, a toast to a job well done.

The final performance

Curtain call

On October 10th, we motored to Brighton, lunched at Wheeler's famous fish restaurant, and walked through Brighton Pavilion, a priceless architectural gem.

We were opening a new concert hall. As we watched the workmen preparing the stage, and setting up microphones and chairs, we received a phone call from Alan Fisher:

"Mrs. Crosby, would you please speak to the gentleman to whom I'm about to hand the phone?"

The gentleman in question was Detective Chief Superintendent O'Hara from the nearby West End Central Police Station.

"Mrs. Crosby, your butler Fisher called us in. I fear there's been a robbery. He informs me that many items of jewelry are missing."

O'Hara's voice dropped to a whisper. "Mrs. Crosby, how long have you known this man Fisher? He appears very nervous. Do you trust him?"

"In answer to your first question, sixteen years. As for your second, with my life, as does your Queen."

I broke the news to Bing, and said, "Sorry, Darling. There went the gold snuff box, but Merry Christmas anyway. We must hope that the thief needed it more than we did."

Oddly enough, Bing was genuinely annoyed. He had admired the box when he saw it at Wartski's, and I had bought it to surprise him.

Insult was added to injury when I learned of the loss of my wedding rings, and of two enamel icons covered with seed pearls, which I had brought over to present to Alan and Norma, who were retiring from our service.

"Forget it," Bing insisted. "To coin a phrase, the show must go on."

Bing made his final stage appearance before an audience of five thousand. The atmosphere was reverent, rather than festive.

At the end, since the fans wouldn't stop applauding, Bing blew them three kisses, and said "I love you," a totally uncharacteristic act.

Then the entire cast hugged one another with tears in their eyes, equally strange behavior for show people who were to meet again within a few weeks for a tour of Japan and Australia.

The following morning, Bing taped twelve songs for the BBC. I had never attended recording sessions, but for some reason I accompanied him to this one. More strange behavior.

That evening, I took some twenty guests to Chow's Chinese Restaurant for dinner. Bing bade us farewell from behind a stack of programs as high as his head.

"Got to finish these," he explained. "I'm off to Spain on Thursday."

Surrounded by guests, I couldn't manifest my surprise. But I had at him when I returned from dinner:

"What's this about Spain? For a man who recently occupied a sick bed, you've been absurdly busy of late. I'm dragging you home for a long and well-deserved rest."

"No, you're not. I've been looking forward to my kind of vacation."

"Well, if you absolutely must go, I'll travel with you."

"That's sweet of you, my love, but I've scheduled a few rounds of competitive golf, and then a whack at the

397

Just before the last round

wily partridge. It will be my first driven bird shoot."

"Mine too."

"No, darling, this side trip is just for the fellows. You go home and take care of the children, and I'll see you all in a few days.

"Oh, all right."

I flew home on October 12, and was busily putting the house in order on the 14th, when Dr. Sullivan phoned:

"You have to be prepared for the onslaught, and I know no better way to say this, so I'll give it to you short and straight. Bing has just died in Spain."

Reporters surrounded the house, and the phones began ringing off the hook. I managed to get a call through to Madrid. César Zulueta expressed his sympathy.

"Tell me what happened."

"It was a warm, sunny day. We went to mass and communion, and then to the Club de Golf . We had completed our 18 holes, and I asked Bing how he felt.

He said, 'I'm fine, not tired at all. I liked the course. Not too many hills to climb.' Then he dropped to the ground without another word.

I thought he had stumbled. When I couldn't revive him, I called a doctor from the clubhouse, but Bing's death had been instantaneous."

A tiny light flickered in my numbed brain. At least he had died as he had wished, swiftly, in his beloved sunlight, not agonizingly in some gloomy hospital. "How well did Bing play?" I demanded. "Did he win?"

Zulueta sounded puzzled. "Why yes, Señora. He won all the bets. It was a very good round."

Thank you, God.

Bing Crosby was dead, and my life had died with him, but, for both of us, it had indeed been a very good round.

My first impulse was to follow him into the dark, but there were the children, and there was the Catholicism to which I had sworn allegiance for his sake.

My existence had lost all meaning, now that its lodestone had disappeared, but somehow it would have to continue.

My mind flashed back to the trivialities which had stolen our last precious moments together: preoccupations with such nonsense as travels, performances, dinners, and thefts.

That was all there would be from now on, a life made up of petty, inane details, but to console me, Bing had left behind his children, his films, and his glorious music.

I hung up the phone, and prepared to confront an alien world.